# EMPOWERING YOUR SOUL

*Buckle Up for the Wildest Ride of Your Life*

**Glenys-Kay**

BALBOA
PRESS

A DIVISION OF HAY HOUSE

Balboa Press books may be ordered through booksellers or by contacting:

Balboa Press
A Division of Hay House
1663 Liberty Drive
Bloomington, IN 47403
www.balboapress.com.au
1-(877) 407-4847

ISBN: 978-1-4525-0756-9 (sc)
ISBN: 978-1-4525-0757-6 (e)

Printed in the United States of America

Balboa Press rev. date: 11/08/2012

*With deep gratitude I dedicate this book*
*to an amazing friend:*


*Pauline*

*This wonderful friend helped me, healed me, counseled*
*me, encouraged me and motivated me.*
*I would not be where I am teaching and healing others if*
*it was not for her dedicated support.*
*She works quietly behind the scenes helping and healing*
*many people, often without recognition.*
*So on behalf of all those she has helped, I say thank you.*


*and*

*in memory of Trisha*
*4.9.46-7.7.12*
*An angelic soul and beautiful friend who valued*
*my teachings so much.*


*True friendship is priceless.*

# CONTENTS

Introduction ......................................................................................................................... ix

The Dawn Of A New Age ............................................................................................... 1

The Universe And Its Laws .......................................................................................... 20

History And Our Origins ............................................................................................. 51

Consciousness ................................................................................................................. 68

Ascension ........................................................................................................................ 80

Birth, Death And Living .............................................................................................. 99

The Energies Of Nature ............................................................................................. 121

Auras And Chakras ...................................................................................................... 134

Our Biology Of Fears .................................................................................................. 142

We Do Create Our Reality ......................................................................................... 160

Relationships ................................................................................................................. 176

Practical Tools .............................................................................................................. 183

The Future ..................................................................................................................... 195

Conclusion ..................................................................................................................... 199

Appendix ........................................................................................................................ 200

*The Truth of who we are lies buried beneath
many layers of negative emotions and distorted
beliefs.*

*We must commit to clearing these and
re-programming our DNA with the
higher codes of light.*

# INTRODUCTION

*It is a lesson to surrender to the words, and trust that when you need to understand more you will discover the means to receive the understanding. Your heart and body understands the words. Trust that that is enough.*

*. . . . The Ascended Masters*

Welcome dear readers, to this book of metaphysics and self-empowerment.

Maybe you have this book in your hands because you have been searching to understand your life and how it works, or perhaps why things are not working. Maybe you have been undergoing this journey of ascension that we talk about so much in this time frame, or maybe you don't know why you even picked up this book to read. In this latter case, then I might suggest to you that you were guided to read it. Perhaps the light shone so brightly on this book that you knew you had to read it. That's what our guides and teachers in the non-physical realms do. They lead us to the next piece of information and understanding that we need.

So whatever your reason for reading this book, I welcome you to my life, my understandings, my truths. Always know you are in charge of what you take as your truth. Don't just believe what I say, because there are many others with truths you should perhaps listen to. Whatever you believe must resonate with your heart, deep down inside, it must feel 'right' to you. That way you know that it is your soul, or your Higher Self, your God Self, talking to you, telling you it is right for you at the time you receive it. Truths change constantly as you learn more, so never set anything in concrete for that will only inhibit your movement forward.

Perhaps you are a healer or a teacher. Perhaps you have a degree in one science or another. In those cases, you probably know much more than I do about specific areas. I am certainly no expert on these matters. I have not studied physics or the sciences in this life, and therefore I feel more open to taking some liberties in these areas, and putting them in a context that makes sense to lay people.

Of course, you may well ask, how does that qualify me to write a book on metaphysics, on health, on manifestation of dreams. I can only say to you that we all qualify to write such a book, to teach such subjects, to heal in many different areas of energy work. Buried deep inside you, in your subconscious and your unconscious, is actually all the information I am going to talk about. So I am not teaching anything new, I am merely reminding you of what you already know.

So, to those who do not perhaps know why they picked up this book, I will explain to you my definition of metaphysics.

To me it is the understanding of the non-physical realms and the beings who inhabit those realms, so close to us, yet so invisible to our eyes. Metaphysics is learning about these beings, these worlds, how they work with us guiding us forward, and how we are part of a wider galactic civilization and a very large, very vast, universe. So I could suggest we are talking about the paranormal: that beyond our five senses. Yet, in many ways, these invisible realms are perhaps more real than our life here on earth.

Metaphysics is also about energy and how it affects the physical body, our lives and our world. Understanding how energy works assists us to make better choices in life.

I have been on my journey, physically and emotionally, for what I would say is a considerable time. We call this our journey of ascension: the ultimate ascension into the higher realms, the higher dimensions of the universe. However, this journey started long ago in earth history, and in this lifetime it started when each of us was born and will continue to the day we leave our earth body. We are always, here and in the other realms, in a constant state of experience, expansion and evolution. And so I bring with this book my experiences through my personal journey, and at times the experiences of those who have walked this journey with me. It is a fascinating journey of life, of living, of learning to live life more fully, creating for ourselves the life we always wanted to live: a life that fits neatly around the "health, wealth and happiness" that most of us have always been striving for.

Why haven't we been able to create this life? What has prevented us from having this mythical health, wealth and happiness? Some have it, then lose it, or throw it away on trivialities. I would suggest that so often we either can't create it, or we then lose it, because we have had absolutely no idea of how the energies of life work.

This is what this book is all about. Helping you to understand how life works, and in that place you can then create your dreams. You become empowered to make better choices.

When you read these pages, please allow yourself to be open to receive the energies that will be transmitted to you through these words. I send my unconditional love for you through these words, these pages. As well as that, you will receive the unconditional love of the Ascended Masters, the Higher Beings of Light, the Archangels and Angels, the Gods and Goddesses, from Mother God and Father God, from Creator, or Source, or whatever you wish to call the Supreme Creator of our Universe. You will also receive the love and energies of Mother Earth, of all her many kingdoms of nature; from the elements of air, earth, fire and water; from the sun, moon, planets, stars and many constellations and elements within the universe you are not aware of. All these energies of love and support, love and wisdom, love and higher intelligence, are directed to earth through what we term the Galactic Centre. You receive them, but you can always choose to accept them or ignore them.

I work closely with the Ascended Masters. However, that is not to say I have great communions with them. I do not! Sometimes I hear them, sometimes I get a few words, but on the whole they seem to make me stand in my own power, my own truth. They don't tell me what to do. They empower me to know I can do it!

I have always said I am not particularly psychic, and I guess that is for a very good reason. We must all learn to rely on ourselves, to know that we have the power to know what to do, when and how to do it.

My journey has covered many ups and down, highs and lows, hard work and challenges. It has very much been about clearing and releasing the emotional entanglements of this current life, past lives, parallel lives and ancestors lives. This is where we must all start, and continue until we have cleared and released all the attachments, the false identities, the negative emotions and beliefs that have been programmed into our psyches throughout many thousands of years of incarnations of both ourselves and our ancestors.

Did you know you inherit all of these from your ancestors through your DNA and that you agreed in this lifetime to clear and release them? They can't do it because they are not in human form. You took on this extended role as part of your contract coming to earth this life time, not only clearing this lifetime's negativities but the whole of your past lives and your ancestors. It's a huge job but do not be daunted by it. It is quite doable although very challenging.

This adventure we are on is challenging. I am sure those of you who have been doing this for some time will agree with me. If you are just starting out, I can tell you it will be challenging for you too. However, be assured that the "end justifies the means". The further down this journey you travel, the more peace you will find within yourself, the calmer the mind, the clearer the thoughts and visions, the more wisdom you access, and finally the more "health, wealth and happiness" you can manifest in your life.

I have used simple language and simple concepts in this book, similar to those which I present in my seminars. If you already have an understanding of much of it, I hope you will discover a few new pieces of the puzzle. Otherwise I speak very much to those with a lack of understanding of what energy is and how it works.

And so, let us begin our adventure into the worlds of the unknown, and allow yourself to be excited about what this book contains: the evolution of the human species and that of our beautiful planet.

With blessings
Glenys-Kay

# THE DAWN OF A NEW AGE

*Regarding 2012, some have erroneously concluded in these changing times that the Earth will be eradicated and we say it will not be, cannot be. It matters not what sensational movies and programmes are broadcast in your mass media about such destruction. The Earth cannot be destroyed and will not be annulled . . . so the transformation of the Earth is absolutely not a destruction, rather a requisite and joyous recreation of itself.*

*. . . . Metatron, Lord of Light*

2012 . . . is it all doom and gloom, the prophesized end of the world?
Or . . . does 2013 represent the beginning of a new golden age of empowerment?

There are many doom and gloom prophecies spiraling out of control around the world. These dire prophecies confuse people and send them into fear, which of course is just what those who control our world want. When the world doesn't end after 2012, they will just set another date, as has happened so often in the last century. I remember sitting in class at high school, sometime around 1960, waiting for the world to end. Obviously it didn't or I wouldn't be writing this.

People quote the bible's Judgment Day and the Armageddon. They read distorted translations of the Mayan prophecies, and then of course they are affected and swayed by the great media storm of fear produced in movies like "2012" and others.

My understanding is that during the Cold War, and even during the 1990s, these prophesized events could perhaps have taken place. Is it so hard to believe that we have changed the course of history by choosing to move on to a Path of Light: the return Home through the process of Ascension? This does not mean that we are leaving the planet after ascension. It means that we lift our vibrations to match those of the higher dimensions of consciousness, and in doing so change life forever on this planet.

All matter and life forms that move into the lower third dimensional frequencies are always guaranteed a path back to the higher dimensions from whence they originally came. The planet was always destined to ascend at this point in her history. Humans may have been required to leave the planet to her ascension and reincarnate on to another planet and undertake ascension in a slower manner. However, the gift from Creator was that humanity could have the opportunity to ascend in conjunction with the planet. This has never been achieved before in the universe, and this makes us a very unique life form in both planetary and universal terms.

2012 is only a signpost in the greater divine plan of the ascension of the planet and humanity. The planet has been transitioning for a considerable time, as have spiritual people around the world. It is not about going anywhere. It is quite simply the lifting of vibrational frequencies of the human and then living with the higher truth, wisdom and intelligence that is the result.

The world will not miraculously change on any given date. Humans and society have been gradually transitioning for many decades, particularly since the closure of World War II. We have seen many changes in social thinking, changes in technology, and changes in travel. These are all part of the release of third dimensional restrictions. However, these moves have been more about technology than spiritual advancement, and this is where we are at now: the requirement to return to our spiritual nature which is inherent in our DNA, but which we have refused to listen to for a long time, due mainly to oppressive religious teachings. Many people don't even want to hear the word "God". Why not? Because of the fear induced by man-made religions.

My understanding is that we will see change and shifts happening within the world's social structures, economies, politics and communication for the next 20 years. Changes will continue to happen for another 10-20 years after that, before we can really start to see the new world we are creating. However, according to the higher realms it will be perhaps 200-300 years before the world moves entirely into what we envision as the Golden Age, the Golden Era of New Consciousness.

Although this seems a long time, in reality it is only a blink of the eye in Universal terms.

People are being guided and encouraged to take on this ascension journey before the intensity of the energies increase, which will only serve to exacerbate the negative thoughts and emotions of people who have not done their work. We are seeing people moving into stress, fear and confusion as they experience a loss of control over their lives—the dissolution of finances, jobs, security and relationships. They are witnessing the clearing of Mother Earth by terrible natural disasters and they wonder what is happening to our world. Nothing makes sense anymore and they worry and fear the future.

As you walk this ascension path, you come to realise what is happening. Knowledge takes away the fear. We are extremely fortunate to receive many wisdom teachings from the Ascended Masters, the Archangels and other Higher Beings of Light that assist us to understand the work of creation alchemy.

It is easier and more profound to do your clearing work prior to 2012. Other people who enter this journey later will have perhaps only the next 5 years to do the work and complete their ascension process. After that the ascension door will shut completely for the collective of humanity, although people can still achieve individual ascension at any time.

For those who choose not to ascend in this lifetime, they will ultimately leave the planet through any of the normal means such as illness and death. Many people are not ready for ascension, or they feel they are not ready, and there is no judgment on this. Some will reincarnate back to earth, such as those people who have endeavored to live good wholesome lives, to be caring and compassionate towards others, but perhaps mistakenly handed over their health to the medical establishment to their ultimate detriment. The elderly have not had the opportunity to understand ascension and they will return to earth for another lifetime. Parents of young children who are bound by the rigors of bringing up their children and don't have time to do their spiritual work, will also incarnate back on earth.

Other humans who are totally disbelieving of any other reality; those who misuse energy, and those who are filled with fear and refuse to move onto the path of light, will reincarnate on to another third dimensional planet, perhaps a parallel earth, where they will continue to experience the lower realms of pain, suffering and fear for another cycle before once again the opportunity for ascension is offered.

"No one will be left behind" is what Spirit has told us, and this has been misunderstood by people. It means that ultimately everyone will return to the higher realms. The Creator ensures that all his/her creations are ultimately returned to the realms of love and light. It does not mean that every human on earth now will ascend. Everyone is given the opportunity but most will choose not to. It is this misconstrued meaning that has allowed some people to sit back and think they don't have to do anything to ascend, that it will happen to everyone as a matter of course. Not so! Each individual must do the work for ascension.

Those who are firmly entrenched in the belief of Armageddon will experience such an event on another planet, or another plane of existence. Whatever you believe is what you create for yourself. It is the Law of Attraction.

Those dark misguided energies that have so ruthlessly plundered and polluted our planet will no doubt find themselves in a parallel world where they will indeed experience the results of their deeds. We can say justice will be served, but it is actually about experiencing what they have created. The creator must experience its creations.

## TRANSITION TIME

*Those humans who readily and enthusiastically step into the unknown, we say to you . . . yes, great things await you, but there is much to learn! This transition is not an idle one. It is an ongoing and very active period of adjustment and learning, planning and preparation, completing and beginning.*

*. . . The Pleiadian High Council*

We are in the midst of a momentous time in the evolution of humanity, our planet, our galaxy and the universe. Because of the enormity of the experiment that is being conducted at the earth level, we are being given a doorway of opportunity that will not be offered again for a very long time. This window of opportunity is operating from 1987 to 2012, a period of 25 years, enabling humanity to wake up out of their zombie-like dormant state and begin to seek the truth. This period of 25 years is what I would call an active transition time, moving towards "ascension" or what is often termed "enlightenment". Ascension means moving upwards in vibrational frequency and enlightenment means taking in a higher quotient of light, so both terms are appropriate.

A cosmic alignment of the sun, planets and stars occurred 16th/17th August 1987, called the Harmonic Convergence, signaling the start of the transition doorway which will begin closing at the December planetary solstice 2012 . . . 21.12.12.

However, the ascension process was actually started back in the year zero, the time of the birth of Jesus. Jesus taught the people about freedom, about peace, about unity, about miracles, and about the time in the future when they would be free from control and would, in his words, "create miracles more than I can do". Jesus was anchoring the energy of love and light into a dark world of control and fear in preparation for the future doorway of evolution. Many humans have carried these teachings and the light throughout the last 2000 years, and I call this the "passive transition" time, although it has not exactly been passive for those of us who were thrown in dungeons or burned at the stake for carrying the light. Nonetheless, it has taken 2000 years to get to this fulcrum point where we are now in the midst of the ascension process.

The end of these transition times coincides with the entry of our solar system into the Photon Band. Scientists have wondered how we can survive the photon band with its very intense photonic light. The photon bands are waves of light, or photons, that travel throughout the galaxy as communication networks. Our solar system travels through the photon bands every 13,000 years, and if we survive it regularly, then why not survive it this time?

Our sun entered fully into the photon band in the year 2000, and each year the planets move more into the band for longer periods of time, before becoming fully immersed. Earth has been moving in and out of the band for a number of years and will enter the photon band fully at the beginning of 2013. This matches the completion of cycles and the beginning of new cycles. We travel for approximately 2000 years in the photon band, at which time the earth becomes free of control and pillage, and whereby with the help of enlightened humans, the earth can clear and return to her pristine state.

The earth, however, cannot enter the photon band with the present amount of toxicity that exists within her body from the abuse of humans. She is presently in the process of clearing much of this toxicity and accumulated debris, and we are seeing this in her fires, floods, earthquakes, volcanic eruptions, tsunamis and tornados around the planet. We can help her as much as possible, so the damage and threat to human life is minimalised. It is time for us to wake up and take responsibility for the poisoning of our home.

Similarly, we as humans also cannot survive in the photon band with accumulated garbage and toxicity in our bodies. It is time to start clearing our own toxic debris, the physical, mental and emotional dross from our bodies. This is the journey of ascension, the clearing and releasing of these accumulated negative energies that we call blockages, distortions and illnesses within our physical bodies. These will only be accentuated by the higher and very intense energies of the photon band.

## CHANGING YOUR LIFE

*"Everyone sees change as so frightening, but what if it is a solution to your problems, or the world's problems".*

This transition to the higher vibrational frequencies entails change, and humans have a fear of change. They don't like change, nor do they like having to change. Even if the status quo is painful, humans will stay in their comfort zone which is not comfortable at all, but at least it is familiar. We have a fear of the unknown. We don't know how change will happen, what change will do to us, or how the changes will affect our life. We don't know whether the changes will be good or bad. Consequently we fall back into our comfort zone, afraid of the unknown and too lazy to change.

The universe exists on change. New worlds come from the constant change going on in the universe. Old systems can dissolve and new ways of living can emerge. Life on earth has changed many times. Civilizations have changed many times. Systems of government have changed many times.

> *Everything we hold as truth is coming up for review and reconsideration.*
>
> *Perhaps we could call these our personal earthquakes.*

Life stagnates without change. Perhaps change can be seen as a challenge, but challenges always cause forward movement.

On a personal level, haven't the various stages of our lives been about change? We have often changed residences, jobs, hobbies, relationships; changed our minds, even. Change is nothing to be afraid of, but is simply the way life happens.

Change is about taking responsibility—responsibility for your life. That often requires work and effort from each of us, but a commitment to change moves us forward.

Information can help to take away the fear. When you have knowledge you can make informed choices.


## CYCLES OF TIME

The Maya people of South America were primitive people who lived simple lives, very connected to the earth and the heavens. The ruins of their sacred temples still exist today, where we can visit and feel the energies of the wisdom and information they left for us to interpret. The Maya people originate from the Pleiades Star System, and here on earth they were known as the Record Keepers of Earth Time. They are well known for their Mayan calendar which recorded cycles of time that the earth and its inhabitants move through.

Many students, philosophers and others have studied at great length the hieroglyphics that were left for us, and the interpretations vary widely. If you are interested there are many books available on these interpretations. If you plan on studying Mayan cosmology, be prepared to spend a great deal of your time involved in this. It seems to me very complicated. I prefer to read the information so readily available and take what I feel is right for me to know.

The Mayans prophesized that our world would end in 2012, and this has been the cause for much doom and gloom and fears of the future. The Maya called it the "end times". However, there has been a misunderstanding of this Mayan prophecy.

Life as we presently know it will end.

But our world will not end. Humans are not going to be destroyed. A new cycle will start. A new beginning, a new way of life, and a new concept of society will gradually come into being. This will be based on peace and unity. Can you imagine a world of relative peace and harmony, without corruption? Without pain and suffering, without abuse? The words of John Lennon's song *"Imagine"* really starts to have meaning.

At the December solstice of 2012, many cycles will come to an end.

The Age of Pisces is completing after approximately 2,160 years. The archetypes we have been working under have been the negative qualities of Pisces: power, greed and control. We are moving into the Age of Aquarius for the next zodiacal cycle of 2,160 years and we are now choosing to work under the benefic archetypal energies of Aquarius which are truth, freedom, creativity and multidimensionality.

It takes us 25,920 years to move around all the zodiac signs in the heavens, there being 12 of 2,160 years each. We are familiar with zodiacal houses because this is what we do when we check our horoscopes. This full cycle around the zodiacs is called a Mayan Great Cycle, and the current one is due to complete in December 2012.

A half cycle of approximately 13,000 years, being a cycle of 6 zodiacal houses, is also an important completion point.

The Mayans had many other cycles which of course are completing at the same time, cycles within cycles within cycles. It can be very confusing, but you only need to know the most important of these time cycles.

Four times around a Mayan Great Cycle, of 26,000 years each, equals 104,000 years which is known universally as an Evolutionary Cycle.

At the end of this cycle evolution throughout the universe takes a new expansion and movement forward. The evolutionary cycle coming to a close has been based on reptilian energies. Reptilian energies have been prevalent throughout the universe and their cycle in this galaxy comes to a close. The next evolutionary cycle, as I understand it, will be concentrating on the human form, a balanced human prototype, which is what we are developing on earth now.

If you want to get really serious, there is a 225 million year Galactic orbit/cycle completing. This is also an evolutionary cycle coming to a close and allowing for a new beginning. This is the time it takes for our whole galaxy to circle the centre point of our galaxy, called the Galactic Centre.

So here we are, in the middle of one of the greatest evolutions of our universe, and most people don't even recognise what is happening and don't even want to know. Our physical bodies are evolving into something more advanced, our consciousness is changing to higher wisdom and higher intelligence, our planet and society are evolving into higher dimensions of awareness and truth, and people don't want to know!! I can't believe how well people have been programmed to not believe in the paranormal just because it can't be seen and proved by science. Ask anyone who has experienced a miracle. They believe. This dense programming is all part of the control measures we have been continually subjected to.

However, in spite of all this, science is starting to "prove" many of the spiritual understandings that the ancients knew and that lightworkers have come to understand. Spirituality is a science: the science of life, the science of energy, the science of love.

## A SPIRAL OF EVOLUTION

We live on earth within linear time: time where we perceive a past, present and future. It is within this linear time that we experience our cycles of life times. The universe does not function within linear time, but works within cycles and spirals of space/time continuums: in other words different experiences in different realities of awareness.

This linear time has us under the illusion of past, present and future: the illusion of ageing and death, the illusion that what we see is the real world, and the illusion that we are separate from God. In the "Now" time of the universe all is one with God.

We are currently experiencing time speeding up: the months and years are moving faster. This is helping us to leave the linear time behind us and adopt once more the cycles and spirals of the universe. We will need to adapt to living in the "Now" moment, that which we call the present. The past will not exist as we currently know it. We will remember it but without living within the emotional reactions we have had to it.

The future will exist around us in potentials. We will not be in the same position as working towards a linear future that was easier to predict. The energy of future potentials extends around us in all directions, and it will be more about choosing what we wish to do in the "now" moment.

Humans have been cycling around and around within many lifetimes to experience, learn and gain the wisdom before moving into the spiral of evolution that we call ascension. Each lesson you master and each negative emotion you release moves you forward on to the next step of the ascension ladder.

We will begin see a greater separation between humanity holding on to the old world paradigm, and the lightworkers of the new world paradigm. The world as we know it will gradually change to the new way of living, the fifth dimensional way of the New Earth—the new world.

Evolution doesn't stop when we reach the fifth dimension. Everything in the Universe is constantly moving up through spirals of evolution. We will continue to work towards raising our consciousness to ever higher dimensions of awareness.

## THE ALIENS ARE COMING !

Well, at this point, you may very well put down this book with the thought that I am one of those weird people that believe in aliens, and you just do not want to go there.

However, I know that most people wonder whether aliens are real or not.

Are they real? Are they going to arrive? Are they already here? Who will they be? Are they friends or foes?

We will eventually find these questions answered. As we move into new cycles there are many dimensional time lines meeting and crossing. This creates portals of opportunity for space visitors of other realms to come visit us. Many of them walk among us even now but we can't see them. Perhaps we will have the visitations so much talked about. You see, the Illuminati control methods have kept us in ignorance of what and who live within this galaxy and the wider universe. Do you know that most of the dictators, presidents and governments of the world are quite aware of these space visitors, who actually visit and talk with our leaders, particularly the big countries that are the main players on the stage of world affairs? Perhaps some government president might introduce them to the world via the media of television—what then? What are you going to think about that?

And so dear readers, the time is coming when you will understand, and then your questions will be answered.

Friends or foe? That depends on your level of consciousness, your level of awareness, and the amount of fears you hold concerning these space visitors. If you fear them, then you may find the ones you meet are to be feared. After all, they are not all happy chappies in love with us. Some of them will be similar to the dark energies of the Illuminati that we have experienced here on earth. Nothing new about that! However these visitors may have a different form to human.

In the main I understand that the early space visitors will be those who have been helping us during our ascension journey, those who we will know as our family and friends from outer space. Most of these will have a human form similar to our own. Nothing to fear then from these beautiful beings.

There will be others from around the galaxy and beyond who will arrive in different forms. Will you be ready to meet them?

I can assure you it will happen and the best way you can be ready for these events which are in the not-too-distant future, is to expand your knowledge, lift your consciousness to higher vibrations of frequencies, let go of all old beliefs and prejudices, and all those controlled thoughts that we have received from the Illuminati. The Illuminati would have little chance to control us if we were convinced that entities exist further afield, many vastly more evolved than we are, and often having far more advanced technology.

This does not make us inferior. Not at all. We must hold on to the inner knowledge that we are Divine Aspects of God. When we know and believe this there should be no fear. No one can control us against our will.

All I can say is that you must develop your discernment and your intuition. You will need these feelings to advise you how to react to those you meet.


## THE ILLUMINATI MATRIX

*The information here about the Illuminati is not given to create fear. It is presented to you so you can understand what is happening and start to take back your power. Don't allow yourself to go into fear, because it is adding to the Illuminati's power and control.*

*We are on the path of light, which is called "the ascension journey", or "the path of enlightenment". This combined energy of humans will create peace on earth, or "heaven on earth". We are creating it here, now. Transition time is the starting process.*

If you have heard or read about conspiracy theories, and either dismissed them, or wondered if they were true, well, in the main, they are true. We have been deliberately controlled, manipulated and lied to for perhaps over 3000 years.

So you need to understand this . . . . we have definitely been controlled.

The "Illuminati" are a small group of wealthy families who have controlled and manipulated the human population for their own power and gain. This is the name they give to themselves, meaning the illumined ones. However, we know that they are far from being illumined, or illuminated. To be illuminated means to take on the persona of Unconditional Love of Source/Creator. They definitely do not do this. They are also called The One World Order or The World Management Team.

I am not into studying conspiracy theories, or even focusing on them at any great length. However, there are probably hundreds of books about these people and many articles available. Even the ascended masters refer to them as being the ones who are trying to prevent us in our ascension journey. We cannot be controlled once we have taken back our power, and therefore they will fail if we do so.

If you wish to, research the internet, read the books. David Icke has written many of the leading conspiracy books, and still lives to tell the tale. In the past if you bucked the system you usually ended up dead, and when David Icke is asked why he still lives, he smiles and says "They don't frighten me. I have no fear. As long as I have no fear they can't harm me". And that's a fact about fear that you should bear in mind.

This information about conspiracies and controls is not to instill fear in you, but rather to warn you of that which you may be unaware of. When you become aware of the control forces at work, then you are in a better position to do something about it. You can begin to take back your own power and this knowledge assists you to do that.

The Illuminati control us in many ways, but their main avenues as I see it are in the Media, Economy, Education, Religion and Medical systems. When I am talking about these areas of control, please know that I am not talking about the grass roots lay people, the teachers, bankers, priests, reporters, doctors, etc. I am speaking of the hierarchy of control forces, those that set in motion the methods of control.

## MEDIA

One of the main ways of controlling the minds of people is through radio, television and magazines, and in particular news reporting. We all know that our news portrays all the chaos, calamities and violence throughout the world. It shows us pictures of death and destruction. It portrays the world as a terrible place to be afraid of. Wars, terrorism, murders, abuse, rapes, and much more are the common news we see and hear every day.

We often ask, why does the news not tell us the good things?

Well, please believe that it is controlled. We are fed a daily dose of negative brainwashing that induces fear into people, and people in a state of fear are easy to control. There is a very easy remedy to this brainwashing . . . . it is called the "off" button.

Newspapers rarely report the truth so don't believe all you read.

Advertisements, both on television and in magazines, are also an excellent control mechanism. Look at all the people who rush around after all the latest fashion trends, the latest diets, the latest props of the modern world, the latest toys and gadgets. These advertisements seduce people into spending money they don't have, perhaps going into debt. When you are in debt, you are controlled. You must go to work, usually doing something you don't enjoy, just to pay the bills. This is not the life you were destined to live as an evolved human on earth.

A home filled with gadgets does not make you happy. Indeed not long after you have purchased the latest toy, you are bored with it. Children are very easily bored with the latest toys or gadgets, simply because they allow for no creativity. Creativity is the fulcrum of life, without it we perish and die. You cannot create your dreams if you spend all your time with gadgets. They are designed to waste your precious time and distract you from what you should be concentrating on . . . . your personal evolution journey.

Women's magazines depict stories of the false lives of the stars of the music and movie industries and lead us to believe that these are normal behaviours. These magazines sell us the need for a wide range of cosmetics, the food plans that will help us to lose weight and become one of the stick figures they portray that we are meant to emulate.

Take your power back and trust your own judgment, not what is handed to you through the media.

## ECONOMY

We are under the control of the monetary system, and it never lets us, or most of us let's say, have enough. We seem to live eternally in survival mode, with only just enough money to get by.

We need the gadgets, the toys, the latest fads, and so we have to work to buy them. We want a new house, new furniture, the latest vehicle, trips abroad. And so we must work to pay for them. They don't come free.

Have you ever wondered who owns the banks? Well, we could certainly look to the Illuminati. Banks are an excellent way of controlling people. Pay the people a pittance, make them pay through the nose for what they need or want, and make people pay taxes to support the war effort, leaving them with just enough to survive on.

That is being controlled!

Imagine, way back somewhere in time, the Illuminati may have been thinking of a new method of control. What can we do? "Let's start up a bank". So they create a building with the word BANK in big letters above the door. No money on hand. Just an idea to make money. Then they advertise and tell the people they will lend them money to buy whatever they want.

Imagine a man sitting on his couch watching TV every night. He sees an advertisement for a flash new 4WD vehicle. He would very much like one but he can't afford it. Every night he sees the same advertisement and wants it even more. Down the track he starts to think he needs this vehicle. He doesn't merely just desire it, he now thinks he needs it. He gets to the point where he just has to have it. This is the so-called brainwashing.

So he goes down to this new bank and asks if they will lend him the money. "Of course, but you will need to give us a 20% deposit in cash, and then pay instalments plus interest every month for 3 years". So the good man hands over his hard-earned 20% deposit. The bank man pulls out his computer and enters a credit entry to Joe Bloggs Car Sales, and then says "Okay, it's all paid for. Just go down and collect it".

This man has to work extra hard, perhaps 50 hours a week, to get enough money to pay his instalment each month. After 3 years he has paid it all, and now owns the vehicle. Great! Or is it? Unfortunately for him he has paid probably nearly twice as much as the original price, and the 3-year-old vehicle is probably worth only a quarter of the original price.

Meanwhile the bank man rubs his hands together and says "Well, that was a good deal. I didn't have any money to start off with, I gained 20% cash initially, and now I have the total borrowed money plus interest. And I didn't have to do a thing except write a computer entry".

We can see from this conceptual story that the media brainwashed this man into the purchase, and the bank controlled him for 3 years because he had to go out to work every day to earn the money to pay them.

Why do you think you pay taxes? Merely to keep the country running smoothly? No. Your taxes are to keep you poor. You have to work hard to earn your money, and then someone grandly takes a big chunk out of it for their own needs. Have you ever thought exactly what that money of yours gets used for? Ridiculous wars, unnecessary military personnel and equipment, dozens of members of parliament who often abuse their privileges and at the same time fight like children. There is not a great deal of either business acumen or sensible leadership amongst them. They take their salaries which we provide, and then dictate to us how we should live our lives. Don't get me wrong here . . . these in the main are good people. They just don't know how they are really being used to control and manipulate the people . . . us!

Here in New Zealand in the eyes of the Inland Revenue Department (unless things have radically changed) you are guilty until you prove yourself innocent. Pay your taxes, or else!

Did you realise that there is no law here in New Zealand that says you have to pay income tax? Great, I hear you say, I won't pay any then. Well, of course there is always a checkmate. In this case you can't work unless you have an IRD number, and once you have that, you have accepted the system! Some people have apparently been waking up to this and refusing to pay tax, so the Inland Revenue has effectively closed that loophole by now giving each new baby born an IRD number . . . long before the child has the opportunity to disagree or refuse. That's control and manipulation of the system we pay for.

## EDUCATION

I am sure we are all aware that education at one time was only for privileged young men, sons of the wealthy who would eventually take over family businesses. The poor were not educated and girls certainly weren't considered intelligent enough to educate. Eventually education was given to the poorer boys but only up until a certain age when they were required to go to work to help support their family.

Nowadays most children in western cultures receive an education, but what sort of education do we get? Is it knowledge that we can utilize in our lives, or is it most often just a lot of useless information that means absolutely nothing to the student and has no influence on their standard of living in the future. Look at how most education systems do not teach good nutrition and exercise to students, do not teach health and wellbeing, do not teach the true history and heritage of humanity, and do not teach spirituality and knowledge of the wider cosmos and the universe. By spirituality I do not mean religion. Religion is not a true teaching. It is a controlled and manipulated dogma. To this we can add the old regime of religious schools with their harsh methods, their harsh punishments and their lack of compassion and love. Children were not encouraged to love God, but were encouraged to fear a God of Wrath.

Education should encourage students to explore the meaning of life. They should be helped to become empowered to make wise decisions. They should be taught integrity, honesty, and compassion for others. Above all their studies should be relevant to highly intelligent young people destined to lead the world of the future.

Intelligent, well educated students pose a threat to the Illuminati. Children are encouraged to become zombies, both with the gadgets and toys, but also the alcohol and drugs so freely available. It's high time adults took power back into their own hands regarding the raising of their children. However, so often the parents are simply too exhausted and stressed trying to work just to pay the bills—no time left for their children!

Today, even the teachers are discouraged by the education system. Both students and teachers alike fight to change the system, but it all appears to come back to monetary issues which of course then relate to the control issues. However, there are now free teachings becoming widely available through the Internet and this is and will continue to radically change education.

We are also aware that many children in third world countries do not get an education: rather, they are abused physically and sexually, and also mentally, emotionally and spiritually deprived. Sending young children out to work long hours with little food or money is slave labour, and the same can be said for the prostitution of children. This should be unacceptable to every sane and intelligent human on the planet. Children should be honoured for their beautiful presence among us.

## RELIGION

If we go back to the years of Jesus, the time of the Roman Empire, where he walked among his people teaching them of the love of his Father, he said that people could become free, they didn't need to be enslaved. His gospels preached of peace, unity and the Golden Age that was coming. He was a balm to the emotional destitution that was so prevalent in those times. It was a difficult way of life and he told the people how it would improve. He said that the miracles he performed, they could perform too.

He created a large following of people who responded to his words, to his presence and to his talk of the Love of his Father.

The Roman Senators did not like this as it was usurping their power and control over the people. The people started not to listen to their rulers, and followed instead the man from Nazareth, the man called Yeshua ben Josef, today called Jesus the Christ.

The Romans did everything they could to criticize his teachings, to ridicule him, to harass him, to discourage his speeches. But they could not succeed. His teachings were too strong, and Jesus did not fear the authorities. So he became a thorn in their side and they needed to get rid of this usurper in their midst. After many attempts to discredit him had failed, they found their ultimate result in a false trial and the crucifixion we know so well.

However, this did not deter the people. They continued to follow the disciples and the teachings of Jesus, declaring themselves free men and practicing the beliefs that he had instilled in them.

So the Roman Senate decided to take the teachings of Jesus and turn them to their own agenda. They set up the Roman Church, set up priests of these churches, and told the people that this was where the teachings of Jesus would be practiced. They established the doctrines that would give them their control back, and the people, eager to follow the gospels, obligingly, and in their ignorance, went to church to pay homage to the Father. For this, they handed over their precious little money to pay the priests to be the instruments of communication for them.

These people, and all people that have followed, have given their power away to the churches and to the priests, and allowed them to determine their fate with God. For 2,000 years the churches have played this role, taking our money, and telling everyone they were not good enough to talk directly to God the Father because we were all born sinners. They introduced the God of Wrath, the image of hell if we didn't obey. Many religions, priests and pastors, cults and sects, have brought people to their knees with their hellfire and brimstone sermons. Fear was instigated so successfully and in such huge measure, that even today many people are frightened of God, of hell, and of not being good enough to receive entry into heaven; too frightened to die even.

Now I need you to understand something very important. The Illuminati was back then, the Roman Senate. Different name, different time, but same purpose . . . to control the people. They certainly achieved that end. Religion has dominated the planet ever since, and definitely not to the spiritual benefit of the people.

The Bible, centre point of western religion, has been written, translated and re-written many times, each time being changed with deletions, alterations and additions that established a wider control over the people. In time the Roman Church became the Roman Catholic Church, and most other Western religions have stemmed from this original source.

The so-called "freedom" of western religion is contained within dogma and doctrines. Religion seeks to control freedom of thought by telling their people what to believe and how to live.

It doesn't take much effort to study religious history. It's all on the Internet and in many books. History records the millions of innocent people who have died in religious wars. Our God of Love, the Creator, had nothing to do with these wars. They were carried out by men in the name of God. Most wars on the planet have been to do with fighting for what each side believed was the true God.

The Popes of the Catholic Church have a long history of debauchery, lust, power and greed, and the laws of celibacy did not apply to the early Popes.

So many gods; every religious culture has their own version of God. Whatever people believe is their truth. There should be no need to fight to prove that you are right and they are wrong. Everybody should be allowed the freedom to believe in the God of their choice, even if it is an incorrect version. It is wrong to suppress people because of their beliefs of their God. There is no right and wrong, only different versions of the truth.

Millions of soldiers, men, women and children were slaughtered for the sake of prejudicial beliefs. It is unbelievable what humans can do to each other. We are only now realising that violence never achieves peace. Only peaceful humans can achieve peace on our planet.

Many Western people have turned to Eastern religions because they seem more real. In Buddhism they relate to the search for peace, freedom and the ultimate truth. Within Taoism is the acceptance that all of life is oneness. Even the foundation of Islam is the love of God, merely subverted and misused according to the whims of men.

It is time to take your power back. You do not need anyone to communicate with God on your behalf. He will listen and talk to you anytime.

If you have a religious faith, please do not feel I am attacking you personally. I have a great deal of respect for those of genuine faith, because after all, that is about the Love of God and you must never lose sight of that. That is where we are all heading: to that Unconditional Love of Source. You do not need a religion to get there unless you choose to. Often people need the companionship and support that a church and its members offer.

I hope I have encouraged you to think outside the box and see a bigger picture.


## HEALTH

Over time the public began to be disillusioned by the doctrines of the churches, and congregations were diminishing in numbers.

So the Roman Catholic Church, albeit the Illuminati, decided to establish another form of control. They left the Vatican as the head of the church, but re-established their headquarters in Washington DC. They set up a system of control that we call politics. Under the banner of politics they set up various state departments of control. Their most effective ones were probably the Military, which pushed for wars and acts of terrorism, the Inland Revenue Service which took in the money from a wide range of taxes, much of which was and is used to support the war effort, and the state departments of the American Medical Association, the American Dental Association and the Federal Drug Administration. Through these later avenues they began controlling the health of the public.

Under the auspices of these departments, they set up the Pharmaceutical Industry, which has been a multi-trillion dollar earner for their coffers.

For centuries natural methods of healing had been in place, but the Pharmaceutical Industry could not patent plants. They needed to take the substances from the plants and convert them to drugs, in order to patent them. This commenced their stake in the diseases and illnesses of the people. If people were cured and made well by these drugs we would live in a disease free society, but we do not. If people were cured and made well then we would all have healthy lives full of vitality and energy, but we do not. They tell us that people today are living longer, but is the quality of life there? If it is, then why are hospitals, rehabilitation units and rest homes so full of half-dead people?

In order to sell more drugs, they set up the Medical Training Schools where doctors learnt about drugs and surgery. Which drug to give for what symptom, and what to surgically remove if there is no response to the drug. Doctors have not learnt about ancient systems of healing. They have not been taught about natural plant medicines, energy healing, and other alternative methods of treatment that in the majority of cases are more effective than orthodox treatment. They have not even been taught nutrition and exercise, although many doctors today take it upon themselves to learn and understand.

Medical Sales Representatives are well trained in selling their pharmaceutical products. Many doctors report being tired and busy and find these sales reps extremely good at getting their products in the door.

I am not saying that all drugs and surgery are unnecessary. On the contrary I believe they are very important in specific illnesses and problems. Mechanical defects, even such as a broken arm or leg, need surgery to correct the breakage. However, it is time that people took back their power and researched the effectiveness and the side effects of the proposed drugs, or proposed surgery. Spend time researching alternative methods. Armed with the necessary research you can then make an informed decision. In many cases, people have gone so far down the orthodox treatment path that they are left with no alternative but to continue.

As if they hadn't made enough money from the drugs alone, the Medical Establishment introduced immunizations. In many instances this prevents the body from establishing its own immune defence. This is especially the case with babies where their immune systems aren't fully established, and immunizations may well prove to be detrimental in the long run. There have been serious problems arising from many immunizations, which parents can often relate to the child's time of the immunization, but which the medical establishment denies. The older immunizations were safer because they were only aimed at a few specific areas. Nowadays, modern immunizations for babies contain ingredients for over 20 different diseases. That is way too much for a baby to safely handle, and the amalgamating of so many chemicals goes against every grain of commonsense that doctors should have. There are homeopathic alternatives that are safer, but of course nowadays we have day care centres, kindergartens and schools refusing to take children who have not been immunized. Young parents are made to feel guilty if they do not wish to immunize their children.

Then we have Ritalin, the controversial drug that you either love or hate. Some people find it very effective without any side effects. Ritalin causes changes in the personality of many people, and especially vulnerable children—changes which may never be reversed. Many children labeled ADD (Attention Deficit Disorder), and ADHD (Attention Deficit Hyperactive Disorder) are given Ritalin to quieten their disruptive behaviour. Perhaps these behavourial problems are nothing whatsoever to do with illness, mental or otherwise. Society should look more closely at why our children suffer from these disorders, which are actually to do with the higher vibrational frequencies and enhanced DNA that these children are born with.

Personally I feel that Ritalin compares with the psychotic drug P, the methamphetamine that is causing such a lot of the violent behaviour throughout society. There are babies being born already addicted to P.

Of course we cannot forget HRT, Hormone Replacement Therapy. This was only an experiment in a laboratory, was never tested and never received approval from the FDA. Yet it was given to menopausal women and then post-menopausal women to prevent hot flushes and other uncomfortable symptoms of menopause. Do your research. You may find out that it comes from mare's urine (as in horses). Do I need to say more?

Currently we have Gardasil being forced on teenagers to prevent cervical cancer.

If you look at the suppression of women, does the following analogy make sense to you. Male and female babies are immunized, which may or may not have serious consequences. School age children also receive immunizations. Teenage girls are given Gardacil. Pre-menopausal women, menopausal women, and post-menopausal women are given some form of hormone replacement therapy, whether they really need it or not. They just trust the doctor knows what he is talking about. Then elderly women, and even today younger and younger women, are given some form of synthetic calcium to prevent bone fractures, which has proved ineffective, and in some people has been the cause of heart attacks and strokes due to calcification of arteries. So we can say that right across the board, females of all ages are being suppressed by the pharmaceutical industry, who are allowed to get away with it.

Then we have the big "C", cancer. People donate so much money to fund the research into finding a cure for cancer. It could be reasonable to assume that the medical establishment probably doesn't want to find a cure for cancer. It's a good control method and a big money spinner through the sale of chemotherapy drugs.

There is no single cause for cancer: it is multi-faceted, and triggered in many ways. Stress plays a big part and suppressed negative emotions an even bigger part. Living a life without joy and happiness possibly plays the biggest part. There are so many things, and people need to start looking internally for their cancer problems, not rely on the medical establishment which does not have a lot of answers.

Chemotherapy and radiation may work on more minor cancer issues caught early, but on the whole these do not appear to be successful. Doctors have been reported as saying that if they had cancer they wouldn't undergo chemotherapy because it doesn't work. However, their problem is they have little else to offer.

With the swing away from dangerous pharmaceutical drugs, people are moving back to alternative methods, back to herbs, homeopathics, flower essences, wholesome nutrition and exercise. This has forced the Illuminati, in this case in the guise of Codex, to bring in controls throughout the world to prohibit the sale of these natural products. Can you believe it? If we don't do what they want, then they take away our privileges.

## OTHER CONTROL METHODS

With the public becoming disillusioned with pharmaceuticals, the Illuminati turned their attention to the food industry. "If we can't control them through drugs, then let's control the food they eat". The fast food industry's unwritten mandate is to make money at any cost.

Processed foods have no nutritional value, but are purported to be a boon to our busy lifestyles. All they really do is de-energise our bodies. It is interesting that medical research is showing us that even with the world wide epidemic of obesity, many doctors are seeing people through their clinics suffering from nutritional deficiencies. These people may be obese, but are actually starving.

There are also addictions such as tobacco, alcohol, social drugs and hard drugs. Many people are addicted to carbohydrates and/or sugars which can lead to diabetes.

Another control mechanism which has made billions of dollars is the petrochemical industry. Our western world is reliant on oil and any threat of oil shortages creates fear in people. They cannot imagine how we can live without petrol or diesel for our cars and planes, and without oil for industry.

We have looked at how we are controlled. Now the question is . . . why?

Firstly, Greed. They want to own all the resources. These people want to have all the money. There is no way they can use all this money but they still want it. They like knowing they own everything.

Secondly, Power. These people love the power. They love the knowledge that they are in charge and everyone is in their service.

Thirdly, the energy of Fear. These people feed on the energy of fear. How do they do this, and why? I will look at this later in the book.

## THE MEDICAL ESTABLISHMNENT

Please note here that I am mostly speaking of the medical establishment of western civilization. However, this medical system has infiltrated most countries to take power away from the people of the world.

As a concept let us go back to after World War II when doctors came back from the war experienced in dealing with war casualties. They had all this knowledge and experience, and perhaps said to the people, "If you give us your bodies to look after, we know what makes them work and we can keep you healthy". People thought this sounded pretty good so they gave over their bodies to the medical people to look after. This was the initial handing over of our power to heal ourselves to the medical profession.

Move on to perhaps around the 1960s-70s, when the medical profession started to think that the mind played a part in healing. So they researched this concept, and the result was that some medical doctors specialized in the mind, and others continued to work with the body. These became two different areas, and mostly did not attempt to correlate their work and findings. Again, we handed over the power of our mind to the medical profession as well as our body.

Perhaps about the late 80s early 90s the new age trend came up with the idea that spirit was a component of the healing process. So began the concept of mind, body, spirit healing. The doctors said, "Well we do know that sometimes faith and prayers play a part in healing, so perhaps there is something in that, but we don't know anything about it. We can't examine spirit, we can't see it, we can't touch it, can't put it under a microscope, we really don't know what it means at all". So they chose to ignore the concept, even ridicule it, and it was left to the alternative therapists to continue with healing modalities that incorporated spirit.

To a certain extent, people took back some of their power by using alternative methods, but whenever something serious occurred then it was off to the orthodox medical practitioners, who by now they, in particular the older generation, have come to believe is "God" as far as treatment of symptoms is concerned. "Give me a pill, doctor, and make my pain go away". By far and large, the medical profession simply looked to drugs and/or surgery to fix a patient. Sometimes it worked very well, but many times it didn't.

> *The fact that we are now faced with such an onslaught of problematic drugs is a testament to the inadequacies, not to mention criminal behavior, of the pharmaceutical industry.*

When graduating, each medical doctor takes an oath which basically says "do no harm". Perhaps it is time doctors took this seriously.

To this point, we had mostly given our power to the medical establishment to look after us. If it had worked effectively as they told us, and continue to tell us, then we would all be running around now fit and healthy, leading full and active lives. Instead, there is a general deterioration in the health of people in the western world and even further afield. People might live longer, but is the quality of life there? The measure of success is looking at the vitality of people, not statistics.

Statistics can be manipulated into anything the establishment wants you to believe, so don't believe all statistics. However, there are a large number of reports and statistics produced indicating that medical mistakes, medical misadventures and medical misdiagnoses are the largest causes of death in the western world.

Moving along in our concept to the mid 90s, energy healing started to come into vogue. The realizations and understandings of cosmic energy and vibrational frequencies had made great inroads. We then had a new concept to consider. To heal, we needed to take into account the physical body, mental body, emotional body, spiritual body, and also now, the vibrational frequencies of cells.

It is time, dear readers, to take back our power and heal ourselves. This can be with the help of a healer, therapist, counselor, doctor, whatever. But take back your power by doing your own research, and do not simply believe everything you are told.

The pharmaceutical industry controls the medical establishment, and they are in this to make money, not for the health of the people. If all the people were well and healthy, they would be unable to make money. So their greed for riches entails them doing everything in their power to keep people sick. In this way, they also have control over people. If you are well and healthy, then you have the intelligence, the stamina and the drive to question authority. When you are sick you are very easily controlled, and manipulated into believing what they tell you.

Please understand . . . the medical establishment at the highest level, is not here to help you get better. They want and need you to be sick. Then they have both the power and the money.

# *OUR DISEASE CONSCIOUSNESS*

*Comments from Dr Ulric Williams, Surgeon and Naturopath, 1890-1971*

- *Abraham Flexner, sponsored by the American Medical Association, recommended that pharmaceutical medicine be taught in medical schools, and that all health care practitioners should be rigorously trained scientists. This recommendation was accepted, thereby excluding preventative medicine, nutrition, alternative therapies, natural healing etc. from being taught. The result has been over 90 years of escalating disease rates.*

- *Hospitals are disease factories. I never became a real doctor until I forgot 95% of what I learned. Doctor means teacher. A doctor's chief duty is to teach people how to be well. Most disease comes from fear. A doctor's first duty is to allay fear.*

- *My first rule of health: Never eat when you are not hungry. Man is the only animal that hasn't enough sense to stop eating when he is sick. If you are well and want to stay that way, half your food should be eaten raw. If you are sick and want to get better, three quarters of your food should be eaten raw.*

- *Other rules: Foods need to be fresh, natural, whole and simple. Food as God made it, not as man mucks about with it. Drink water. The most important food is oxygen. Exercise in fresh air. You are what you eat: you can't expect your body to run well if you put rubbish into it.*

• *On the spiritual dimension: Our whole Self needs peace: peace comes from thoughts of love, faith and forgiveness. Faith means expecting good things to happen instead of expecting bad. Love means seeing good in all things, even things we don't like. Forgiveness means saying "If I forgive this person, God can use my forgiveness to put things right." Forgiveness means saying: This person did the best they could with the knowledge and awareness and understanding they had at the time, I set them free from my condemnation." Throw out the resentment by forgiving people who annoy you.*

• *The world is a beautiful and wonderful place. If you don't see it that way you are looking at it upside down.*

• *No disease is incurable, but some patients are, because they don't want to change. They go down to death like sheep in a slaughter race, just because they will not change. You cannot hope to be healed unless you throw out all fear and all resentment. These cause hormones to be secreted in the brain, which are very potent and very toxic in excess.*

• *All disease comes from one of two places, either an unhealthy way of life with poor diet, drinking, smoking and lack of exercise. Or else it comes from unhappiness in the mind and spirit. Disease in nearly every case is merely the effect upon our bodies or minds of psychological or physical barriers to health. The diseases will go when we ourselves take the barriers down.*

• *You don't have to do anything to get better, all you need is to stop doing what is wrong. If you really want to know what that is, your divine intelligence will tell you. Your body has a healing power that will heal you when you stop making yourself sick.*

*Taken from New Zealand's Greatest Doctor: Ulric Williams,*
*by Brenda Sampson, 1977.*

# THE UNIVERSE
# AND ITS LAWS

*All any scientist can do is lift up one small corner of the veil that*
*covers the truth of this world, and then try to express it in words*
*that the general population can stretch their minds around.*

*"The Secret Life of Water" by Masaru Emoto*

**WHAT IS TRUTH?**

During the 15th century people thought that the world was flat, and that if they sailed to the horizon they would fall off. This was the 'truth' of the day. However Ferdinand Magellan's ships sailed around the world in 1519-1522 and proved that it was round. So the beliefs of people had to change to accommodate new information. It was of course already understood that the earth was a sphere but the people were kept in ignorance by the church.

In the 16th century people believed we were the centre of the universe and that our planet was stationary and the sun moved around us. In 1543, Copernicus, an astronomer and canon of the church, realised that in fact the earth and planets traveled around the sun. However, this new information was not revealed until he was on his deathbed, in a book he had written on his findings. The church at that time wanted people to believe that this was the only world that existed, and that we were the only beings in the universe. As a canon of the church, Copernicus knew his life would be in jeopardy if he went against the doctrines of the church. When this news was released the church ridiculed the information and it took a long time for science to validate his work. Today we know that indeed we travel around the sun, along with all the other planets. Once this work was scientifically acknowledged, then people had to change their beliefs. We were not the centre of the universe at all.

To bring this concept closer to home, imagine you are standing on a beach on a beautiful clear day. The sky is blue, the sea is flat, the horizon in the distance is a straight line between sea and sky, indicating no waves and swell on the water. There is nothing on the horizon: not a ship in sight. Now if someone handed you a telescope and when you looked through it, suddenly you could see a ship on the horizon, you would have to change your belief that moments before there was no ship there. Now you know there is because you can see it through the telescope.

So this brings us to the understanding that what we see or perceive, creates what we believe. What we see and believe, we accept as our 'truth'. When we receive new information our belief, and therefore our 'truth', has to change.

So truth for us is not set in concrete. It changes according to what we believe. We can never say "this is the truth, the only truth, there is no other truth". Your 'truth' will always change according to your beliefs and your perceptions, and in that, your perception is based on your level of awareness. When you have a higher level of knowledge and wisdom, your perception of what is the truth will be different from that of people existing on a lower level of awareness. So the perception of truth varies, and this does not make anyone right or wrong. Our individual truth is simply based on our level of awareness.

Always be open to new information. If your mind remains closed to new things this can prevent you from moving forward.

As I have already stated, please do not just take my beliefs, my 'truths' and make them yours, simply because you can't be bothered to research any further. That's laziness, and the universe does not support laziness. Read, listen, ask questions, and then keep what resonates with you and discard the rest.

There is one Truth, and one only Ultimate Truth. That is, the Unconditional Love of the Creator. This is the foundation of the universe and everyone and everything within it. This Truth is the only Truth you should totally believe in, and that it never ever changes. This is what your journey is all about: a return to the Ultimate Truth of the Creator, a total belief in Unconditional Love which connects us all within this vast universe.

## COSMIC ENERGY

So, what is energy? Where does it comes from, where does it go, how is it created?

We are inclined to think of energy as just physical energy . . . the energy to get up in the morning and do our work, our sports, looking after family, or home and garden perhaps. We often don't feel we have enough of this physical energy to do what we really want to do. We also understand that energy is used to power our houses and farms, our communication networks, even the cars we drive. However, energy is much more than that.

I use the term cosmic energy, which to me is the totality of energy within the universe, used in a myriad of ways. Cosmic energy can be called Source energy, Creator energy, God energy, spiritual energy, white light, higher dimensional energy or photonic energy and perhaps many other names in different cultures.

Cosmic energy comes to us from the sun as solar energy, from the moon as lunar energy, from the stars as stellar energy, from the planets as spirit energy, and from Source as creation energy. We actually receive some form of cosmic energy from everything within the galaxy, and perhaps the wider universe, and so a passing comet will emit rays of energy which we will then receive here on earth. We also receive energy from Mother Earth and her many kingdoms.

Everything that exists must be created from cosmic energy. Cosmic energy is actually light, which exists as photons we call electrons or atoms of energy, or perhaps quarks or quanta in science. The electrons spin: fast, slow and at trillions of frequency speeds in between. It is the vibrational frequencies of the spinning atoms that dictate the denseness of matter (the density of form).

These photons of light, the electrons, travel around the universe in what we term as waves, waves of light. Each photon contains information. These waves of light represent the communication system of the universe, a universal "Internet", and this is the role of the photon bands. Cosmic waves, or rays, can therefore be defined as "cosmic intelligence".

As humans we are also made from cosmic energy and we exist as groups of electrons, atoms and molecules. These spin and create vibrational frequencies that we radiate outward.

Many people are familiar with what is known in science as the Schumann Resonance, and science tells us that this resonance cycles at 7.8hz (cycles per second). This is the base resonance, or vibrational frequency emitted from the core of our planet, which we can say is the pulse or heartbeat of Mother Earth. Science has in recent times discovered that the Schumann Resonance has altered, now cycling at 12hz, and the Ascended Masters have suggested that it will rise to over 13hz.

Energy is infinite: it never dies nor is it completely destroyed forever. Energy can only change in some way, such as transforming (changing form, structure, or function), transmutation (similar meaning, although we use this term when we are talking about changing dense dark energies into the energy of light and love), translocation (a shift in time/space), transduction (stepping down the vibrational frequencies, as in telephone communications), fractualize (split/divide into smaller parts), or refraction (as in a prism, splitting into different facets/vibrational frequencies seen by us as colours).

Energy merges and melds, and this is a normal occurrence throughout the universe for many different reasons. There are no secrets in the universe and all information is shared. When one light being or master wishes to access the wisdom or information from another, if agreed to by both parties, they simply meld together, whereby the information is downloaded as energy packets, they then separate and the transfer has happened.

Energy has a completion point. All creations have a finite time span, reaching a point of completion. This may be a star, a planet, life forms or civilizations. These go through a transformation of energy. These completed systems enter into a black hole where the energy is transformed into neutral energy, which is then birthed through the white hole on the other side. This rebirthed energy exists as the energy of potential, awaiting creation into another form, perhaps new galaxies, planets or suns within the universe.

A black hole exists in the centre of every galaxy and is a vast spinning vortex. The universe has to have a means by which completed energies can be renewed. Black holes are not something to be feared, but exist to carry out a very necessary function within the universe.

Cosmic energy is fluid, malleable, changeable. It is in continual expansion, contraction and evolution. This is how the universe and life exists. If it is not fluid and flowing without restriction, then energy gets stuck. This is what humans are currently working through—unblocking stuck energy so life force energy flows again through our physical bodies.

All these changes of form or function is called alchemy. Alchemy is known as the science of turning base metals into gold, but it is also the transformation of anything and everything into something else.

The Spiritual Science of Alchemy uses the mind to alter energy, therefore thoughts change or manifest the creation desired.

We are energy beings made up of atoms that spin, which create vibrational frequencies. Our physical body and our aura, which is our non-physical body, exist as energy. We can therefore carry out all of the above changes, along with everything and everyone in the universe.

Humans, both individually and collectively, together with the planet, are currently undergoing an Alchemy of Consciousness: changing the consciousness of ourselves as third-dimensional humans and that of our planet to a fifth-dimensional consciousness.

## VIBRATIONAL FREQUENCIES

Vibrational frequencies can be dense, heavy and slow, and then move up a scale of infinitesimal graduation, getting lighter and faster. As the spinning atoms move up this scale, they become invisible to the naked eye. Laser rays, x-rays, gamma rays and microwaves are all rays of light of fast spinning electrons creating higher vibrational frequencies invisible to the eye. The colour spectrum is an example of our visible view of vibrational frequencies; each colour being a graduated scale of frequencies giving us the variety of shadings we see. There is a far vaster range of luminescent colours within the universe: we just can't see them.

We understand the difference between tuning into an AM or FM radio station. They operate on two different bands of frequencies, and you cannot tune in to both at once. You must be on the right band for the station you wish to hear. Each station on these bands has its own frequency.

When microwaves first came out they operated in a frequency band between 650khz and 850khz and in this range of unseen frequencies your food was cooked. When cell phones became available, the authorities had to find a band of frequencies for them to operate within, and it is my understanding that microwaves were moved into a higher band of frequencies between 850khz and 1050khz and because the spin of the unseen electrons is faster, your food is cooked faster. Cell phones were placed in the band 650khz to 850khz. When you are using your cell phone, or you have it at your ear day in and day out, or keep it close to your vital organs, please remember this range of frequencies cooks your food. What effect is this having on your organs, your ear, or indeed your brain?

## OUR UNIVERSE

Energy never dies, only expands or contracts, and evolves. Therefore the universe is infinite—eternal, either expanding outwards into new experiences, or contracting back to the whole.

The universe is teeming with spinning electrons, or atoms as I prefer to call them for non-scientific people. We can therefore say our universe is atomic, or even nuclear. Everything created within the universe, including humans, is made up of those very electrons/atoms and that makes us atomic as well. That may sound frightening, but it is just saying we are made of energy . . . the same energy that created the universe. Divine intent behind atomic creations is safe, whereas the negative intent behind nuclear weapons on earth is destructive and devastating, and has an effect on everything in the universe.

There are thousands of universes, and universes within universes. There are multiverses, parallel universes and alternate universes, collectively known as the Omniverse. We cannot possibly comprehend these vast fields of energy. Universes are set up for many reasons: varieties of experiences, expansion and evolution. You do not have to know or understand about these many other universes. It is quite enough attempting in some way to understand our own.

We are told to imagine that our universe is about the size of four rugby fields and that our entire galaxy would fit on to the head of a pin with room to spare. So the vastness is unimaginable, probably making each of us feel very small and insignificant. Not so! In the vastness of this universe we are actually extremely important, each one of us.

Even though we are given the four rugby fields analogy, the universe is actually a toroid, a toroidal shape, a shape like a doughnut with a hole in the middle. The hole in the middle represents the God Matrix, the centre of the universe and home to the Spiritual Hierarchies. Around this centre are layers and layers of experiential realms, or dimensions as we term them. So the vastness of the universe is contained within these many layers.

Within this universe are literally thousands of galaxies, suns/solar systems, planets, worlds, civilizations and life forms. Galaxies are the form of creation in which various worlds and life forms can experience life in a myriad of alternate ways. It is obviously ignorant of us to assume that we are the only life in the universe, and even more so, the speculation that we are the most intelligent life form. Why would we say that, unless we ignorantly assume there is nothing "out there" but empty space. That seems illogical no matter how scientifically knowledgeable you may or may not be. Many civilizations in the universe are ancient, we are probably one of the newest.

We need to understand that humans are not the only life form that exists. There are civilizations and intelligent life forms that exist throughout the universe, many not of human form. The reptilian form has been the predominant form in this galaxy through the last Galactic Cycle, known as the Reptilian Cycle.

Remember the movie Star Wars? Remember all those different creatures that were seen in the movie? This was the start of the education of humans in regard to the existence of other life forms in the universe. Star Trek, Star Gate and a myriad of sci-fi movies have been downloading this information to us ever since.

However, many entities existing in our galaxy are based upon a similar human form to our own.

Anything that lives is part of God, an important part of the Universe. Life forms do not need to have a physical body: many civilizations are homes to "beings of light". Civilizations can also be created for forms we would call animals, insects, etc. Just think, the dinosaur age was probably a civilization. We need to shift our focus from thinking the universe is just about us.

Science suggests that our planet Earth is about 4½ billion years old. The higher realms inform us that it has been inhabited ever since its creation. We are known as the Fourth World, and are presently moving into what the Maya people term the "The Fifth World".

The universe is based on Base-12 Math, which means that there is always a multiple or division of 12, each one also containing many levels and layers of 12. There could be 144,000, there could be 12 x 12 x 12, there could be 3 x 4, or 2 x 6. Everything is based on 12. 144,000 is a sacred geometrical number related to ascension and the 144 Crystalline Grid.

There is not just one planet Earth: there are 12 Earths in an overlapping concentric circle, with no doubt hundreds of Earths in parallel and alternate realities. Each of these Earths would operate in a slightly different time/space continuum and within a slightly different band of vibrational frequencies.

Within Sacred Geometry our planet is based on the number 3 (a division of 12). We are familiar with many things in 3's. One, two, three, go. The holy trinity: Father, Son and the Holy Spirit. Witches are known to work with the number 3. Synchronicities in our lives are often seen in sequences of 3's—both bad luck and good luck.

Universal systems use light, sound/tones, and colour. It operates on Sacred Geometry such as signs, symbols, codes and sacred keys, etc. We are constantly bombarded with signs and symbols, the greatest in recent times are the crop circles found particularly in the south of England, but also in other parts of the world. These are communications from the beings we see as Orbs. They are not necessarily telling us anything other than that they are close by.

The Beings in the non-physical realms communicate to us by mental telepathy, visions, dreams, music, signs, seminars, and through people, or by placing certain books in our path. These can all be sent to help us on our journey of discovery. As we reach higher levels of vibration these higher beings can also meld with our energy field to transfer information.

What we experience and learn here on Earth is learnt by every realm in the universe. Nothing is lost, everything is shared.

## CREATION ALCHEMY

Scientists have felt sure that life began with the "big bang" theory, but they haven't gone as far as understanding what created the big bang. In some respects it is understandable how they arrived at that theory, but they are only interested in facts, not creation energy.

Our religious texts have always told us that we were created as a thoughtform of God. How correct they were, without actually understanding the creation they were telling us about.

Perhaps that thought of God created an instantaneous explosion of creation energy that commenced the life of this particular universe. We may never know exactly how that creation happened, but we can use concepts that help us to make sense of the bigger picture.

I have already mentioned alchemy. Alchemy is recognized in science as taking base metals and converting them into gold. Alchemy is how the universe operates. Alchemy means changing something from one thing to another, or taking neutral creation energy and creating something entirely new.

Thoughtforms are what makes alchemy happen. We therefore understand that "thought creates reality", but more importantly it is the intent behind the thoughtform that manifests matter.

Manifestation is therefore hologramic . . . "thoughtform with intent" is creation.

Our universe was created from a thoughtform, which means that this universe is a hologram. It is a hologramic (holographic) universe. The Creator had a desire to create another universe. Creator visualized what he wanted and created it from Source energy, or what we term neutral energy, also known as the Energy of Potential. This energy of potential is the "stuff" of the universe, the so-called "nothingness" out there in space. The creation of a new universe is Creation Alchemy.

The Creator called out through the Omniverse to any higher beings of light who would like to come and help set up this new universe. From vastly evolved universes came the Beings of Light who would head this new creation.

The Creator endowed this universe with three of his attributes, that of Unconditional Love, Divine Will and Power, and Creative Intelligence. These three attributes endow us with free will and choice and the ability to create intelligently and responsibly, all within a matrix of Unconditional Love for all.

These three attributes became an energy matrix which we refer to today as God, the God Matrix. The foundation of this universe is Unconditional Love, and therefore everything that is created also has this as the foundation energy, including us as humans. These three attributes supply us with a divine template for life within this universe.

The Great Beings of Light that head this universe created the galaxies, worlds and civilizations, so that life could be experienced in a variety of ways. These were co-creations with Creator, as all creations must be.

## THE HOLOGRAMIC UNIVERSE

Everything in the universe is created by a thoughtform and is therefore hologramic, and therefore everything and every life form in the universe is also hologramic.

Science knows how to create holograms. Indeed scientists have known about holograms for many decades, and both experiment and use them in many ways in order to help them understand the nature of life.

In very simple terms a hologram is created by splitting a laser beam in two, then bouncing one beam off an object and directing it to collide with the second beam, thereby creating a mirror image of the original object. This image is identical in every way to the original object. Perhaps this "collision" of beams is what could be seen as the "big bang" theory of evolution. The image is actually photons of light, very fast spinning atoms from the split laser beam, and as these fast spinning atoms gradually slow down they become denser in form. They could be slowed down to become a solid object that looks just the same as the original, but is actually an "illusion". This illusion appears real.

The interesting thing about holograms is that when you break the image into pieces, perhaps hundreds or thousands of pieces, each one will always contain the complete picture and function of the original hologram. Every fragment contains the whole.

Perhaps we could say that the Creator bounced a holographic image of the universe from another universe. We certainly don't know, and don't need to know. Perhaps the great Beings of Light bounced images of suns and planets from others, to create what we have here within our universe. Again, we don't know. The vastness of creation is incomprehensible to our minds.

However, what we need to accept and understand is that this universe is hologramic, and therefore everything that has been created within it, is also hologramic. That includes all life forms including humans, our world and everything within our world: all holographic. The main understanding of this is that every creation contains within it the Divine Template, those three attributes of the Creator. In the nature of a hologram, when the energy of the universe is fragmented into pieces, each one contains that Divine Template, the three Creator attributes. As humans we contain the Divine Template of the three Creator attributes. Each human DNA is endowed with Unconditional Love, Divine Will & Power, and Creative Intelligence.

Every sun, star, planet, world, civilization and every life form no matter what that life form is, are all endowed with this Divine Template, whether they actively choose to work with it or not.

Our universe is a "free will" universe. That means that we have free will to create what we wish. However, all creation must be a co-creation with God, and must serve the highest order and cause no harm.

We can say the Universe and the God Matrix are the macrocosm. The Milky Way Galaxy of which we are part, is a hologram of the universe. Our planet Earth is a hologram of the galaxy and the universe. Humans are a hologram of our planet, our galaxy and the entire universe. Each cell of our body, including our brain, contains the whole. We are a microcosm of the whole universe.

As a hologramic microcosm, everything we say, think and do affects the entire hologramic universe, and everything within the universe affects us. All is connected.

*Humans live in a world where there are abundant symptoms of a disintegrating hologram: an old holograhic system that is not able to integrate the incoming elevated cosmic light particles. The collective reality of the planet is shifting and the ability of humans to move into a co-operative and harmonic alignment with the new holographic Earth is what will take the New Earth from template to form.*

## CREATION BY THOUGHT

As everything in the universe is created by thought, we could say that creation is "conscious thought with creation energy", or: consciousness and energy creates. Consciousness is the engine of all creation—all matter and anti-matter.

Thought creates reality through waves of conscious energy. Therefore consciousness is "light" in waves of energy, or vibrational frequencies, that is changed into particle form by thought.

The following is a simple perspective:

1.    The universe is made up of electrons—what science might call quanta or quarks, the smallest discernible matter, or what we would call the sub-atomic particles.

2.    The electrons make up the atoms, or photons of light. Light carries information around the universe.

3.    These photons of light travel in waves. These waves of light are flowing throughout the universe but are invisible to our eyes. They are what we call anti-matter, the fast spinning atoms.

4.    The observer effect, which is well known to science, affects the invisible atoms to become particles when observed. Hence the particles become visible. The observer effect is the thought that is manifesting the particles into form.

5.	The thoughts of the observer change the anti-matter particles into particles which have density, and are what we call matter; the slower spinning atoms.

6.	We can state then that atoms respond to thought.

7.	Space and matter would be said to be congealed thought.

## DIMENSIONS OF THE UNIVERSE

I see the Creator as a different entity to God, but we often interchange these titles and that is okay. However, the Creator created our universe and gave to it its attributes of Unconditional Love, Divine Will and Power and Creative Intelligence.

Unconditional Love is Divine; nothing like we have experienced on earth. It is not romantic love; not even the love of mother and child. It is the highest form of Bliss and Grace bestowed to this universe by the Creator. Divine Will and Power means we have freewill at all times to choose what we want to experience—dark or light. Creative Intelligence gives us the ability to create using our intelligence responsibly.

Our universe consists of dimensions, each one a band of vibrational frequencies. Each band consists of thousands and thousands of graduated frequencies. Of these many dimensions are 9 dimensions that we as humans, and our earth, actively work within.

Around these 9 dimensions is a 10$^{th}$, which contains the Spiritual Hierarchy of the universe; or we could say, the bosses of universal creation, the Elohim. It is interesting that the Collins Dictionary defines hier/hiero/hierarchy as "divine" or "holy".

The 11$^{th}$ dimension is what we could term the Creation Dimension, the Void. The Void is potential energy awaiting manifestation into form.

Around that is the 12$^{th}$ dimension, which we would refer to as "God". Now God is not a man sitting on a throne or on a cloud watching over us. God is an archetypal energy field containing the three attributes of Unconditional Love, Divine Will and Power and Creative Intelligence. This is available to everyone and everything that exists in this universe.

Above and beyond that there are thousands upon thousands of dimensions that we do not need to concern ourselves with at this present time.

Each dimension is a different band of frequencies, different levels of awareness, different levels of experience, and different levels of consciousness. The higher up the levels of awareness, the higher the levels of understanding and responsibility.

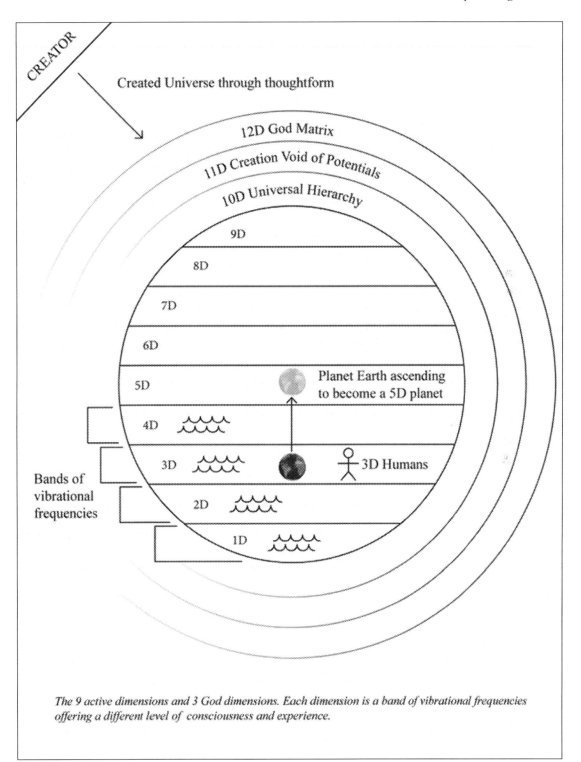

CREATOR

Created Universe through thoughtform

12D God Matrix

11D Creation Void of Potentials

10D Universal Hierarchy

9D

8D

7D

6D

5D

4D

Planet Earth ascending to become a 5D planet

3D    3D Humans

2D

1D

Bands of vibrational frequencies

*The 9 active dimensions and 3 God dimensions. Each dimension is a band of vibrational frequencies offering a different level of consciousness and experience.*

We often conceptualize these dimensions in a circle and moving upward in a pancake system. However, this is not how they are at all, but it helps our mind to perceive an image that is otherwise difficult to grasp. These dimensions are all around us, horizontal, vertical, all different angles. There are no physical boundaries, all dimensions just merge into each other. However, there are energetic barriers that prevent anyone who is not capable of being in a higher dimensional frequency from moving into that band. No dimension is superior to another. They are only a different level of experience, with a different level of awareness, or consciousness.

The frequencies are denser, starting from the Schumann Resonance, or heartbeat of Mother Earth and continuing upward through to about the fifth dimension, at which time the band of frequencies become less dense and of a lighter frequency. The further up the dimensional levels, the lighter and faster the vibrations, until at the level of the eighth dimension they simply become light, with no denseness of matter at all.

Life in the fifth, sixth and seventh dimensions can make a soul choice whether to exist with a form or not. At the eighth level all beings, or entities, are light without form. From the fifth dimension upwards, the Light Beings are aware of the Mind of God. They know and understand that they are part of the "whole" of creation. They co-create with God.

Planet Earth and humans exist in the third-dimensional band of frequencies. This is our physical realm. The fourth dimension is the non-physical realm of earth and is where we exist in between incarnations on earth. When we die in the third dimension, we transition into the fourth dimension before returning once again in physical form into the third dimension.

Our third-dimensional earth, along with any other third-dimensional planets, is where life forms incarnate to experience life separate from God. Levels of awareness therefore do not encompass the big picture of the universe. We are aware only of our own plane of existence.

We are at a point of evolution whereby the earth and humanity are transitioning to the fifth dimension after December 2012. The planet's cycle of evolution is moving her into the fifth dimension whether you know it or not, and each of us as a human has the choice whether we wish to ascend with her into the higher dimensions.

It does not mean we are going anywhere, leaving the earth, or anything else you may have heard about ascension. We are staying here on the planet, but our level of density is transitioning to a lighter density and the higher vibration of the fifth-dimensional band of frequencies.

So if the planet is moving into the fifth dimension, what then happens to us? We must move with her, and to do this we must undertake the work required to clear our emotional energy fields and lift our vibration to match hers.

Anyone who does not wake up to the spiritual nature of this evolution and expansion, will find life becomes extremely difficult. Nothing will work like it did previously. The physical body will not be able to cope with the higher vibrations and will break down in illness and disease. Ultimately death is the choice of the physical body to escape the higher vibrations and return to the fourth dimension.

## OUR SPACE VISITORS

We have believed that all we see is all there is. It is time to wake up and understand we are part of a wider galaxy and an even vaster universe.

There are many Universal Beings working with us and through us to help humanity and all kingdoms of life to ascend into the fifth dimension with our planet. As in any collective, there are some beings who do not hold our highest good as their priority. It will become imperative that you use your discernment in the future as the visitors from other realms start arriving after 2012. Up until this time the Creator has placed Earth in isolation so that we could get on with the work of evolution and ascension. Our ascension into the fifth dimension while retaining a physical body has been an experiment for humans, and we have been allowed to get on with the job relatively uninterrupted by beings from around the Universe. We have had some interference from within this Galaxy, but on the whole we have been left undisturbed.

You need to know and understand that we have always had Space Beings visiting our planet—we just haven't been able to see them. After 2012 when the isolation is lifted we will indeed be visited, and many of these will simply be our family and friends from other worlds. We are "aliens" ourselves. Most of us are not indigenous to earth and have come from other worlds.

As a galactic consciousness, we work within the 3 God Dimensions and 9 active dimensions. We have many non-physical beings from these realms assisting us at all times through this cycle of ascension.

For our simple understanding we could define these dimensions as follows:

$10^{th}$, $11^{th}$ and $12^{th}$ Dimensions are the realms of the God Matrix, the higher Universal Beings of Light and the Elohim Councils.

The $9^{th}$ Dimension is the realm of the Galactic Centre, the centre of our galaxy, and the home of the Spiritual Hierarchy and higher Light Beings of our Galaxy. It contains the library of knowledge, wisdom and experience of all realms within this galaxy.

The $8^{th}$ Dimension is the home of the Galactic Federation. You may think the Galactic Federation only existed in Star Wars movies, but it is real and plays a very active role throughout the galaxy. The Galactic Federation comprises of over 50 member worlds of this galaxy, who work extremely hard to achieve harmony among all worlds and life forms. After our collective ascension to the fifth dimension we will be accepted as a member world of this Galactic Federation.

This dimension is also the home of the Orion Star system. The Orion beings hold the template of earth intelligence for the time when we are ready to assume our roles as intelligent creators in this galaxy. This dimension is also the realm of the star system Arctures, the home of the Arcturians who work closely with the Sirians in carrying out the scientific work of this galaxy, particularly relevant to our ascension to 5D.

The 7th Dimension is the realm of the Andromeda Galaxy and the photon bands. These photon bands are the galactic information highways of light, and spiral around our galaxy receiving and transmitting information. The Andromedans are assisting us through this ascension as their galaxy is the complementary twin galaxy to our Milky Way Galaxy. This is the band of frequencies we would refer to as Ultra-consciousness.

The 6th Dimension is the home of the Sirius Star System. The Sirians hold the light body template for our 3D world. The Sirians are very much the scientists of this galaxy, and are known as Masters of Energy, Technology and Sacred Geometry. They are benevolent beings who are the stellar parents of many human life forms. The Sirians have always been very closely connected with earth and its inhabitants. They work from the non-physical realms, and in some cases in physical form, helping the earth and humanity to ascend. This band of frequencies is the band of Hyper-consciousness.

The 5th Dimension is the home of the Pleiades Star System, and the stellar home for much of humankind. Astronomers refer to the Pleiades as having 7 stars within its constellation. What they don't realise is that our sun is the 8th star of the Pleiades Constellation. The Pleiadians contributed their stellar code to our evolution, what we term star seeding, and as such are our Stellar Parents. The Maoris of New Zealand recognise that they originated from the Pleiades Constellation and this is celebrated during Matariki, the Maori New Year. All Pacific Polynesians have the Pleiades as their origins. As our stellar parents the Pleiadians are very much assisting us through this ascension journey; a journey they undertook and completed 104,000 years ago. The Pleiadians hold the template of love for earth and humanity until we are ready once again to embrace the Unconditional Love of the Creator. The 5th Dimension is what we call Super-Consciousness—that of your Higher Self.

The 4th Dimension is the realms of our earth archetypes, held by the people of the planet Nibiru. We experience life on earth under these archetypes. The 4th dimension is also the realms of mass consciousness, and is what we term the astral realms.

The 3rd Dimension is that of Planet Earth, humanity, the animal and plant kingdoms, and the life we have created here.

The 2nd Dimension we refer to as being the home of the devic kingdom, the elemental kingdom and the mineral kingdom. The Devic kingdom refers to the fairies or the fey folk, the gnomes, goblins, leprechauns and all the other little folk. These may have a form that we perceive, or they can exist as energetic entities. The elemental kingdom consists of the elements of earth, air, fire and water, and the mineral kingdom which contributes to the make-up of our biological body.

The 1st Dimension we would refer to as the solid planet which we call home. The core of the planet is of a Sirian crystalline matrix, the atoms of which spin one way, and surrounding this core is another fluid molten core which spins the opposite way. This spinning rotation holds the planet balanced on its axis.

Geometric structures are held in the even numbered dimensions. Experience and ascension is carried out in the uneven numbered dimensions.

When we move into Fifth Dimensional consciousness, we will gain access to 5D, 6D and 7D. We must then undergo further initiations to move into 8D awareness, from where we have access to 8D and beyond.

## THE INNER EARTH

Our earth is not solid, even though it appears to science to be so. The crust or mantle of the earth is approximately 3 kilometres deep, varying in depth in different locations. There are vast spaces, caverns and tunnels throughout the inner earth. At the centre is the core crystal, and around it is the molten lava that we understand as being our core.

There are many different beings living in our inner earth. These would be on different dimensional frequencies and within different time/space continuums.

The Lemurians that ascended when the Motherland was flooded live inside Mt Shasta, California, and number 1½ million. They are fifth-dimensional and work very closely with Lightworkers. When the collective consciousness of humanity has lifted enough they will come out and walk among us. Their main city is Telos, a beautiful city of light containing many temples that we can visit with our consciousness. Telos is ruled by a king and queen, and the people live happy and harmonious lives of thousands of years. They are our ancestors and look just like us although of course with a lighter density.

The civilization of Agartha is very ancient, long before our time. They have a human-like form and are somewhat green in colour, due no doubt to the copper content of the inner earth. They are very evolved, higher dimensional beings who do not wish to walk on the surface of the earth among us, because they consider we are very primitive violent beings. They are working closely with the higher realms to help the planet and her kingdoms, including us, through this time of ascension. Their main city is Shamballa, and they are ruled by a benevolent king and queen. They do make limited contact with a few people who channel their messages.

We are aware of their presence following several visitations by Admiral Byrd in 1947 and again in 1956. Admiral Byrd was flying on an assignment over the north pole and connected with a dimensional time shift where he flew into Agartha. He was treated very well by the Agarthians and allowed to leave. He then spent many years plotting the co-ordinates so that he could repeat the visit, which he did in 1957.

He returned and wrote books of his visits. However the Air Force suddenly shut down all further information and reference to Agartha—another cover-up of something we were not supposed to know about.

The Greys, the extra-terrestrials that we hear so much about, have a base in the inner earth with permission from the governments at the time, which probably were the United States and Soviet Russia, and perhaps Britain. In return for information these Greys have been existing alongside us for many decades. They have been responsible for cattle mutilations and abducting people. Apparently their race is dying out and they are trying to figure out how human biology operates, in the hope that the knowledge may help to save their race. These Greys are not particularly friendly to humans but seem to cause no major harm within our world. However, the people abducted suffer emotionally and in their fear, many choose to leave by suicide.

Many of our space friends have bases in the inner earth, such as the Sirians, Pleiadians, Arcturians, Orions, and no doubt others. They have always been able to come and go from earth, and are here presently helping the earth and humans with this ascension process.

Prior to the destruction of Atlantis there was a tunnel system in the inner earth whereby these many beings could travel around the inner planet quite freely. However, the destruction of Atlantis caused part of the tectonic plates to collapse, and so at this time the tunnels do not completely circumnavigate the planet.

However, the tunnels are still there and available to those who use them. Of course the Illuminati use them, as did many of our governments of the past, maybe even currently.

The U.S. military base known as Area 51 in the Nevada Desert is also a vast underground network used by the military. My understanding is there are about 50 levels to this base and many undercover operations are carried out there, including large laboratories. Area 51 is where the Roswell stories of alien space craft landing and being captured originate. There are many such craft and even space beings that have disappeared into Area 51. This area is well protected by the military and no one is allowed near or they will be shot. No planes are allowed to fly over.

Does this sound like an innocent operation?

# WHO IS GOD?

*The Father can never be identified outside of your wondrous being. To even attempt it is unfair to yourself because you are going outside of what you are, to describe something which emanates from within you.*

*. . . . Ascended Master Ramtha*

Who or what is God? Is there a God? How big is God?

Religions have fought over God for thousands of years; every religion believing theirs must be the only true God. These religions fight from a limited human perspective, knowing that there is a higher power in the universe, but being unable to conceive of a bigger and vaster picture of God.

So, who is God?

Imagine you are standing on the eastern shores of the vast Atlantic Ocean. You are looking across the ocean to the western shores. Can you see the other side? Of course not, the ocean is far too large. This ocean is full of molecules—what we know as $H_2O$ water molecules. How many molecules would be in this ocean? We could never ever know, so vast would be the number. Trillions and trillions and trillions and trillions.

Imagine that this ocean is God, and that every water molecule is an angel. Does this give us some idea then of the vastness of God, and the vast number of angelic entities within the universe. Every water molecule is connected and they are all part of the big ocean. If the tide moves on the western side, then the eastern side knows about it. If there is a large swell somewhere, all the water molecules know about it. If there is a typhoon, then all the molecules feel it. They are all part of the same ocean; they know about each other; they communicate with each other; they feel everything that goes on within their ocean world.

The water molecules are aware of all sea animals and plants within their world, and they co-exist together in harmony.

So in terms of angels in the universe, we are all part of the same ocean of God, vast beyond our imagining, but all connected and interwoven together—all feeling and knowing everything that happens to that ocean. Because we are all part of God, we are actually God as well. How could it be otherwise?

We are all the ripples; the waves of the ocean. These waves can represent the continual movement of the universe and the flow of life. The ocean is never still, always in a state of change.

We are filled with the ocean of God, and this reflects the meaning of "I Am God Also".

Now, imagine a glass half full of that very same water, bobbing about on the surface of the ocean. Let us say that what is inside that glass is our world. It is filled with the exact same water molecules, the same angels as the universe. It is still part of the ocean because it contains the same things. But what if the glass turned opaque and couldn't be seen through? It still contains the same water molecules, or angels, and is still part of the ocean, but those molecules or angels inside can no longer see the rest of the ocean, or the universe of God. They can still see the sky, the stars, feel the sun, feel the movement of the ocean, and therefore those molecules know there must be something bigger outside their world, but they cannot see it, and their view of their world becomes limited, restricted by the boundaries of the glass.

However, inherent within all the water molecules, or angels, in the glass, is the divine knowledge that there must be more, and they just need to search for that knowledge and understanding.

The angels outside our world can see into our glass. They can travel through the glass and visit with us because they are not bound by the limitations of our glass, or our limited belief systems. They are interdimensional and have the freedom to move through the veil that we conceive of as being in place around our world.

As humans start to wake up and move into understanding the interdimensionality of things by moving onto the path of ascension, they realize they are still part of the vastness of the ocean, or God, even though they are still in the glass. In time, they can learn to move through the glass and become one with God and the trillions of angels once again.

They never left the ocean—they only thought they were separate.


## THE ANGELS OF GOD

The Creator created the Source Energy of God which we can call the "Mind of God". In this Source Energy of God, the God Matrix, stands the hierarchy of our universe: the mighty Elohim and all its many Councils of Light.

From this God Matrix, the Elohim created everything and every life form in our universe. All the multiverses, realities, galaxies, worlds and living creatures including humans, come from this "Mind of God".

This means that everything in the universe is a particle of Source Energy. Always connected, and always interwoven into the tapestry of life: Cosmic life, Galactic life, and human life.

So how were Beings of the universe created?

We could look upon the Source Energy of God as a gigantic field of light and love, and each atom of light and love that exists came from within this field. When this God Matrix wished to experience Itself, we could say it exploded, like an atomic explosion. In our simple terms we could conceptualize it as a fireworks explosion, and from this an infinite number of God sparks issued forth.

These sparks of God constituted life in the universe. As each of these sparks, or atoms, experienced life outside of the God Matrix, they became conscious of learning, of experiencing, and ultimately of creating. So that which started as a creation of God, became creators in their own right; co-creators with Source, with God. From this came life in the universe: worlds, galaxies and a variety of life forms.

As energy can be split, or fractualized, so each of these sparks continue to divide, creating more and more of themselves, each one connected, and containing the original attributes of God and Creator. We can therefore say that the universe is filled with divine sparks of God continually expanding and evolving to experience more and more of a variety of life outside of the Creator. The Creator is always connected to each and every life form, and is continually absorbing the experiences gained outside of Itself. This is often referred to as the inbreath and outbreath of God, each inbreath taking back into Itself the wisdom and knowledge gained, and on the outbreath breathing more life back into the universe of Itself.

As our universe is a holographic thoughtform of God, that makes each spark a hologram of God, we are therefore, each of us, a hologram of God: a spark of Source Energy.

So, who are these sparks of God? We know them as angels. Each spark, or atom of light, is an angelic essence, each moving through the universe experiencing more of itself. Each of us is an angel, we are one of those sparks of God, presently incarnated on earth in human form to have the experience of human life on 3D earth. We have always been angels, are still angels and always will be. When we are finished with our earthly life experiences we will return to the higher realms from where we came, returning to our angelic essence having gained wisdom from our sojourns here on earth.

The Angels helping us on this ascension journey operate from what we term the "Angelic Realms" just outside of earth reality.

The energy field of God is the macro of our universe. Humans on earth would be the micro aspect. However, this does not make us unimportant or inferior to anything else in the universe. In reality, the micro of anything is always the most important, because even the smallest of atoms can make a difference to the macro. Science experiments and evidence corroborate this. This means that one thought from a human here on earth can have an impact on the universe.

## A CREATION STORY

The God Matrix consists of Divine Feminine Energy and Divine Masculine Energy, represented by God and Goddess: complementary energies that cannot be one without the other. God/Goddess carry the template for the existence of life in the universe, and are represented by what we would call Mother Goddess and Father God.

All fragmentations of life from this God matrix are Sparks of God, Divine Expressions of God, or called Expressions of Existence, all playing in the playground of the universe.

In the beginning these aspects of God were learning about light, how energies worked, what they could do and become. The Divine Feminine Energy was the creation energy which had the visions and ideas, and gave birth to and nurtured new energy forms. The Divine Masculine was the active principle that acted upon and with these new creations. The creation energy, the Divine Feminine, as the foundation of all things, was allocated two thirds of available energy, and the active principle, the Divine Masculine, was allocated one third.

As the Feminine energy created, so the creations were constantly destroyed. Galaxies, worlds, civilizations and life forms were created from fragmented aspects of God/Goddess, and they seemed always to be in a constant state of destruction.

The Goddess felt perhaps she wasn't doing a very good job of creation, due to the vulnerability of destruction. She offered the God energy to take over two thirds of the energy, and retained one third for the creation aspect. Goddess hoped that this may work better and prevent further destruction.

However, that did not appear to work well either, for still creation was constantly destroyed. There appeared to be an imbalance of energies which neither side could comprehend and overcome. In time the Goddess felt that the God energy wasn't making a very good job either, and so she took back the two thirds once more and they tried again. Still the universe consisted of creation and destruction.

The Goddess carried guilt and shame for perhaps not creating intelligently. This legacy is carried within the feminine energies of humans.

They changed once more, the God again taking two thirds.

The universe was stuck: at a standstill. Eventually if no forward evolution could be found, this particular universe might have found itself in a state of dissolution and returning to Creator Source.

So a plan was eventually hatched by all the higher beings of the universe, in agreement, to see if a solution could be found to this imbalance.

A planet called Earth was created in the far corner of the universe. This was to be an experiment to find a balance that would ensure creations could endure through cycles and spirals of evolution. Representatives of all the families of the universe were to take part in this experiment.

Our earth is that plan.

We are that plan.

Throughout its 4½ billion years, earth has been inhabited by light beings through many separate civilizations, each one endeavouring to find the qualities of balance and endurance. Most of us have been involved in those civilizations. Again, each one was ultimately destroyed due to the dark energies and misuse of creation energy. Earth was about reliving what had been experienced in the universe to try to find an answer. Much was learnt and understood through these sojourns into form on earth.

In order to implement this plan into our current world, the Spiritual Hierarchy set up what is called the "Order of the Arc"—an elaborate code of energy, or gateway, which prevents outside interference in this plan. This is an Order of the Archangels, all those families of angelic light that assist us here on earth. The Order of the Arc is a code which we initially collected as we came through the so-called Wall of Fire from Home. Only we hold the keys to this Order, which ensures we always have a route home.

Only a small group of angels incarnated on earth to work on this plan. That small group is us . . . . and, oh dear, we volunteered!

There were queues of angels wanting to come to earth to participate in this experiment, but only the most evolved were given the opportunity. We volunteered for this mission. No one forced us to come to earth. We knew what was involved, and how challenging and difficult it would be, but we came to see if we could find the solution that would enable the universe to expand into a new evolution, a new universe.

However, coming through the Order of the Arc to incarnate on earth meant that we forgot our origins, forgot our past, and forgot who we really are, because we could not implement a plan if we were aware of what we were trying to achieve.

Our current earth civilization now thinks it has found the answer. This answer lies in each human form achieving a balance of Divine Feminine and Divine Masculine within each individual human body. This creates a balanced civilization and therefore a balanced world. The human body will always exist with the polarities of masculine and feminine, but in the future this will be balanced, allowing for the immortality of the human body, but also allowing for the world of earth to endure throughout its current cycle of evolution, before deciding whether to continue this civilization, or end it and start again on a new plan, a new play, a new game on the gameboard of life.

## THE NEW EARTH TEMPLATE

*When you enter into a harmonious relationship with all of life, you will participate*
*in the alchemy of creation—your thoughts, your intentions and your beliefs will*
*assist in co-creating the new holographic Earth.*

There are many labels for levels of the universe, but I am using terms described by Ascended Master Tobias channeled through Geoffrey Hoppe. This is a simple concept for us to understand.

Outside of the God Matrix, we have the First Circle, what we would call "Home". This is the realms of the Spiritual Hierarchy, the Gods and Goddesses, the Elohim, the Lords and Ladies of Light and the Archangels.

Outside of this is the Second Circle, the experiential realms containing all the created galaxies, worlds, civilizations and life forms. This Second Circle is about experience, expansion and evolution through many different planes of existence.

Humans on earth are creating the Third Circle. This is the new expansion of the universe. It is what we term "The New Earth"—the new world we are in the process of creating with our thoughts, words, actions, intents and desires; a world of peace and harmony, a world of balanced humans. We are creating the template for life in this Third Circle. This is the concept of bringing "heaven to earth" or recreating paradise on earth. Heaven is not somewhere we "go to". It is a state of consciousness where life is experienced as loving, abundant and without limitation.

Only those angels and light beings who have descended into the density of third-dimensional earth, experienced life and transcended the lower realms of fear and negativities, will be able to live on this New Earth.

These balanced humans will be the prototype humans of a new balanced race which will be seeded throughout this Galaxy, and perhaps other worlds within the universe.

Our galaxy may not be able to fill the head of a pin in terms of the vastness of the universe, but can you now see just how important we all are to the implementation of a plan to move the whole universe forward?

This, folks, is why we are here!

## DIVINE FEMININE ENERGY & DIVINE MASCULINE ENERGY

These divine energies are nothing to do with gender/sex.

Divine Feminine Energy and Divine Masculine Energy are the two complementaries of Source energy. Everything in the universe operates on polarity, which means that everything has an opposite, but those two opposites work together as complements. Such are these two energies of God, the Divine Feminine and Divine Masculine energies.

The Divine Feminine energy represents creation, creating new ideas, giving birth to them, nuturing them. The Divine Masculine energy represents the actioning of those ideas; the strength and action to make those ideas manifest and experienced.

The God Matrix energy is divided into these two energies, God and Goddess, represented as Father God and Mother Goddess. These are the two principles of Source Energy working in tandem. Everything in the universe and our world is based upon this same polarity of the two energies. Everything is based, always, on two opposite but complementary energies.

So we have the Gods and Goddesses. We have Archangels with a complementary partner working alongside them. We have those such as Jesus and Mary Magdalen, Bhudda and Lady Quan Yin. The universe contains matter and anti-matter, gravity and anti-gravity. Atoms move in particle form or wave form. Cycles move clockwise and anti-clockwise, and planets move direct or retrograde. All are the same energy manifesting in complementary polarities.

We talk about Father Sky and Mother Earth, Grandfather Sun and Grandmother Moon. All planets have corresponding complementary planets. The twin complement planet of Earth is Maya of the Pleiades constellation, which is also going through an ascension process.

The Divine Feminine Energy is represented by the Goddess of Creation, Isis, also known as the Cosmic Mother. In our world this Divine Feminine energy has always been represented by the Priestesses of the Temples of Light. The Divine Masculine Energy is often worshipped by many cultures as the Sun God, Ra.

Our human energy field also contains these energies of Divine Feminine and Divine Masculine, again nothing to do with gender. Each of us contains these two complementary energies. The work of ascension is to balance these two energies within us.

## EARTH AND DUALITY

As well as the polarity of Divine Feminine and Divine Masculine energies, Earth also has a process known as Duality. This means that we always have two opposites, but instead of working in tandem as twin energies, they work as opposing energies.

We therefore live within a world of black and white, up and down, right and wrong, in and out, start and stop, rich and poor, and good and bad. This is life on Earth. It is designed that way, so that angels participating in human life can experience what it is like to work within opposing realities, a reversal of the normal process of the universe. It allows humans to experience the shadow side of life. Often this means experiencing evil, manipulation, control, pain and suffering. It is not a punishment from God that we are sent to earth and go through pain and suffering. We choose this experience because of the wisdom we can gain by understanding both sides of duality.

Duality has also led to much separation between men and women, often portrayed as a "them and us" mentality. We see infighting within families and relationships, imbalance between the rights of men and women, and the imbalance of masculine power and the degradation of women.

We each contain the Divine Feminine and Divine Masculine energies and they should be balanced within us. We are moving towards this with our Ascension process.

To help the world realise that sex/gender are equal in the eyes of God, we have had lesbians, homosexuals, transvestites and transgender people setting the stage for us to understand that the love of God has nothing to do with gender or sexual preference. These people have had a difficult time in our world of rigid thinking, and have given much of themselves to be a catalyst for change in society's thinking. Their role was to break down the stereotypes of sexuality.

In the higher dimensions, beings are what we would call "androgynous", neither one sex nor the other. They contain a balance of masculine and feminine energies and have no need to express themselves as one or the other gender. However, that is a matter of choice for the being concerned.

Both our external world and our inner world of Self will exist within this duality, until we learn to transcend it by working through the Ascension process.


## SEPARATION CONSCIOUSNESS

Because of the duality of Earth, working in reversal to the Love and Light of God in the higher dimensions, we are part of a separation consciousness which leads us to believe we and God are separate. It is a "me" and "him" mentality that has removed our divine power, so that we can experience fully the effects of duality. This separation has been fostered by religions throughout the ages and also through much of society today.

Ascension is about remembering that we are "One with God"—there is no separation. We are divine sparks of God Source, always connected to God and everything and every other being in our world, our galaxy and the entire universe.

It is not possible to fully integrate the Divine Feminine and Divine Masculine energies in human form while still within separation consciousness. As we raise our vibrations to the higher dimensions of life we lose that feeling of separation.

Once we have moved into the fifth and higher dimensions we become balanced as a human, and then resume our multi-dimensional nature, or angelic essence.

## ARCHANGELS

Although we perceive archangels as one entity, in reality each archangel is a group of angels who have come together for a specific purpose and so become an angelic matrix. At this pivotal time in our evolution, thousands of archangels surround our world to help humanity, Mother Earth and our galaxy through this transition and ascension.

We perceive archangels often with a masculine gender, but as with all angels or matrices, they are genderless. However they do permit themselves to be seen with a form which we perceive as similar to a human form. They appear predominantly as the Divine Masculine energy which is the active principle they represent. We consequently see, for example, Archangel Michael as male, his energy matrix representing the Divine Masculine energy. The same applies to all of the archangels that we perceive.

As with all life in the universe, archangels always work with complementary partners, representing the Divine Masculine energy and the Divine Feminine energy. Not as in genders, but in God/Goddess energy.

There are seven primary archangels working with earth for this ascension process. Each archangel overlights an aspect, or a quality, of the Creator carried within a "love" matrix. So we have Archangel Michael and Lady Faith, Raphael and Mother Mary, Gabriel and Hope, Uriel and Aurora, Jophiel and Christine, Chamuel and Charity, Zadekeil and Amethyst. These are some of the more well known of the archangels because they are working very closely with us during this time, but there are many many more archangelic families involved in our transition work.

We each are a facet or expression of one of these archangelic families.

## ASCENDED MASTERS

When angels have lived on earth, attained higher levels of consciousness and successfully completed their path through ascension back to the higher realms, they gain the title of Ascended Masters. To be an Ascended Master means they have transcended the darkness of earth duality and ascended to higher levels of light. No one can become an Ascended Master without having experienced human life on earth.

This process of ascension is what is termed Christed, or a state of Christos, Christ Consciousness. The term Christ or Christos does not relate simply to Jesus of our bible stories. Christ means "the light", so when Jesus died and ascended to his Father's house, he became Jesus the Christed One, having received "enlightenment" by moving through the Ascension process at the time of death.

Just prior to the last stages of ascension, there is usually a moment called "the dark night of the soul", where the last of negative energies are released before transcendence. This accounts for Jesus on the cross calling out "Father, why hast thou forsaken me". He received forgiveness from himself and from the Father, and with a smile on his countenance let go of life and transcended to his Father's house.

Many thousands of Masters have traversed the challenging path of duality here on earth, of course Jesus being the most well known, but also Mary Magdalen, Mother Mary, Buddha, Lady Quan Yin, Lord Kuthumi, St Germain, El Morya and so on. Of course many of the ancient myths and legends of Egypt and Greece told us stories about those who had traveled similar paths. Their ascensions were done individually. We are doing it now not only as individual ascensions, but as a collective of humanity.

All of these Masters are helping us through this Ascension process because they know it, have made it through, and can provide us with wisdom and tools to help. These Masters are available to any of us through individual communication with them in the higher realms; all you need do is ask and they will attend you. Of course you must be open to receiving their help and this may not come in the form of spoken words. They may send you a book, direct you to a seminar, instigate a dream, or other signs that are relevant to where you are at the time. Take notice of their answers, because they may not be what you expect.

We all now have the opportunity of Ascension within our current lifetime. This is a Divine Decree from Creator that all may have the opportunity within this current ending of many cycles and the beginning of new ones. However, Ascension does require commitment and work; it is not given for free. You need to be prepared to examine your beliefs and perceptions, examine who you really are, release all negative aspects of living, and heal all inner wounds and traumas. It is not an easy path, but we are always told the rewards are immense.

We can become Ascended Masters ourselves, still walking the earth with physical bodies.


## OUR JOURNEY TO SELF-MASTERY

*Your task is to discover mastery within yourself to the degree that you meld with your divinity. That is ascension.*

We are told we are on the Path to Self-Mastery where we will become Ascended Masters while still living in a physical body on earth. This path is that which we term our ascension journey: ascending to the higher levels of vibration. To achieve this we must learn self-mastery—to have power over our emotions and our emotional reactions, learning the Laws of the Universe and living them in our daily lives, transcending our four lower bodies: physical, mental, emotional and spiritual, utilising higher intelligence and wisdom in all choices, expanding our compassion for all by recognising that we are all connected, and standing in Truth at all times.

As I have already said, this journey can be somewhat daunting and challenging. However, if you commit to this journey and do the work you can achieve the status of ascended master in this lifetime. Some people will find it too difficult in the chaos of the world we presently live in, and will choose to achieve this in a future incarnation.

To be an ascended master on earth means we will have the same powers as the ascended masters we presently work with in their non-physical form. We will be able to do what Jesus did, and remember he told us that "you will be able to do what I do and more".

However that cannot happen until we clear our physical, mental, emotional and spiritual bodies of all the debris of third dimensional living. We must learn, understand and embody all the Universal Laws into our everyday existence.

We must understand how to conduct ourselves as fifth-dimensional humans. If you carry your negative dross into the fifth dimension you will affect that dimension with your negativity and that simply will not be allowed to happen.

Hence, there is a great deal of work to do.

# COSMIC LAWS

*Understand these Laws do not exist simply to annoy you; they have an important purpose. Without them the universes would be places of great chaos. These laws, which you need to make yourself familiar with, are what keep the whole cosmos running smoothly, planets harmonious and abundant, and humanities experiencing limitlessness, peace, love and true brotherhood. You must become these laws incarnate!*
*. . . from "The Seven Sacred Flames"*
*channeled by Aurelia Louise Jones*

In order for the universe to function harmoniously for the experience, evolution and highest good of all sentient beings and all life forms, there are codes of conduct that must be adhered to by all life in the universe. The Spiritual Hierarchy of the Universe and our Galactic and Planetary Spiritual Hierarchies are charged with the implementation of these laws.

In our free will universe, life on this planet has been allowed to proceed according to the consciousness of humankind, and we now realise this has ultimately been to our detriment, albeit for a higher cause of learning and experiencing the dark side of energy.

We have forgotten the Cosmic Laws that we inherently know. They are imprinted in our DNA, but we have buried them under hundreds of layers of distorted and negative beliefs and emotions. It is now time, and imperative, that we remember and relearn these Cosmic Laws. We must integrate these back into our four bodies, the physical, mental, emotional and spiritual, and embody them in our daily living. We cannot proceed to the fifth dimension if we do not understand the protocols and codes of conduct that the higher realms require.

When we live within these laws life becomes much simpler and flows with ease and grace. There is no more pain and suffering and we experience abundance of all the good things in life.

I don't know how many Cosmic Laws there are, but I would presume there may be 144, perhaps more. These Cosmic Laws are being channeled through different messengers, but I have been following the teachings of Ascended Masters Lord Kuthumi-Agrippa and Mary Magdalen as channeled by Michelle Manders of *www.palaceofpeace.net*

I am summarising here what I consider to be the foundation laws that we need to embody. I can assure you these can and will be life changing.

## LAW OF FAIR EXCHANGE

This is the foundation law through which all energies pass. The fair exchange of energy is not limited to the exchange of money, or how we extend it in giving.

It is vital that you understand you must have a fair exchange of energy with yourself in relation to certain areas of your life. You have four areas, or quadrants, in your life that you must pay attention to: Self, Home/family, Work/career/creativity and Relationships/friendships,. When these four quadrants are in balance your life flows harmoniously. You need to consciously consider these quadrants and how they are playing out in your life. Are they balanced, are there discordant energies in any area, what areas are over-compensated and which are under-compensated?

Nothing is for free, there must always be an exchange of energy to keep things in balance. However, we have been brought up and conditioned to give: to give to other people, to always be in service to others, but without accepting energy in return. This just depletes our life force energy and because it is not recognising our own needs, the body gets run down and what we term burn-out can occur. This fair exchange does not have to be one of money. It can be an exchange of healing sessions, produce or just helping one another in various ways.

Many healers feel they should not have to charge for healing because it is a gift from God to share. That thought is wonderful, but there must still be some form of energy exchange. Maybe it is simply in the form of a hug. When money is exchanged for a service, money is the energy, the tool of exchange.

We also have a great deal of trouble accepting from people, whether it be gifts, compliments or service. We try and pass compliments off by deflecting their meaning, literally saying we aren't worth what is being said about us. It is time we learnt to receive and say thank you without feeling guilty. Perhaps that wonderful compliment deserves a hug in return. This is a true exchange of energy.

## LAW OF FREE WILL AND CHOICE

Every moment of every day allows you to make choices utilising your free will. However, through the restrictions and limitations of society it has become almost impossible for us to be aware that we have choices. Religious teachings and government controls have disempowered us and strengthened the feelings that we are not in control of our lives and that we have no choice.

This cannot be farther from the truth. You do have choice but you must understand how this law works, and with the clearing and healing of your karma and emotional blockages you will attain the power to choose the life you wish to live.

You must choose every day to become more empowered and take every opportunity which comes your way to choose to do something differently. Fear is the paralysis that keeps us in limitation. With this law you will develop a higher knowledge and intelligence to interact with life in a different way, to make choices that support the highest good of you and your soul's journey.

Even when you feel you do not have a choice, there is still a choice to be made. Are you going to do nothing, or are you going to choose to take the only action you can at that time? So there is indeed still a choice to be made. If either available choice is not a suitable one, you must still choose, and in that you must surrender and accept the best that that time has to offer. Maybe in hindsight you will find that the choice was a good one after all, but you couldn't see "round the corner" at the time.

You can always utilise free will to transcend any emotional reactions to a person or situation. Free will means you choose how you are going to react: positively or negatively.

The partnership of spirit and humanness, or our divine self and human self, is the ascension path. When we choose through our humanness every choice reflects our fears; when we choose from spirit we make an intention to stand in our power. Make your choices divine for the highest good of yourself.


## LAW OF ATTRACTION

Much has been said about the Law of Attraction and many books published about it. The main concept you must understand is that you attract to you whatever resonates to your vibrational signature. If you are an angry person, you attract anger or angry people to you. If you are depressed you attract situations into your life that will depress you, or attract other depressed people into your life. If you are a victim, then you attract circumstances or perpetrators to you that enable the cycle of victimhood to continue.

It is as simple as that. If you wish an abundance of money in your life, then your vibrational frequency must match that higher resonance of abundance. Poverty frequencies attract more poverty, prosperity frequencies attract more prosperity.

In other words, you are magnetic, and you magnetically attract what resonates with you, either negative or positive.

Daily affirmations and prayers will not attract what you want unless the vibrational frequencies match. These are merely mental activities, often just wishful thinking. This Law is a highly sophisticated system of universal principles which command certain actions from those tapping into it and wanting to apply it. The first step is making the commitment to better understand yourself, or how else are you going to raise your frequency to that of abundance.


## LAW OF DISCERNMENT

We are now receiving ever more intense light and higher energies and it becomes very important to be discerning about what you allow into your space, what it is that you allow yourself to be part of, what kinds of people or the environment you wish to be associated with, what thoughts, words and actions you wish imprinted upon you and your life.

Through discernment you are able to question aspects of your beliefs which perhaps you may not have questioned before. Don't become paranoid or neurotic about this; that's a mental attitude. Just use your feelings to guide you as to what is appropriate for you.

We often call this feeling our gut instinct, and it kicks in immediately upon meeting a person perhaps for the first time, or when entering a new situation. Your immediate gut feeling is telling you the truth, but so often our left brain logic kicks in and doubts what we have felt. It is time to allow ourselves to accept the truth of that first reaction.

On the journey, you learn to use discernment about healers, teachers, information, courses or books you read. Anything you take in must resonate with you—it must feel right. It doesn't matter what anyone else feels, you only need concern yourself with what your gut reaction is telling you. Honour what your body is telling you. Even if something or someone resonated with you some time ago, that dynamic may have now changed. Perhaps your vibrational signature has moved higher, and the old dynamic no longer fits. That's okay. Don't force yourself to accept something just because you used to. Change is continually happening.

We have often been lead to feel guilty about things, things we have or have not done. Understand that when you stand in your power and truth, utilising your discernment, there need be no guilt.

## LAW OF ACCEPTANCE & SURRENDER

The power of self-acceptance, the power of surrendering to self, is perhaps the magic of life. Allow yourself to surrender and to trust the multitudes of higher energies directing you where you will best perform and shine your brightest.

Acceptance is not giving up, and neither is surrender. Acceptance takes courage. When you accept whatever it is you face, you allow a higher dynamic to begin flowing into your life simply because the acceptance process opens you up to find different ways to manage your life. The creative mind is opened and you find potential solutions. Surrender, knowing there is no need to move into fear.

Finding a means to an end requires the acceptance and the surrender, accepting that it is safe to surrender, and surrendering because you have accepted this fact. Through acceptance you allow Spirit to serve you, for in surrendering you allow the sacred waters of life to carry you along its natural course in the direction of your true destination.

If you do not understand and embody this law, fear and desperation take over. When one tries to force and control situations in times such as these, very often it exacerbates the negative aspect of that situation. However, applying acceptance and surrender empowers you to see into a future potential.

This law will reveal to you the simplicity that lies within trusting and having faith that by accepting any situation and surrendering to the outcome, the most important and best solution will come.

## LAW OF CHANGE

Change is the one and only constant in the universe and the Law of Change offers new opportunities in your life through accepting and allowing change to happen. You need to make peace with change, which is the one thing in life guaranteed, because energy is never stagnant.

The Law of Change requires you to be flexible and to be in the present moment, ready to "go with the flow" on the new pathways that change evokes. Through the wisdom you have gathered, you see that you have the power to make choices to transform areas of your life, particularly relating to negative belief patterns.

Change empowers you and guides you. You are saying yes to life. You must have faith that that which best suits your life right now will come to you. You will be attracted to opportunities which allow that to happen, and that which you seek, desire and need will come into being.

Think about the changes you desire in your life. How do you experience change? What is your definition of change? What emotions and feelings do you associate with change? All of these questions will reveal things to you which will make way for the Law of Change to weave its magic for you. Surrender to the Law of Change and you will see your life take on new meaning, new directions, and new relationships.

> *Change is the nature of reality but certain laws remain forever in place.*

## LAW OF LOVE

Within the worlds of creation everything is based upon the energies of love, and these energies create dynamics which influence millions of levels of consciousness. Humans do not understand the qualities of this energy of love. This law strips away all the old concepts of love.

Absence of love results in darkness and ignorance. The absence of the true understanding of love is what results in experiences motivated by greed, fear, and the desire to control.

Everything is bound together by this sacred law whether individuals are aware of it or not. Love is what creates change. It is the energy facilitating the evolvement of humanity's consciousness.

This is the time of reconnecting on a much deeper level with the emotional body, allowing the process of sensing a deeper inner power and light which enables you to face your shadow, to integrate these powerful systems of light, and to observe your life from a wiser and more emotionally mature perspective. This more acute awareness of life and utilising wisdom opens the portals of fluid love in every cell of your body. This propels you further into the dimensions of love, highlighting every process of regeneration. You are generating the new light of love which enables humanity to evolve beyond the old world and truly accept the concept of rising in love, rather than falling in love.

Trust that this force of love is not the energy that we have come to accept as the energy of love. All of us have experienced a love misguided, an energy misinformed, and a creative power misdirected.

This Law helps to clear past mistakes in love, whether they were inflicted upon you, or you inflicted them upon another. This Law brings the opportunity for all to be forgiven.

Do not be afraid to look at the wounds of your past. All you need to do is open your heart, open your soul and release the pain. It is time to sacrifice all the parts of you that have been bound to disillusionment as a result of a negative experience with love. This is not limited to romance, but relates to every single area of life. Once released, these wounds of the past will not control you again.

Embrace the qualities of this new energy without question, without cynicism, without doubt, without fear, and allow yourself to experience something called love in a whole new way.

## LAW OF TRUST

*Trusting in the universe requires faith. Faith is believing that the universe knows what it is doing, and that it assists us in every way possible to achieve our highest potential as a human on earth. Our faith allows us to surrender and accept that the universe works on our behalf.*

Most people have had to deal with betrayal, deception, abandonment, abuse and other debilitating experiences, both in this lifetime and past lifetimes. This has resulted in an inability to trust, either Self or others.

A lack of trust results from fears and ultimately these fears will decimate your ability to fully live your life. Understand that if you do not trust other people, they simply live up to your expectations. If you do not trust others, this is an indication that the issue you have is with yourself: trusting Self.

We seem to have no trouble trusting our weaknesses, our ability to fail, and our inability to attract love into our lives, yet we cannot seem to trust our inner courage and strength and our intuitive abilities to know what is right for us. We doubt ourselves at every turn.

Utilising the Law of Discernment we must learn to trust our inner guidance, trusting that we are always safe and protected and trusting that abundance will flow into our lives. This takes work and effort to release all the old wounds and the defences we have built up to prevent being hurt once again.

As you release the pain and negative experiences you gradually rebuild trust in Self and in life. As this strengthens, you allow new opportunities, new people and new experiences to enter into your life. The greater your ability to trust yourself, the greater your ability to trust life.

## LAW OF ASCENSION

We often carry fears about this journey we are undertaking. We do not know what the future holds, but as we face the future, our past comes to meet us with great intensity to clear the old beliefs and fears. We need to transcend these fears of the future, at the same time as clearing the old fears of the past.

The Law of Ascension offers doorways into deeper realms of our consciousness. As well as locating the old darker aspects of ourselves and transmuting them into light, we are more and more accessing the higher aspects of ourselves. This is actually the goal of ascension.

To do this means dying to the "old me/old world" and being reborn into the "new me/new world".

We have shut down many of our feelings because we simply didn't want to go there: didn't want to enter into our darkness, but it is only by doing this that we access our higher aspects of light.

Ascension is embracing LOVE in its fullness. The Law of Ascension asks us to love our self, and to make choices which empower us.

We can achieve and accomplish amazing and very wonderful goals and dreams in this lifetime if we apply the Law of Ascension. The Law of Ascension offers us turning points in our journey. At certain stages of our clearing and integration, turning points give us the opportunity to take a huge step forward on the path but it is always our choice whether we accept the opportunity. It is a choice between continuing our fated path or moving into our destiny.

If you do not choose to accept this opportunity you must remain in the cycle of pain and suffering until you reach the point of making a better choice: a higher choice for a better life for yourself.

The Law of Ascension comes under the auspices of Ascended Master Serapis Bey and you can call on him for assistance at any given time.

## LAW OF FORGIVENESS

The Law of Forgiveness plays a vital role in life and teaches us another level of unconditional love.

The wounded parts of us inside often motivate us negatively on a subconscious level. These aspects block our ability to transform our life into what we truly desire, and also impedes our ability to forgive. Sometimes the forgiveness process consists of forgiving Self more than asking another for forgiveness.

Every time we feel guilt, anger or resentment toward another requiring our forgiveness, we are giving our power away and leaking our energy.

You give your energy to your guilt or to the anger and resentment you may be feeling. This debilitates you and blinds your vision, resulting in the inability to forgive. This requires deep soul searching on your behalf, because there may very well be a part of you feeding off the guilt, anger and resentment, even though it costs you aspects of your personal power. What do these feelings do for you? What are you getting out of them? Does the anger and resentment simply remind you that you are alive?

There is an increasing anger being expressed by people throughout the world as this imbalanced energy comes up for release. The opposite energy, and the antidote for anger, is forgiveness.

The time has come to surrender to the power of forgiveness. Know the energies of forgiveness reciprocate one another, freeing all parties concerned. You do not have to wait for others to forgive you.

You are asked to open the doorway further into the worlds of your subconscious and unconscious, so that you are not motivated by invisible forces shoving you from pillar to post, exacerbating your fear, anxiety, confusion, and at times delusion and illusions you have accepted as your reality. It is your spiritual, intellectual and emotional intelligence which will bring you the power to lead your life motivated by love and wisdom.

## LAW OF MANIFESTATION

The essence of manifestation is rather simple, but humans find it complicated, perhaps because we feel we have not been able to manifest our wishes and dreams in the past. However we are now entering a new life, a new energy, which supports the manifestation of our needs and desires. This does not come without work on our part. The more we release the negative blockages and distortions the higher our vibration, and this then supports manifestation of abundance in our life.

You need to understand that you create your own life, every single day. Your thoughts are powerful forces of creation, but they can create a negative life or an abundant life. The choice is yours. Energy flows and grows where it is directed. Are you focusing on creating negatively or positively? Are your thoughts of fear or love?

Manifestation is not just an intellectual process of visualisations and affirmations. Manifestation involves your body, mind, heart, emotions and spirit. You must align your consciousness with the higher dimensions of the new life you wish to create for yourself.

If you have made the choice to change your life by doing things differently, and therefore manifesting a different outcome, you need to step into your inner strength and courage, to have faith, belief and trust that you are co-creating with the higher realms of love, light and wisdom. Follow your inner guidance and all will be well. Your future lies with your thoughts.

*Glenys-Kay*

## LAW OF WISDOM

Wisdom is not something given to us, it is something we have to earn through experience. In each lifetime we gain wisdom from our experiences and lessons mastered. However, as they are often so deep in our subconscious, buried beneath many layers of negative experiences, we do not recognise that we have this inner wisdom, and so continue on our path of darkness. The Cosmic Laws assist in the clearing and releasing of these blockages, allowing us to access all our ancient wisdoms.

Wisdom is the ability to be still, to be centred in the heart, to observe what is currently challenging us, and then to make a wise choice how to deal with the situation rather than the old knee-jerk reactions we are so fond of. Wisdom is something that is applied in each and every moment of every day.

The confusion that currently reigns throughout humanity's consciousness is because we exist in-between two worlds, the old world of 3D, and the new world of 5D and beyond. This confusion allows people the opportunity to consider which world they desire to be part of, the world of illusion, or the world of reality.

Wisdom allows us to straddle both worlds, making conscious decisions for our highest good, and the highest good of all others. Wisdom incorporates the foundations of love, truth, trust and integrity, and is the force that will enable us to transcend all the lower emotions of the ego.

*These Cosmic Laws are summarised here with permission from Michelle Manders, channeler for Ascended Masters Kuthumi-Agrippa and Mary Magdalen who are bringing the Cosmic Laws to earth for the wisdom teachings they embody. They are vitally essential to the ascension of humanity. For further information on these Laws I recommend you visit www.palaceofpeace.net*

# HISTORY AND OUR ORIGINS

## LEVELS AND LAYERS OF PERCEPTION

When we are considering the history of our civilization, we need to understand that people have different perceptions of our history. This may depend on their culture, their level of awareness and consciousness, their present situation, and their beliefs and perceptions of the world around them.

Throughout historical dialogues there are common threads, so people tend to agree on the principles, but they may vary in some of their perceptions.

So first we need to look at the levels and layers of life itself.

Our world uses numerology, or in fact, sacred geometry, to structure life. If we look at the number "zero", it designates a point of perception, which can be accepted as the "observer" of what is happening. This can then be understood as the "reference point".

The numbers 1 through to 12 are the structures of life, 12 being understood as a completion point. However, all the numbers have endless levels and layers of themselves, and there are countless levels and layers consisting of time lines, dimensions, worlds, alternate and parallel realities. So your perception of history is dependent on what level or layer of awareness you are on. In other words what is your point of perception? History is different according to where you stand and your perception at that point. For example, if you drowned in the Atlantis floods and were looking at it from that perspective, you would feel differently to an ancient Egyptian who was very spiritual and connected with the unified fields of earth and universe. If you look at history from the perspective of each culture, each would offer a different perspective.

At present we see history through a very limited and controlled perspective.

As well as all these levels and layers of history, we must also understand that there is never one sole reality. All things exist on other dimensional timelines: other frequencial structures of reality. Earth is our 3D reality and we believe what we perceive with our eyes. However, this is an illusion because everything exists in multidimensional form: in different time/space continuums.

For example we have the fabled Avalon. Nobody has been able to locate the Avalon depicted in myths and legends. Avalon was a fourth dimensional place that also had a parallel 3D timeline. Avalon was the non-physical form that existed around the Glastonbury and Tor region of south England. People could not see it, but the priests and priestesses who lived in Avalon were able to move between the dimensional timelines, but for other people to enter Avalon they had to access it through the "mists of time", at a higher dimensional level of awareness.

The same can be said for the mythical "Camelot". People searched for this beautiful place, but did not understand that it was a multi-dimensional place that could only be accessed by people of higher spiritual awareness. It was also accessed through the "mists of time" in the forests not far from where the story of King Arthur and the Knights of the Round Table happened in our 3D timeline. One was physical in our perception, the other was non-physical. King Arthur and the Knights of the Round Table was also a storyline that was enacted out in both 3D and other realms.

These often occur at a conjunction of timelines, where two or more realities intersect and bleed through.

The pyramids on our planet also exist in simultaneous multidimensional realities. There is not just one of each pyramid, but many of them. We see one, but many exist in the etheric realms. These pyramids appear or disappear according to the consciousness of the people and the requirements of that era of civilisation.

## ZERO POINT

We have had several zero points of note in our history. After the 9/11 terrorist attack on the Twin Towers in New York, the area was called "Ground Zero". It was at that point in our recent history that the tide turned for humanity.

In actual fact, the terrorist attack implemented by the Illuminati was meant to have created a huge wave of fear around the world, making people once again more controllable through fear of further terrorist activities. This fear of course happened, but unfortunately for the Illuminati they misunderstood the depth of human empathy for one another in times of chaos. Indeed the fear was there, but it was superimposed by a wave of love and compassion that flowed around the world as a result of this terrible act. Probably much to their disgust, the attack actually increased the amount of light and love throughout the world. Since then the Illuminati have tried in vain to increase fear by instigating further acts of terrorism which have not been so effective. Humans have had enough of war, violence and terrorism, and are now shifting their allegiance to spiritual matters of love and compassion and seeking to live in peace and harmony.

Another zero point of history was the time of the birth of Jesus. The Roman Senate, as the minions of the fourth-dimensional Nibiruans, knew all about the ending of cycles in 2012, and instead of allowing humanity and the planet to be raised up into the fifth dimension and out of their control, they decided on a take-over plan to completely dominate and control the earth and its inhabitants. During the visit of the Nibiruans, around $3600_{BC}$, they started putting in place their control mechanisms.

Julius Caesar set up a new calendar, the Julian calendar, which was to count down to the year zero at which time the planet Nibiru was once again to visit earth. This year zero on the calendar was then to be the implementation of total world control.

However, this year zero also coincided with the birth of Jesus. Jesus came as a fully twelfth dimensional Avatar to anchor the higher dimensional grids of light into the planet, and to teach humans about their divine origins. So the last 2000 years began a battle by the Illuminati to instigate their world domination. Unfortunately this has been at the great expense of millions of souls who suffered and died at their hands throughout many religious and political wars on the planet.

This "zero point" in history was actually the turning point of humanity towards their true origins as divine essences of the Creator.

We can say that the deaths of John F. Kennedy, Martin Luther King, Princess Diana, the bombing of the Rainbow Warrior, the fall of the Berlin Wall, the ending of slavery in America, were all zero points where life changed for humanity.

These zero points are therefore times of new perceptions, new awareness, and consequently new beginnings. They can be said to be "the point of perception" of life. They can also be understood as the "reference point" from which to see the future.

The solstice of 21st December 2012 is a zero point, a time when many cycles will be completed, and the beginnings of a new cycle, a new earth, will move forward; one that will gradually create peace and harmony on earth. Year Zero with Jesus began the countdown to 2012 and Ascension.

Atoms of light, as said previously, flow in a wave-like motion forming spirals of evolution. If they are observed, they can then take on the form of particles. These particles are called dense or dark matter (solid matter or perceived matter).

The atoms that make up our world have been spiraling in a clockwise direction, causing the atoms to become solidified as matter. At or around the 2012 zero point, the atoms of light will reverse their spiral and begin to spin anti-clockwise, creating a lighter planetary body. This is the ending of the old cycle and the beginning of a new cycle.

The atoms of each of our human cells will also reverse their spin, causing the human body to become less dense, to take on more light, and to ultimately become a "light body". This light body has less denseness and vibrates faster.

At the end of the Mayan Great Cycle 21st December 2012, life on earth will never be the same. A new cycle will have commenced.

Zero point!

## OUR SOLAR SYSTEM

Our sun is the pivotal point of our solar system, and without it we would not survive. It directs heat to earth for life, but it is apparently not hot at all . . . it is simply light. Light is sent to earth in solar waves at a frequency which we feel as warmth. Our sun is actually a portal to the Galactic Centre and to the centre of our universe, known as the Great Central Sun, or the God Matrix/Source as we would call it. As we know, light carries information so the waves of light emanating from the Sun contain information from the Great Central Sun, from the higher dimensions of the universe, and from all the different star constellations of our galaxy.

We know we have our Sun, and spreading outward from it are the planets of Mercury, Venus, then Earth, Mars, the Asteroid Belt which is in fact the remnants of the planet Maldek, then Jupiter, Saturn, Uranus, Neptune and Pluto. This makes ten planets, the most recently discovered being Pluto in 1967. Scientists have recently begun accepting the presence of Chiron, a small planet with an elliptical orbit of 65 years around the sun.

However within Base-12 Math there should be 12 planets.

Scientists do suspect the presence of an extremely large planet, which they have termed "Planet X", but they have not been able to confirm its presence.

This large planet is in fact the planet Nibiru, an enormous red planet, slightly smaller than Jupiter, with an elliptical orbit of 3,600 years. This means it only visits earth's atmosphere every 3,600 years, passing by for a period of about 200-400 years. It was well known in ancient history that these people visited us from time to time. They were known as the "Shining Ones", "the Gods who came down from the Sky", or "the Gods who from Heaven came".

The Egyptians called Nibiru the "planet of a million years". Nostradamus quoted its presence when he said "there appeared in the sky a great red sun which slowly traversed the heavens".

This just shows how much of our ancient history has been hidden from us and distorted in the minds of people.

## NIBIRU AND THE ANNUNAKI

The planet Nibiru was originally part of the Sirius star system, orbiting around Sirius B, but was somehow thrown out of its orbit and ultimately drawn into the orbit of our solar system. It orbits between Earth and Sirius and so actually acts as an intermediary between the two. Its first visit to Earth was over 500,000 years ago and it has returned every 3600 years since. Its last visit coincided with the "year zero" at which time world domination was on their agenda, and the same time that Jesus was born in Bethlehem.

The people of Nibiru, the Annunaki, are the archetypal energies that exist in our fourth-dimensional realms.

The Annunaki are very ancient beings originally from the Orion Star System. They have high intelligence and excellent scientific and technological skills. However, there is a group of these beings who have moved away from their divine origins, saying they do not need God in their lives. They have what they need in their sciences and their technologies.

Having landed on Planet Earth after the cosmic event that sent their planet hurtling into the wider galaxy, they have considered they own our planet and have used it for their own means. They have based our world on their own negative energies and have corrupted and manipulated humanity. They have fostered the separation from God concept through their various control methods. Many of the so-called truths we have believed have originated from the Annunaki to pre-empt their power base.

Needless to say they are part of us, and have played a role in causing us to turn away from their dark power and authority, and return to the Love and Light of God.

They are reptilian with human-like forms, although it is said the forms are more metallic than our earth biology. They are cold-blooded as reptilians are, and do not have a wide range of emotional expressions as humans do.

They are brilliant geneticists and through their intervention in our natural evolution, they became our parent race.

At the birth of our planet, angelic energies arrived on earth as completely new souls, never having experienced life in any other form and in any of the worlds throughout the universe. They existed as "light entities", and lived in harmony with the earth and nature. They created many of the plants, trees and animals, and became part of the animal forms to experience life in what they had created. Some of them ultimately took form in the family we know as the ape family and natural evolution was creating a more upright animal that could walk on two legs and use hands as tools.

The Annunaki had been coming to earth to mine for our mineral resources, particularly for gold which they used to protect their planet during their long elliptical orbit in deep space. Many of the Annunaki were fed up with the mining activities they needed to undertake, and therefore looked at the animal inhabitants of earth to see if any of them could be genetically modified to work the mines for them.

A geneticist by the name of Ninharsag started the genetic manipulation of the ape form to supply workers for their mines. She used genes from her brothers Enki and Enlil and her own to change the DNA of the ape to hasten its evolution into humanoid form. This took quite some time and much trial and error, but eventually she achieved the purpose, and so our humanoid form continued on its natural evolution from that point. The ape/humanoid was merely biological, not divine in matrix.

This means that our heritage contains reptilian genes as well as the mammalian genes from our ape ancestors. An interesting combination that has worked extremely well for us. Even though we have a lot of reasons to be annoyed with the Annunaki, we also have a lot to be very thankful for. In the universe, genetic manipulation is quite common and not frowned upon providing it is done for a higher intent and purpose. Ninharsag did alter the genetics to produce miners for the Annunaki but in the process she became attached to the development of her "offspring".

The Annunaki are cold-blooded, but we inherited the warm blood of the apes. The Annunaki has a very poor emotional body, but we inherited the emotions of the animals to feel pain and to feel joy.

The Annunaki's main mining activities were in Africa, primarily in the area we know today as Zimbabwe. Scientists have uncovered ancient skeletal remains in Africa which they have carbon dated to about 450,000 years ago. They named this skeleton "Lucy". From her DNA they have found that all humans have descended from her, and in fact all animals have the same DNA.

At a later date, some of these workers were shifted to another continent where they mined extensively in what we now call Mexico. These workers were the original Olmecs of Mexico.

I understand that Nibiru has a wide range of people of different worlds, many of whom work in the higher realms as evolved beings. It is only a small minority of rebels who actually cause the problems here on earth. These people are patriarchal and have promoted violence, bloodshed, corruption and evil here on earth. Their thoughts are transmitted to us by what we could call mind control, through various methods including the media, politics and religions. These thoughts are vibrational frequencies that affect us making us feel negative, depressed, angry and poor, which in turn cause illness and disease. Although we have been unfairly manipulated and controlled, we have allowed this to be so by being gullible and not standing up for our own interests. This is seen even today by humans believing everything that is told to them by governments and religious leaders. We have refused steadfastly to use our own discernment in what we have taken as our truths. Many of the so-called truths we have believed have originated from the Annunaki to pre-empt their power base.

To use an analogy, these negative thoughts are streaming above us in a "river of life", and automatically being downloaded into anyone who is vulnerable enough to allow it. We need to learn discernment, the art of deciding what we wish to allow into our individual consciousness, and what we won't allow in. It is our fears that allow the acceptance of these negative streams of energy into our auric field.

Mass consciousness is however a two-way stream of thoughts. Our thoughts go out into the field of mass consciousness and can have an effect for better or worse. If the critical mass of our thoughts are negative, then mass consciousness becomes even more fearful. If the critical mass of our thoughts and beliefs are in Love and Light, then the field becomes changed in that direction.

So, do we wish to accept the Annunaki downloadings of negativity, or do we wish to change our beliefs to Love and Light, and send that to them?

Do not look on any of this as right or wrong. Nothing in the universe is right or wrong. That is a perception of the duality of our world. Everything is as it is. If we don't like it, then we have the means by which to change it. Live within the Love and Light and you will help to change the world.


## STAR SEEDING PLANET EARTH

Humanoid evolution continued for a further 450,000 years, and the workers continued to operate the mines in preparation for the Annunaki's visit every 3,600 years.

However, about 100,000 years ago, the Spiritual Hierarchy felt these humanoids had the potential for evolving into stellar beings, divine beings that could become part of the galactic family. To achieve this they added a stellar matrix to our DNA. This was a cellular imprint that was encoded in our Mitochondrial DNA, called the "star seeding" of humanoids.

This DNA modification entailed the stellar consciousness of star beings to be implanted into the biological ape/humanoids on earth. It was the implantation and activation of stellar essence, in other words our divinity, which would allow for further evolution into ascension.

Five hundred stellar beings were either chosen, or volunteered, to implant their energies into the earth humanoids in this manner. These were the Pleiadians, and this is a reason that so many people feel very connected to the Pleiades. At that time on earth there were about 20 different ape/humanoids evolving. The Star Seeding was carried out on only one of these forms, the form that was considered to be the most upright and intelligent and had the most chance of successfully evolving into a divine human.

These star beings from the Pleiades visited and lived on earth for many generations, seeding the ape/humanoids in the normal biological manner which ensured that the DNA carried the seeds of divinity for all future time. Natural evolution continued. Gradually the other humanoid species died out, leaving only the strongest and fittest, the one having received the star seeding. This is the human of today.

At later times there were a number of stellar implants of Sirian origin, and smaller numbers from Orion, Andromeda, Arctures, Alpha Centauri and maybe others.

The ancestry of many humans on earth is the Pleiadian families, and therefore they are our parents and ancestors.

The timing of this star seeding was also important. Apparently it takes 104,000 years for the evolution of a life form into a higher evolved being. This 104,000 years was to coincide with the ascension of planet earth into the fifth dimension, December 2012.

# LEMURIA AND ATLANTIS

The civilization of Lemuria started about 50,000 years ago and was well established around 35,000 years ago. The Lemurians were very spiritual and connected to their stellar heritage by a strong connection to the cosmos and God and living in harmony with nature. The main continent of Lemuria was in the area we now know as the Pacific Ocean. Many of us know this as our "Motherland", the land of Mu. This civilization flourished for 20,000 years. Most angelic essences that incarnated into the civilization of Lemuria did so only once, and there were about 3½ million in total. They did not reincarnate over and over again. The reason for these incarnations was to establish on earth the Akashic Records. These records keep the memory of every angelic essence that has ever lived on earth in human form, their thoughts, memories, deeds and abilities mastered. All of this was in preparation for what the star seeding had commenced: the evolution and ascension of humans at the end cycle of 2012.

At a later date, and at the same time as Lemuria, there existed a civilization called Atlantis, but this was one of the Ancient Atlantean civilizations, not the Modern Atlantis people think about today. It existed in the area known now as the Atlantic ocean. This was a grand civilization incorporating both spirituality and technology. However, the Atlanteans gradually came under the influence of the Annunaki, and became warriors, seeking power and control. The Lemurians were generally scoffed at for their spiritual nature and simple way of life.

Around the time of $15,000_{BC}$ the planet was going through one of her weather cycles, and waters on the planet started rising. The main area of Lemuria was based in the valleys around the mountains of Hawaii. As the waters started to rise, the Lemurians knew they had to do something to save themselves from an eventual flood of their homeland valley. They became seafaring people and migrated to other lands, in particular Micronesia, the Easter Islands and New Zealand.

However some Lemurians had also evolved into light beings of a higher vibration and about 20,000 of them elected to ascend and pave the way for the others to follow. The ascended Lemurians moved to the area known as Mt Shasta in California, United States, and eventually moved into the mountain and currently still reside within it, waiting for humanity to lift their vibrations high enough so that they can come out and walk freely amongst spiritual humans. This is a fifth-dimensional city and not accessible by humans at this time. They presently number about 1½ million and retain their human form, but are more blue in colour and a lighter density. Their main city is called Telos and their High Priest Adama does make contact with some awakened humans offering information and guidance for ascension.

Many of the Ascended Masters work from Telos, alongside the Telosians, assisting humanity through this ascension time.

Some Lemurians elected to stay on their Motherland and as the waters rose, so they climbed and lived higher up the mountain. The highest peak of Hawaii today is the last ancient remnant of the Motherland of Mu and there are some families living there today who are living descendents of the Lemurians.

Some Lemurians migrated to the Atlantean cities, where they were treated as the lowest form of life. Modern Atlanteans did not believe in a God, they only believed in their own power, whereas the Lemurians lived very simple spiritual lives. They were treated badly and often used as slaves and killed at the slightest provocation.

There is very little to be physically found of the land of Mu. The buildings and temples were submerged under the ocean and the strong currents and erosion have removed them from our history. However the etheric fields of these temples still exist at the bottom of the ocean and can be accessed by higher consciousness. There are artifacts that were aboard ships that lie on the ocean floor. Some of these artifacts have been found, but have been hidden away because scientists can't explain them, and the Illuminati do not want people to know of this history.

Modern Atlantis is the one we normally refer to as Atlantis. It was a flourishing civilization by $15,000_{BC}$, based on Annunaki science and technology—no God required in *their* lives. They were a seafaring nation and traveled widely throughout the world. As well as their main continent they had outposts scattered far and wide.

In any culture throughout history there are always two sides, two viewpoints, two modes of action. We exist in a duality world, so this is normal. Atlantis, although very controlling and technological, also had a side where many people lived beautiful spiritual lives. It is all relevant to the level of awareness of each individual and where they exist in relation to the reality that surrounds them. The main cities of Atlantis were very beautiful, the land was green, and many of the temples and buildings of commerce were white marble. Many statues were situated around large plazas where businessmen would gather to discuss their various businesses. Everywhere you looked, there was beautiful white marble.

The main city of Atlantis was powered by a large crystal satellite that hovered above the city, often called their second moon. This power source was watched over by a sect of Scientist/Priests called the Atla-Ra. They were highly intelligent scientists who took their responsibilities very seriously. However, the power elite of the Atlanteans wanted the control for themselves and eventually convinced the Atla-Ra to show them how to use the satellite. The Atla-Ra were not easily convinced but the Atlanteans put forward such a sincere case that the Atla-Ra gave in. However, in time the Atla-Ra were stripped of most of their powers and the Atlanteans took over control of the satellite.

We know from our own ancient memories just what happened after that. As the Atla-Ra priests foretold, the Atlanteans misunderstood and misused the crystal power for their own warring purposes, and one terrible day about $10,600_{BC}$ the satellite exploded and the shattered remnants rained down upon their continent. This vastly disturbed the tectonic plates, and earthquakes, tsunamis and volcanic activity occurred. There were huge lightning storms, thousand mile an hour winds, and the lands quaked under the oppression. Over time the continent disintegrated and slid beneath the ocean. Most Atlanteans did not survive this cataclysm, and those who survived had to seek shelter underground in the caverns of the earth.

The Atlanteans caused their own destruction and the memories of this still haunt us today. Most of us were part of it in one way or another.

After the destruction of Atlantis our solar system traveled through the photon band in the Age of Leo for 2000 years. This allowed the planet time to slowly heal from the trauma.

After emerging from the photon band and the waters had subsided, about $8800_{BC}$ the remnants of humanity once again set up a civilization. This was in the area of the Middle East and from these beginnings grew the ancient civilization of Egypt. Ancient Egypt was once again built upon the attributes of stellar communication and sacred geometry, with technological assistance from the Sirians and Arcturians. This culture was in full swing around $7000_{BC}$. At this time the planet Nibiru returned and the use of their technology once again expanded. The Sumerian culture arose from Ancient Egypt, and then the Assyrian and Akkadian cultures, and from that point many civilizations sprang up across the middle east and beyond.

In 3600$_{BC}$ the Annunaki once again visited, and this time set up residence on earth. The Annunaki had previously not taken on permanent human form on earth, but at this time they were given permission to immerse themselves in the reincarnational cycle of earth. This was for several reasons. Duality always involves two sides, and this was no exception. The Annunaki are our parent race and in their higher dimensional realms knew that we would need help to move forward into the ascension process prior to 2012. However, the 4D Nibiruans (being the human incarnation of the Annunaki) had in mind the complete domination of earth and its inhabitants, thereby making us their slaves for the next cycles of time. This visit started the wheels in motion, both for our progression into ascension, and for their attempt at world control. Either one would win the battle, but if the Nibiruans won it could very well mean the end of this earth civilization due to their plunder of earth's resources and the pollution of our environment. They knew this but still continued with their plan; their idea being that if they couldn't have earth then nobody else would have it either.

The incarnation of Nibiruans was credited to Inanna, the Nibiruan Goddess and the Goddess of Ancient Egypt, also known as the Sumerian Goddess Ishtar. Inanna was a Nibiruan scientist who felt their culture was in need of learning emotional feelings, as humans on earth had. This would help them to evolve over a period of time, because without feelings they could not connect with their spiritual natures which had atrophied throughout their history of separation from Source.

There is also seemingly an idea that the more evolved beings of Nibiru knew that they were emotionally deficient and that their war-mongering ways were not conducive to harmonious life in the universe, so their incarnation into human life was to enable them to experience emotions, and to start their own evolution into higher consciousness during this ascension process of Earth.

The Spiritual Hierarchy of the Galaxy and the Planet were also concerned about the destructive nature of the rebellious Nibiruans. A meeting was arranged with the Annunaki Councils where it was put to them that they needed to incarnate on earth to learn from earth humans the value of emotions and spirituality. The Higher Selves of humans were agreeable to allowing them to incarnate, and we have been assisting them in their journey of evolution since that time.

Modern Egypt arose during this next time frame, and it was very different to Ancient Egypt. It was Nibiruan based, patriarchal in control, and ultimately became the Roman Empire so well known to us in history.

During the period prior to Year Zero, the Nibiruans had virtually thrown a Net around us, keeping us in ignorance of our history, our stellar origins, and the true reality of our world.

## HISTORICAL FACTS

At this point, it is prudent to discuss how we know all these details of our obscure history. As already explained, history is recorded from the beliefs and perceptions of the recorder, so although most details have a similar vein of truth, they may differ according to the level of awareness of the culture at that time.

The Bible, for example, has been used for 2000 years as a reference for the teachings of Jesus. However, the original transcripts were written for a culture that existed 2000 years ago, totally different from the society we live in at the present time. The Bible has also been translated and re-written many times, with additions and deletions made according to the ruler of the time. It is now time for people to search for their own truth rather than relying on an old book now out of date, and one that has been open to change throughout history.

Religious texts such as the Torah, the Qu'ran, the I-Ching and the Book of Genesis, have threads of truth running through them. There are important works of the disciples, particularly the Gospel of Mary Magdalen and the Book of Enoch that have been entirely omitted from the bible, but are now available as separate texts.

Indigenous cultures such as the Maya of South America, the Olmecs of Mexico, the Dogon of Africa, the Aborigines of Australia and the Polynesians of the South Pacific islands always told their histories orally and these became our myths, legends and folk tales. Most of these have truths running through them even today.

> *From The Book of Enoch the Prophet . . . Chap. VI: Verses 9-12*
> *First translated by Richard Laurence 1821*
>
> 9.  *The elect shall possess light, joy and peace; and they shall inherit the earth.*
> 10. *But you, ye unholy, shall be accursed.*
> 11. *Then shall wisdom be given to the elect, all of whom shall live, and not again transgress by impiety or pride; but shall humble themselves, possessing prudence, and shall not repeat transgression.*
> 12. *They shall not be condemned the whole period of their lives, nor die in torment and indignation; but the sum of their days shall be completed, and they shall grow old in peace; while the years of their happiness shall be multiplied with joy and with peace, forever, the whole duration of their existence.*

Why do so many of our fairy stories have dragons in them? People never give serious thought to this fictitious character of children's bedtime stories. Dragon beings were some of the original beings that came from the far corners of the Omniverse to set up this universe that we currently reside within. Dragons are therefore our ancient creators.

One of the cycles we are completing is a galactic cycle of 225 million years and this has been a "reptilian" cycle. The Annunaki are reptilian of origin and so we have much to remember about our reptilian origins. Medical science also tells us that part of our brain, the cerebellum, stores our ancient memories . . . they call this our "reptilian" brain. Our long spines are also similar to that of reptiles, and we even have a stub of a tail. Some babies are born with a short tail which needs to be surgically removed.

The Mayan Calendar of earth records is still a source of stellar truths. It talks of cycles and spirals of time, and the positioning and movement of planets, moons, suns and stars pertaining to evolution in our Galaxy.

We also have ancient texts such as the Emerald Tablets of Thoth the Atlantean, and the Dead Sea Scrolls discovered in Qumran and Nag Hammadi on the shores of the Dead Sea; the first one discovered in 1947. These scrolls talk about life in the era estimated to be $170_{BC}$ to $47_{AD}$. They describe the communities of Essenes living around the area of the Dead Sea at that time. There appears to have been a community of Essenes living family lives, and a community of ascetics that consisted of only celibate male priests who spent their lives rigorously following the teachings of their "Teacher of Righteousness". The scrolls probably do not accurately portray our history as these are fairly localized interpretations of the day. However they do give us a good insight into their way of life.

If you are searching for the most original and ancient texts of creation, then the Sumerian tablets appear to be the oldest available to us. They originate about 7000 years ago. There are thousands of clay tablets found in Mesopotamia, printed in cuneiform, the original language of those times. The Book of Genesis, the Story of Creation in the Bible, closely mimics the Sumerian tablets and is probably where the information in the Book of Genesis originated. The information in these tablets is not widely known, no doubt because they tell the true story of our creation and the Annunaki, the gods of Nibiru who came to visit from afar. They are the shining ones of the bible, the Anakim: "Those who from heaven to earth came". Genesis calls them the Nephilim: "Those who have come down from the heavens to earth".

The Annunaki taught the Sumerians their cosmology, their technology and the creation story, and taught them the language to record this. The Sumerian culture was advanced and we are only learning now what they knew 7,000 years ago.

Archeology and anthropology contribute to our knowledge of our past by way of artifacts, ruins, cave drawings and skeletons. They offer information about the lives of the people of that time. One of the most interesting unearthed was the skeleton of "Lucy" in Africa. This blew the modern theory, instigated by the church, that humans only began around 1000 years before Christ. There are so many ruins that have been discovered, and anyone searching for ancient truths would do well to study them.

Astronomy and cosmology show us the movement of the heavens, and that we are not alone in the universe. Astronomy is one of the oldest sciences, and drawings from ancient cultures show humans holding a telescope up to the heavens.

Astrology brought forward from the Mayan culture shows us the emotional influences of the heavenly zodiac moving us through cycles of expansion and evolution.

The sciences of Quantum Physics, Metaphysics, Mathematics, Geometry, Medicine, Earth and Environmental sciences offer us much information on how our world works and interacts between the universe, the world of animals, and the world of humans. If we can understand the basics of quantum physics and quantum mechanics, we will understand the workings of the interdimensional universe that is part of us and surrounds us moment by moment through all time/space continuums.

Throughout history we have had many prominent prophets, seers, visionaries and shamans who have been able to see into the past and future and tell us their visions. Many of them have been time travelers who could access the higher dimensions and other realms. The prophecies of the past have come to an end, and it is no longer worthwhile looking to their visions of our future, because since the year 2000 all future events are only potentials and nothing is set down as definite. In the past our linear time line enabled these prophets to foretell the future. After 2012 our linear time disintegrates and therefore the future becomes interdimensional and unable to be predicted ahead of time. We will learn to live in the 'now' moment, creating our futures as we go. At the December solstice of 2012, we will all participate in the choice of a potential future for earth, albeit this will be at a soul/Higher Self level and not at a conscious level. However, we do know we are seeking peace in our world and this will be the future we manifest.

To help the seeker of knowledge, there are literally hundreds of thousands of books to choose from. Discernment is always a requirement of spiritual knowledge. Find the books that speak of love, of unity, of truth, and of peace. Any book that speaks of fear and doom and gloom behooves the reader to put it aside and look for something that resonates with Truth. There are many books, magazines and articles available from very knowledgeable writers.

The Internet is also a good source of information, but once again be discerning where and who it is coming from. The Net is a really good way of moving a great deal of hidden information around the world, and is a source for light, as well as being used by the dark forces trying to persuade you otherwise.

Many speakers come forth to tell of their physical and emotional experiences with paranormal events, their visits and communication with higher beings, their visions, dreams and near death experiences. Be open to the new information that can come from these spiritual or new age people. What seems like fantasy can often be real.

In this same vein, movies are often channeled information, to set in motion the acceptance of the unknown, or the non-physical realms. Movies such as Star Wars, Stargate and Star Trek have allowed us to see into the unknown worlds around us in a way that has not frightened our senses, so laying the foundation for their existence and appearance in our world of the future. Even The Matrix was a good new age movie, and in more recent times Avatar achieved box office success.

Regarding hidden agendas of the Illuminati and other control forces, there have been many whistleblowers over the last 50 years or more, who have spoken up about what they consider wrongdoings. Many of these people have unfortunately been killed, strangely enough, but many more are coming out of the woodwork to tell of the underhand dealings that have been hidden from the public. Expect to see more of this, as the energy of Truth that is now expanding on earth will not support their agendas.

There is an amazing amount of channeled material from higher beings of the non-physical realms that is available to us all. Again be discerning and choose that which resonates with you in Light. Often this is the only avenue we have to become familiar with our history, the workings of the universe, and the present evolution of earth and humanity. Present channeled information is up to date and factual, and if it resonates with Love, Light and Truth, then those Beings are working alongside us to help lift us up to a level of higher vibration that is required for us to move through the Ascension Gateway.

Most importantly we have our own current memories, DNA cellular memory, past lives, and intuition. We can access our Akashic Record of the past, and we have access to our Higher Self who has all the knowledge that we require. All the answers to our questions are already within us: we just need to learn how to access them. This can only be done by clearing the debris from our energy field and lifting our vibrations up to meet our Higher Self. It is time for us to become our own prophet, our own visionary, our own guru. Look to yourself for the answers you seek.

There are many teachers, speakers and workshops available. Be open to hear other points of view. Don't limit yourself to just what you know. There is always more knowledge to be gained by expanding your vision of the universe.

# MOTHER MARY

*Your divine birthright is to live in Light, to take yourself lightly, and to allow others to feel lighter when they are with you. That is your assignment, and you may take it or not. In other words, the choice is up to you. But you have found that as you go through a day feeling happy about something, feeling that you are truly okay—because you are—others can feel your joy, your happiness, and then they are uplifted.*

*. . . Mother Mary*

The Divine Feminine we know as Mother Mary was a high level multidimensional stellar being, a high priestess of the Temple of Isis. She presently resides in the 9th Dimension holding the feminine energy of love for all humans. On earth she was an embodiment of the Goddess Isis, which means she carried the highest level of this Goddess energy.

Mother Mary incarnated with a specific role to play. She was to give birth to a star child. Religious teachings have called this the "Immaculate Conception", that Mary was divinely inseminated by God and this led to the term "Virgin Birth".

High Initiates Joseph and Mary were married. Joseph was an embodiment of St Germain, carrying a high level of Divine Masculine energy.

Joseph and Mary had a biological conception and gave birth to Yeshua, later known as Jesus. It is more than likely that during conception an additional infusion of the highest level of Divine Masculine Energy and Divine Feminine Energy was imprinted on that conception from the highest realms. This could account for the human concept of the so-called Immaculate Conception.

Yeshua had a fully operating 12 strand DNA, the 2 biological strands and 10 layers being his interdimensional DNA. As well, he would have received his mother's mtDNA, the stellar codes of Divine Feminine energy, which when linked with his own Divine Masculine energy made him a fully integrated and balanced human, a fully multidimensional being at birth.

Mother Mary's role was to nurture her son Yeshua into adulthood, at which time he was to carry out the role he came to earth for. She was there to hold the higher energies for him, along with Mary Magdalen, during his times of teaching and then his crucifixion.

Mother Mary is an Ascended Master and is the Divine Complement, or twin flame energy of Archangel Raphael, both very much involved in assisting the healing of humans, particularly in regard to these lies and distortions.

Mother Mary has confirmed this information with me and said it is vital that the lies be exposed. She told me that the Roman Senators of that time were suppressing women, making them possessions of lowly worth. However, because she was the Holy Mother of the Holy Child, they could not say that of her, and so they didn't know how to deal with her presence. They decided to use the Immaculate Conception and Virgin Birth to lead the people into false truths. This was a manipulation on their part, designed to help gain control over people who were worshipping this holy birth.

The religious account of Mary riding into Bethleham on the back of an ass surely points to the Illuminati/Roman Senators mocking and deriding the holiness of this birth.

Astrologically, the signs were there in the heavens for the visionaries of the time to read of this imminent holy birth.

# JESUS AND MARY MAGDALEN

*When I first met Yeshua and our eyes met, I understood that we had been destined for each other. Our times alone were the most precious times I ever experienced. Whenever I speak of Yeshua even now I am overcome by my love and the feelings that I hold for him throughout all time.*

*. . . Mary Magdalen*

Yeshua ben Josef and Mary Magdalen were both stellar beings, twin flames, divine embodiments of Lord Sananda and Lady Nada. They represented the God/Goddess aspect of balanced Divine Feminine and Divine Masculine energies. They were married and indeed it is said in the bible that Jesus attended a marriage in the synagogue. The bible just neglects to say that it was his own marriage he was attending.

These two high dimensional beings represented the Sacred Union of Relationships.

Mary was pregnant at the time of the crucifixion and ultimately gave birth to a daughter, called Sar'h, or Sa Ra, or as we would know it today, Sarah. To hand down Mary's stellar mtDNA through the future bloodline, this birth had to be a daughter. Sar'h was a star child who has continued the divine bloodline of Jesus for 100 generations to this day. We do not know who Sar'h married but her daughter married one of the early Knights Templars, and so today there exists a family bloodline of Christ but it is kept very well hidden for obvious reasons. They would not be safe if this knowledge was made public and their identities will continue to remain hidden.

The church sought to discredit the bloodline of Christ as they didn't want people to know of the possibility that he was still represented on earth through his family bloodline, so they convinced the people that Jesus was celibate and never conceived a child. The fact that Yeshua grew up in an Essene community gave them this leverage. However the Essene communities did support marriage and families. It was the ascetic Essenes, a male order ensconced in their monastery, who were celibate. Yeshua was not one of them.

The church wanted to denigrate women to worthless possessions, removing the knowledge that the Divine Feminine is the creation energy and very powerful. Women then became mothers of men, or prostitutes for men. Their Divine Feminine energy has been made subservient to the male patriarchal governing bodies throughout the last 3000 years.

Yeshua's role was to teach the people about the love of his Father; that they could be free, they could heal, they could create, and they could change their lives. Just prior to beginning his teachings he went into the desert for 40 days and 40 nights to be in isolation to prepare himself for the times, and even the ordeals, that lay ahead.

He was a twelfth-dimensional teacher who could create miracles which is well recorded in history. His teachings were that we could do the same.

People are upset that he was crucified alongside robbers, but we must remember that those were the ways of death at the time. However, symbolically it certainly aligns him with the poor people and not those of the ruling class.

Yeshua has said he has had enough of hanging off a wooden cross for 2,000 years and wishes people to take him down. Jesus on the Cross is about pain and suffering and that is not what he represented, then or now.

Leading up to this ascension journey of our times, people have started to move towards more New Age and spiritual teachings. To counteract this, the Illuminati made the movie "Passion of the Christ". This movie effectively brings people back to the manipulation that if Jesus suffered on the Cross, then so should you people suffer. What a delusion!

Yeshua now works from the higher realms trying to change the distortions of truth around his life and teachings.


## JESUS AND CHRIST CONSCIOUSNESS

Yeshua/Jesus was a 12th dimensional Avatar not only of those times but for the Age of Pisces and his sign was of course the fish.

He lived his early life as a simple man, living and working with the people of the times. He learnt what they wanted for their families, he understood their dreams, he knew they desired a change in their life of servitude. When he entered fully into his role as Master Teacher he understood his people. He taught them they didn't need to be controlled and manipulated. He said that freedom was available to them. He showed them miracles and said they could do the same. He told them about their Father God. He led them into spiritual thinking and encouraged them to accept their Father into their daily lives.

He was born Yeshua ben Josef, son of Josef, until after his crucifixion when he became the Christed Self, Jesus the Christ. As he was hanging on the cross he went through the dark night of the soul, and was heard to say, "Father why hast thou forsaken me". Immediately after that he was immersed in the love and light of God and transcended his human body, becoming one with the light. This is the meaning of becoming Christed. In doing this, he paved the way for us to follow in his footsteps and become Christed Humans.

During the last supper he established the Eucharist, and with the breaking of bread and drinking of wine he laid down the foundations of Christ Consciousness for the future. The bread represented the flesh of Christ, and the wine the blood of Christ. This ceremonial ritual established the Christ Light, the Christ Consciousness, into the blood of all humans who followed him throughout history, until the time came in the future when they would wake up and realize they are divine beings, an aspect of God represented in human form on earth. So the Christ Light, the Christ Consciousness, exists in each and every one of us, carried forward from generation to generation as an interdimensional aspect of our DNA.

Each cell of our blood is encoded with the word "God", and this coding will ensure that all humans who wish to, will wake up from their dormant state of duality and choose to search for the truth about themselves and their history. The future of earth lies in the hands of those lightworkers who have moved into the higher dimensions of wisdom and knowledge.

To continue his teachings and to make sure his Christ Light was anchored firmly on earth, Jesus walked the earth after his crucifixion, living in many countries around the world. Many cultures talk about a Master Teacher living among them, often for months or years at a time, and although churches discount this as nonsense, each of these beings will have been a divine embodiment of the Christed Jesus.

## MARY MAGDALEN AND GODDESS CONSCIOUSNESS

Mary was the daughter of a wealthy shipping family in Mesopotamia and recognised as being extremely intelligent and knowledgeable at a young age. Her name was actually Mariam and she was often known as Mariam of Magdalen. She is also given the title of The Magdalen. Unlike Yeshua, who prefers that as his name, she is happy to be called Mary.

Mary was a high priestess of the Temple of Isis but received different training to Mother Mary.

After the crucifixion Mary continued to tell the disciples about further teachings of Jesus, but because of the patriarchal society of the times they rebelled and considered her a threat.

It became necessary for her safety and that of her unborn child to disappear, and she traveled firstly to France and then on to Egypt where she was hidden by the priests and priestesses of the Isis temples. She finally settled in Wales where she lived in a cottage by the sea. She tells of the visits she had from Yeshua each year, when he appeared to her in his light body.

Mary Magdalen carried the Divine Feminine Energy or Goddess Consciousness and anchored it here on earth. In interdimensional terms, she was responsible around $300_{BC}$, many years before she and Jesus were incarnated on earth, in setting up the Order of Magdalen. Many of the priestesses of the Isis cult were initiated into this Order in preparation for their role after the crucifixion, of continuing to hold and anchor the light of Goddess Consciousness on earth. Their role for the last 2000 years has been difficult, with many of them experiencing torture, death, being burned at the stake or thrown in dungeons, often for simply being the healers, herbalists and visionaries of their times.

By 2012 their role in this service will have ended, but most will willingly take up further services for humanity by once again becoming healers and teachers.

## GOD/GODDESS CONSCIOUSNESS

God Consciousness is the complementary twin energy of Goddess Consciousness.

The Feminine aspect is the creative force, the creative source, the nurturer, and the template for Love. The Masculine aspect is the anchor, the initiator, and the activator for the Divine Feminine energy and represents the Light aspect. In a complementary relationship therefore, the Goddess is the creator of ideas and the God aspect carries those ideas into manifestation.

To move into the higher levels of consciousness, it is necessary that each person clears their energy field of negative energies and distorted beliefs and fully awakens both the Divine Feminine and Divine Masculine aspects within the heart chakra, and then balances them into divine union within Self. This is a requirement to move through the Ascension Gateway, and we cannot move through this gateway without these fully balanced and integrated Divine aspects of self.

# CONSCIOUSNESS

*Ancient wisdoms teach that Light and Consciousness comes out of Dark and Unconsciousness, and that one cannot exist without the other. There is a constant pulse between these two energies—the life wish or the death wish.*

Can you imagine yourself and your life encapsulated in a small cocoon? Everything inside this cocoon is your little world: the world you have created for yourself. It contains your family, friends, home, work, community, sport and hobbies, etc. Everything about your life is contained within this cocoon. This cocoon is bound by your ego personality. This ego judges your life and the world you have created for yourself. It tells you that life is hopeless—it is about pain and suffering, clashes between people in your life, financial stresses, that abundance is never yours. There is often very little love in this little world. This little world is so contained that you cannot see outside of it. You cannot see any other reality.

In this little world, you never look to yourself for the cause of your problems. You only look at everyone else and blame them for the situations you find yourself in. Blame the rich people, or the government, or the system for the lack of wealth in your life. It is always someone else's fault.

Whatever is within this cocoon becomes your perceptions, beliefs and truths. In other words, this is your individual consciousness, your personal level of awareness.

Can you now imagine a bigger circle, one that contains perhaps your country? Within this circle we have beliefs about who we are as a country, about our people, about what we want and think and do. Within this bigger circle, our country can blame everyone else in the world for our problems, blame things on outside influences, everybody else's fault. This bigger circle contains the consciousness of our country.

Now imagine a larger circle again. This is our world and contains within it the consciousness of the people of the world. Who are we blaming as a world? Is it everyone else's fault that the world is in such a mess? I didn't do it . . . so someone else must have. Maybe it was God. Laying blame again on something outside of ourselves.

Outside of this circle, there is a larger one, a universal picture. This contains the consciousness of the universe, where the big picture of eternal life is viewed. This is the awareness of the spiritual and eternal nature of life within the universe. God's Divine Plan is carried out by the life forms containing the higher intelligence, the higher wisdom, and the higher Love of God.

Outside of this again is the circle of God, the God picture, carrying the eternal spirit of God.

Now . . . God sees the big picture. He sees and knows all. He "looks through the eyes of God" at every atom of life in his many worlds and universes. Every atom of life is a spark of his creation and loved by him eternally.

He has the big picture . . . the Divine Plan of Eternal Life.

What picture does each of us see? Do we see only our own little picture of stress, worry, and lack, or is it possible for us to look at our individual life, our world and our universe through the eyes of God? Can you see the big picture? In doing so our lives and our world start to make more sense.

Within our little picture, we worry about the price of milk and bread or the cost of petrol. Understand that there are people in the world who do not even know what milk and bread taste like.

It is time for us to expand our awareness, our consciousness, and to incorporate the big picture of eternal life, which includes our human life here on Planet Earth.

In viewing life from the bigger picture we can often see a solution to our problems, which we are unable to see from our limited perceptions within our little ego oriented cocoon. Viewing life from the bigger picture is "expanding our consciousness: our awareness".


## LEVELS OF CONSCIOUSNESS

We all have an individual consciousness, which means "level of awareness". Whatever level of awareness you are on is how you perceive your life, your world, and the wider universe. If you exist on a lower level of awareness you will not be conscious of the wider dominion of the universe we live within.

Whatever our individual consciousness, we are always influenced by "mass consciousness". This is a stream of energy that contains all the thoughts and beliefs of humanity, and which is dominated by either positive or negative energies. "Critical mass" will always be the dominant factor and we all know that the state of the world we live in at present indicates that mass consciousness is in a state of deep negativity. Unless you decide otherwise, this has an effect on your thoughts and actions.

Our thoughts are based on our perceptions, our beliefs and our truths, and these are influenced by our attitude to life—who we think we are, what we do, and how we interact with other humans and our world. These influences can stem from our parents, friends, workmates, religions and schools, and in fact anything that we have heard from other people and believed.

Outside of our individual consciousness we also have a family consciousness—the perceptions, beliefs and truths of our family. We are influenced by the family that we live within and adopt their beliefs as our truths without ever questioning whether those beliefs are truth or not.

We also have a work consciousness. Where you work will have policies and procedures, perhaps work philosophies in place that you believe. They become part of your life. Corporations and government bodies are a good example of this, where the people who work within these offices often become brainwashed into the mentality of power, greed and manipulation. Most people genuinely believe that what they are doing is right because they have never stopped to question whether the policies are right or wrong. They simply continue the tradition of the office. Soldiers can be an example of this. They fight for their country, genuinely believing they are helping to save the world without ever stopping to think if what they are doing is the right thing. "Is peace ever attained through more and more violence?"

Education, or school systems, have a consciousness of their own. Different schools have different philosophies or different beliefs, as in religious beliefs or the way of teaching. The education system supports competition which causes separation between pupils, instead of encouraging them to work together and achieve their aims in a unified manner.

All tribes, cultures and religions have a consciousness of perceptions, beliefs and truths. This only adds to the interest and diversity of our world and should not be looked at as "they must be wrong because we are right".

We have a global consciousness; the way people perceive our world, our environment, our industry, and our reliance on oil products. Do we care, or just simply believe it is someone else's problem? Our global consciousness currently reveres people with money, people with high IQ, people who are beautiful, people who are tough and successful, sports heroes and movie stars. It appears to look down on people who are poor, not so good looking, have lower intellect, different colour skin and different religious beliefs. Is this really how we wish to see our world? Would it not be better to appreciate everyone for what they individually represent, and what they each can do for the world?

## MASS CONSCIOUSNESS

The duality of mass consciousness means that there are opposing energies. Within mass consciousness is a quotient of Love and Light, and opposing it is Dark and Fear. The Love and Light is the Divine Aspect of God and contains within it the divine attributes of our Creator. Up to this point the Dark and Fear have held critical mass, which means we have all been affected by the negative and dark energies filled with fear. As more and more of humanity fell under the spell and manipulation of these dark negative energies over many thousands of years, so the light quotient receded to a low level.

However, during this transition stage more and more people have become aware of their true selves as children of God, or divine sparks, so the quotient of Love and Light has increased and is continuing to increase exponentially. It has surpassed critical mass and so the dark energies are losing their grip of control in the world. The Light quotient has affected mass consciousness and therefore decreased the power of the dark controllers.

When the critical mass of Light and Love quotient is reached and surpassed, more Love and Light is available to humanity. As people begin to feel this Light, whether consciously or unconsciously, their attitude to life starts to change. People begin to seek answers that have been hidden from them. They seek their spirituality. They begin to take back their power and say no. They begin to question authority. They begin to want to see changes to the systems that control us. They want to see an equality of wealth. In other words, people are starting to wake up to freedom.

Thus, mass consciousness is changing from negative and fear based, to a spiritual based consciousness of Love and Light. This causes people to re-consider their truths, beliefs and perceptions.

As stated previously, the thoughts and beliefs which are our mass consciousness are held in the fourth dimension, under the auspices of our Archetypes, the Annunaki of Planet Nibiru.

# SEPARATION CONSCIOUSNESS

*The separation from "All That Is" is an illusion which only exists in the lower worlds of the third and fourth dimensions. When this illusion of separation is released, pain can be healed and the illusion no longer has a foundation to hold onto. Then you can begin to remember your true multidimensional Self and ground that Self in the third dimension.*

Separation consciousness comes from mass consciousness where we all believe we are separate: a "me and him/her" mentality, an "us and them" mentality. It is where we believe we are separate from our Creator, from God. It causes us to not care about the world we live in. It causes us to fear death because we may have nowhere to go. It causes wars and acts of violence, because we are separate from the Love of God. In separation consciousness we are lost, always seeking to find a way out of the hell we seem to have created in our world, and not knowing where to go to find the solution.

The solution has always been to reunite once again with the love of God; to recognise that Love is everything. There is nothing else. God is Love and we are made in his image, so we too are Love.

Religions have taught that we are separate from God. Governments have perpetuated this belief because people who believe they are separate from the Love of God are easier to control and manipulate. When you take back your power and reunite with God, you free yourself from the relentless demands of this 3D world and its leaders.

The way our world has been set up supports separation consciousness. Each country has a boundary that we cannot penetrate without huge protocols, rules and regulations. Countries have different languages which prevent us from communicating with each other. Each country has a different religion. We have negative attitudes of racial differences, but we are all humans on earth, regardless of skin colour.

All of these perpetuate separation consciousness.

# UNITY CONSCIOUSNESS

This is where our journey of ascension is taking us. To the place in our hearts where we can recognise that humanity is one race, one family of peoples, regardless of skin colour, beliefs, where we live, and what we do. Unity is understanding we are all one in the eyes of God. What you do, think, believe and say affects everyone and everything in our world, and not only in the world, but in the entire universe.

We need to overcome the idea that we are separate from others, separate from the universe, and separate from God. We are all one, we are all children of God, represented by our individual lives and consciousnesses.

# ALCHEMY OF CONSCIOUSNESS

To expound the meaning of consciousness I will use a sparrow as an analogy. One sparrow has an individual consciousness: it knows who it is, where it lives, what it eats. That sparrow is part of a family, and is therefore part of a family consciousness: the family knows who they are, where they live in a particular tree and part of a particular garden, what they eat and where to find it.

All the sparrows in the same city are part of a wider sparrow consciousness. They know they all live within this city, they are all part of a wider family of sparrows, they all sleep in trees, they all eat similar food. On from that all sparrows within the country have a country consciousness, and then beyond that all sparrows throughout the world are part of a global sparrow consciousness. They all know what they are, they live in trees, they eat similar food, and therefore their perceptions, beliefs and truths on a global level would be similar.

Most people have heard the story of the 100th monkey phenomenon. On an island off the coast of Japan lived a family of monkeys. One day one of them started going down to the water and washing his fruit before he ate it. After a time other monkeys started to do the same, until eventually all the monkeys on the island were washing their fruit in the water before eating it. Then scientists noticed that monkeys on neighbouring islands started doing the same, even though they had no connection and no contact with the original monkeys. This occurred because of the critical mass achieved, or what is known as the 100th monkey, in the mass consciousness of the original monkeys. Once the dominant thoughts of their consciousness was reached, then those thoughts travelled via vibrational frequencies of light, or thought transference, to the other monkeys on other islands and so their thoughts and actions changed accordingly.

Thoughts are awareness. Awareness is consciousness. Consciousness is energy. Energy is light.

Everything is energy and has its own consciousness: not just humans or animals—everything. Even a pen, a chair, a house and a garden; all of them have a consciousness. They are aware of what they are and where they are, what they are made of and what they are for. That chair you sit in remembers everyone who has ever sat in it. It retains the energy as part of its consciousness: it is aware of itself. A pen or a chair might not have an eternal soul such as humans have, but that does not mean they have no conscious understanding of their life and purpose.

The trees in the forests understand what they are and what they do. They contain a high level of consciousness and will transfer their knowledge and wisdom to anyone who seeks a higher level of awareness.

All creatures contain consciousness. The whales and dolphins are blessed with a very high level of consciousness and know what their role in this world is, and it is a sacrilege to have them slaughtered to the degree happening even today.

Dogs are called "man's best friend". They are indeed because they are part of a consciousness that always seeks to serve and love their human companions.

The animals that provide us with food have a consciousness. They are blessed to know that they are here to serve and provide food for humans. They do not have a problem giving their life to sustain ours because their consciousness understands the need for this. However it is time that humans learnt once again to honour these animals and treat them with dignity, respect and gratitude.

And so, what is alchemy consciousness? Alchemy means to change one energy into another. It does not matter what the energy is, if you are changing it in any way, it is an alchemical change. Alchemy is a scientific term, but can be understood as any level of change.

Milk production undergoes an alchemical change. The cows eat grass, their body changes it into milk, which is then given to us for sustenance.

As individuals we are undergoing an alchemical change. We are changing our 3D bodies for 5D bodies. Our world is alchemically changing from a 3D planet to a 5D planet. This is called Ascension, or the Alchemy of Ascension.

As we move through this Ascension process, we are moving into the higher dimensions of living. We are expanding our level of awareness. We are acquiring our knowledge and understanding of the bigger picture: the expanded God picture. So consciousness is our level of awareness and understanding of the bigger wider picture.

## NEW EARTH CONSCIOUSNESS

*When man frees himself from this restrictive consciousness, with its laws and plans and rules, he will find the joy and peace of being that will allow him to love himself and the whole of mankind and allow all to be in the freedom of their own willful designs.*

*. . . Ascended Master Ramtha*

New Earth Consciousness is the energy of the new world we are in the process of creating. Our journey of ascension is about changing our thoughts, beliefs and truths into ones of Love and Light and a unity with God, which will become the basis of our future world. We are not ascending anywhere, we are not going someplace else, we are changing the world we live in.

With every negative belief and truth that we change into love and light, we help the world to establish a new way of living; this exciting new world of our future. It won't happen overnight, but it will happen, because we have surpassed the critical mass of humanity that wants to see change in our world. We all want freedom, and that is where we are heading.

This new world has a new energy consciousness—a new vibrational frequency that moves beyond anything that has ever been in place on Earth before.

We are in transition, transforming our old earth/old world from 3D consciousness to new earth/new world 5D consciousness, or more correctly, multidimensional consciousness. Planet Earth is becoming fifth-dimensional and we are returning to our original angelic state of multidimensionality.

To transition both ourselves and our world means we cannot take any old systems, old rules, old methods of control, old beliefs and truths, old fears and negative emotions with us. They must all be cleared from us individually and from our beloved planet. Mother Earth is going through the same transition and purging of old energies as we are. She cleanses herself through the elements of fire, air, water and earth, and so we need to recognise that the tsunamis, the earthquakes, volcanic eruptions, and floods and fires, are all part of her process of clearing. What she is clearing is the debris of humanities' gross misdeeds to their environment and to each other over eons and eons of time.

We need to understand that when we create violent deaths, wars and pollution, and have complete disregard for the animals and nature of our world, this energy sits in the elemental kingdom within earth, which in turn becomes toxic to our environment.

Mother Earth loves us and nurtures us, but we have allowed ourselves to be led into destructive and disrespectful ways of living. She must now cleanse herself in readiness for her own transition to the fifth dimension.

On an individual basis we too must look to our inner selves: to the old beliefs and truths that have settled into our unconscious being. We must also cleanse and purge ourselves of these negative energies because they cannot and will not exist in the higher dimensions. If you insist on retaining any old energies of whatever type, then you will be unable to live in the higher dimensions on our new planet earth.

As part of this ascension process we will gradually lose the duality of our world. This duality has meant that our world has been about the two energies always opposing each other. Our new world will be one of Triality: the trinity of the Divine Masculine energy, the Divine Feminine energy, and the Higher Self. This can also be seen as our light side, our dark side and our higher self. We can also look at it in terms of a problem, our divine self, and the solution. Whatever our situation and thoughts, we will always be able to see from a higher perspective, a higher intelligence and wisdom, and access what we need to know and do.

In the past, religions have promoted the trinity of the Father, the Son and the Holy Spirit. They were very much aware they could not function without the complementary energies of God/Goddess, and so they disguised it to appear as a patriarchal trinity. The churches did not inform their people that this trinity in fact meant Father as God, Son as the Divine Masculine energy, and the Holy Spirit meaning the Divine Feminine energy. In ancient Egypt, the Holy Spirit was always known and recognised as being the Divine Feminine aspect of God.

## OVERLAY OF THE NEW EARTH

*There are many Lightworkers who have chosen to venture into the unknown, and then to emerge into the realms of the New Earth. They spread their light by bringing new information to assist the expansion of awareness and a deeper enlightenment to the divinity within each human.*

To create the new earth, we are presently creating a new 5D consciousness overlay. We could say that this sits around the present earth and contains all our thoughts of Love and Light and how we wish our new world to be. As we send out thoughts of peace on earth, freedom from control, freedom from poverty and instead an abundance for all, a life of joy and laughter, and a life filled with creativity and passion, so these thoughts manifest in this etherical field of our new world. This overlay contains the attributes that we wish to base our future lives on.

This overlay is called "The New Earth", which is about creating Heaven on Earth, or Paradise Earth as some refer to it. It is returning us to our original angelic essence, further enhanced by having experienced the lower dimensions of duality.

Our mission is to incorporate the spiritual aspects of our divine nature and meld it with the physical embodiment of our life here on earth.

At pivotal times in this evolutionary journey, the non-physical realms take a poll, so to speak, of our intentions for the new cycles about to begin. So it is important that we focus our thoughts on how we wish our new world to be. As we "feel" this new world into manifestation, and believe we will create our dreams, so it will come to be.


# GOD CONSCIOUSNESS

*Love is not an emotion, it is an omnipotent resonance. Love is the building block, the core DNA of everything, and consciousness is the engine of all creation—matter and anti-matter.*

Consciousness exists through all things: living forms, sentient beings and inanimate objects. This consciousness represents the level of awareness of the life form or object.

If we were to look at the levels of consciousness of the universe, we would understand that the consciousness of God must be the top level of consciousness, and this we might be inclined to think of as the "Mind of God". This Mind of God contains all the thoughts of creation and the experience, expansion and evolution thereof. The Mind of God contains the three attributes that the Creator has endowed our universe with: Unconditional Love, Creative Intelligence and Divine Will and Power.

So the Mind of God containing these three attributes flows through everything and every life form in this hologramic universe: every electron, every atom, and every cell of our human body. As the Mind of God carries this attribute of Unconditional Love, this God Consciousness is therefore aware of every life form in the universe and loves it unconditionally.

The Mind of God, as represented through the God Matrix and the higher Beings of Light, creates intelligently, responsibly and creatively for the highest good of all.

As this Mind of God, or energy of God Consciousness, flows throughout the Universe, we could say that the Universe itself is "the Mind of God".

So what we call God Consciousness is a stream of consciousness that emanates from God, or Source: a stream of awareness of All That Is.

We could therefore say that "consciousness" can be defined as "Mind connected to God".


# CHRIST CONSCIOUSNESS

This new world has a new frequency of Love and Light which has never been present on earth before. This new frequency is called "Christ Consciousness". Christ consciousness exists throughout the universe, but we have a new frequency, or a new level that has not been available before.

The man we call Jesus came to earth to establish this new frequency of Love, and he anchored it into the energies of the earth as a seed for humanity to take up, expand, and evolve with into the new world that was divinely planned for earth and humanity. It was always going to be a slow process but evolution does not happen overnight, not anywhere in the universe. Structural creations can manifest instantly, but evolution of life forms needs to be taken slowly or the intake of higher vibrating frequencies would cause the death of the life form.

Our physical bodies are evolving slowly, but much faster than normal evolution. The faster process is in our consciousness. Our consciousness is concerned with changing our beliefs and truths and that can happen reasonably quickly, but our ego personality does take time to adapt to new beliefs. Change is always a frightening concept to our ego as it means the ego has to let go of the control it has had in our lives. We need to reassure our ego that we are merely moving to a heart based existence but we still need our ego mind to action our spiritual beliefs.

The definition of Christ Consciousness is "the Divine Seed, or Spirit of God, the essence of Divinity". It is the energy of Truth and Authenticity. Christ Consciousness carries Christ Intelligence which is the "Word of God". It is the embodiment of the Law of God.

We all contain Christ Consciousness within our cells and DNA, and this means we are a blend of Divinity, Angelic energy and Humanness.

Due to a distorted understanding we believe that Jesus is the Christ. However Christ Consciousness is the part of the God Matrix, or God Consciousness, that actions and embodies the creations. There is a Universal Christ in the Universal Spiritual Hierarchy, and Lord Maitreya is our present Planetary Christ.

God Consciousness is the foundation of the Universe—which is LOVE—the Divine Feminine creation energy.

Christ Consciousness is the active principle—which is LIGHT—the Divine Masculine energy.

## QUANTUM CONSCIOUSNESS

Every electron, atom and being in the universe knows they are part of the whole. Everything is interconnected and woven together as a "tapestry of existence". We humans are part of this tapestry: each of us an integral piece of the web.

Quantum is being aware of that connection. We have that awareness, whether we remember it or not. We are starting to remember that we are part of the Quantum Unified Field, as science might call it, and therefore part of the Oneness of Creation. This quantum connection is within our DNA.

## GALACTIC CONSCIOUSNESS

We are part of this Galaxy, and therefore an integral part of Galactic Consciousness. From there our solar system also has a Solar Consciousness. Arriving in the fifth-dimensional realms will gift you with the ability to remember your friends and family throughout the solar system and galaxy. We are becoming galactic humans.

## PLANETARY CONSCIOUSNESS

Humans, animals, all life forms, all kingdoms, the inner earth realms and Mother Earth make up a planetary consciousness. We are not separated from these other realms: we are all interconnected and if we remembered and honoured this, we would not poison our planet and our resources—other life forms depend on them. Our Planetary Consciousness is looked after by the Planetary Spiritual Hierarchy.

Humanity has what is called a collective consciousness of humanity, which is a collection of all our thoughts and beliefs that we are currently actioning in our lives within this world.

All groups have their own group consciousness.

Mass consciousness exists in the fourth dimension and is where all our thoughts and words go that are not actioned within our lives. Thoughts do not just disappear into nowhere. If you think a thought, then it is a creation in its own right and must either be manifested into form or it goes into mass consciousness. So many of our thoughts are negative: ones of fear and anger, poverty and helplessness. These amass in the 4D mass consciousness and constantly bombard us with those same negative energies.

## INDIVIDUAL CONSCIOUSNESS

*Everything that you need, everything that you want, everything that you choose to create, every potential of every moment is already within you. I'm not talking about in your physical body, although it is there also. I'm saying it's in your consciousness. Your consciousness is your awareness, but so much of your awareness has been shut down, on purpose, and it's been actually for a reason. It wasn't a mistake. It wasn't a mistake at all. It was part of the learning and the growing of the human.*

*. . . Adamus Saint-Germain*

If we define consciousness as "awareness", then our individual consciousness defines our individual "awareness of Self": what we are aware of as "Self". Your knowledge of Self is your level of awareness, which is then your vibrational signature.

As long as you exist in the little picture of Self you are existing at a "limited" level of awareness or consciousness. Our journey is about expanding our consciousness to become aware that we are part of the wider universe.

We could call this limited awareness of Self superficial. This limited Self believes the physical body and brain/ego are all there is. This has been our third-dimensional life. The person with the limited belief of Self usually does not seek the deeper truths of Self.

However, each step you take on this spiritual ascension journey, when you learn something new about yourself, and you understand and integrate it, then that step lifts you up to the next level of awareness and consciousness.

Before we can achieve these higher levels we need to go deep into the many layers of the sub-conscious to discover who we really are.

I have stated that dimensions are levels of awareness/consciousness, and we talk about them being outside ourselves in other realms of existence. However, these dimensions exist internally as well as externally. We must search, discover, understand, integrate and balance our internal dimensions to enable us to access the dimensions of the many external worlds.

Individual consciousness is our God Self, our Spirit, connected to the Mind of God.

We have a Lower Mind—which is restricted consciousness, and we have a Higher Mind—which is expanded consciousness. What are our conscious thoughts? What are we creating for ourselves?

We create according to our level of awareness. If our awareness is one of pain and suffering, poverty and fear, lack of love, then that is what we create for ourselves. As we clear and release negative emotions and beliefs and lift our awareness, our positive conscious thoughts create abundance.

Become consciously aware of your thoughts. Are your thoughts positive or negative?

## SOUL CONSCIOUSNESS

What is the "soul"?

The soul is our immortal and divine creatorship. It is the "I Am God Also". Energy never dies, so the soul is immortal, eternal. Our soul is a fragmentation of God, an aspect of God, and is connected to All That Is, as well as retaining individuality to experience expansion and evolution.

The soul contains our cellular memory of all experiences and the wisdom gained.

This soul is part of the wider universe. This vastness is hard for us to understand, but we must come to the remembrance that we are galactic humans. Human civilization on earth is moving into becoming a galactic civilization. As souls we are known as travelers and gypsies, ones that traverse the many worlds of this universe.

When we die and leave our body, we become our soul consciousness once more. This soul consciousness is a field of energy: our energy matrix containing our divine essence. In other words, we become a "matrix of light" which consists of colours, tones and vibrational frequencies. This is how we are seen and recognised in the higher realms. Our soul consciousness does not need a form. The physical body, our form, is not who we are. We can exist without form in the higher dimensions of light.

We also need to understand that not all life forms have a soul. It is not necessary to have a soul. If life forms do not have a soul they have Spirit and consciousness, as does all life, but they do not reincarnate into the same soul consciousness as we do. Many of these beings may have a form that lives perhaps for many thousands of years, but without the divinity and without being a fragmentation of God essence, they are not eternal.

## INTEGRATED CONSCIOUSNESS

From here you can understand:
Your Individual Consciousness is one with the Collective Consciousness of Humanity,
which is one with the Planetary Consciousness
which is one with Solar Consciousness,
which is one with Galactic Consciousness,
which is one with Cosmic Consciousness,
which is ultimately God, All That Is.

## TO SUMMARIZE CONSCIOUSNESS

What is consciousness?
It is interdimensional—beyond space and time.
Consciousness contains the whole.
Consciousness is awareness.
The higher the level of awareness, the greater the authenticity and responsibility.
Consciousness is conscious thought with creation energy, at the highest level: God.

# ASCENSION

*Enlightenment is for you to discover within. Indeed it is already in you, in your Beingness, your subconscious and your DNA. Spiritual enlightenment is not about following any Guru or Channel, but rather for you to find through personal discernment and your inner guidance. It is around accepting and KNOWING that the Divine Self is the spark of God within you, and that you are an intricate and eternal portion of Creator God. There are tools to help you along the way, there always has been and always will be. You are not alone. But Dear Ones, you have appointments to keep in this very special era of Ascension. Perfection is in play.*

*. . . Archangel Metatron*

Our third-dimensional (3D) biological body used to have to die to return the soul to its lightbody, or angelic form. Because this was at a higher frequency level, there was no other way for lower dimensional humans to access it except to have the biological form die.

There have been instances in our history where people have de-materialized their body and returned to their higher dimensional lightbody. It is recorded in the bible that the prophet Elijah returned to heaven in an explosion of light, witnessed by Elisha. This was a de-materialization of the body. There is no body left, no physical vessel left to bury. It is an acceptance at a very high level of Self that knows and believes that we are all the energy of God. We are not just flesh and bones, we are energy. Therefore if you increase the energy vibrations of the body to the higher frequencies, the body will simply dissolve back into the source field from whence we all come. After seeing this vision, Elisha became a prophet himself and continued the teachings of Elijah.

Ascended Master Ramtha, channeled in the US by a lady called JZ Knight, also claims to have de-materialized his body, recorded in his channelings and books. He said he always wanted to become the wind, and so in reaching up to the higher dimensional frequencies he also de-materialized his body and became his dream of being the wind.

St Germain, one of the ascended masters currently assisting us through our ascension process, says he often materializes and de-materializes his presence here on earth at will, even today.

There are many other masters who have transcended this reality and are able to materialize form on earth. Many of these actually live on earth in a higher dimensional state which we do not see.

The Creator has gifted this lifetime to us to complete all our karma and all unfinished business at a rapid rate in order to qualify for ascension.

With the current ascension process, we do not have to die to access our fifth-dimensional lightbody form. This is a new experiment for life on earth, and we are well on our way to achieving the Divine Plan that decrees we can ascend if we choose to, into the higher dimensions while still retaining our physical body. Once we have done this, like St Germain, we will always have access to our physical vessel, and will be able to materialize or de-materialize at will. Do not expect this to happen anytime soon. It will take a long time for the human form to evolve into something so complex.

We will become biological 5D humans. To achieve this, we need to clear our physical vessels of our negative and erroneous beliefs, to clear our emotional reactions to our world, and to create our own individual overlay that will become part of us as we ascend into the higher frequencies of light.

## OUR DESCENT INTO THIRD DIMENSIONAL REALITY

We commenced this journey as angelic entities in the higher dimensions, moved into the fifth dimension, then lowered our vibrational frequencies to live within the third-dimensional reality.

In descending through the vibrational frequencies we lost our Spirit (the love of God), our Higher Truth, our Freedom (our power), our Wisdom, our Abundance, our Knowledge, and above all, we lost Trust: trust in both ourselves as aspects of God, and trust in God and the Universe.

On our journey back to the fifth dimension and higher realms we must re-gain these attributes that have lain dormant within our cellular memory for so long. To do this requires love, compassion and forgiveness for ourselves and others.

The zero point of 2012 is the furtherest point of descent. From this time onwards everything moves forward into the fifth dimension, and life will never be the same.

## ASCENSION IS A CHOICE

*The definition of our ascension is "transcending third-dimensional reality". It is transcending the four lower bodies: physical, mental, emotional and spiritual. These are presently based on third-dimensional constructs which in turn create our third-dimensional perceptions, beliefs and truths. Ascension means completing our earthly cycles and moving to higher levels of consciousness.*

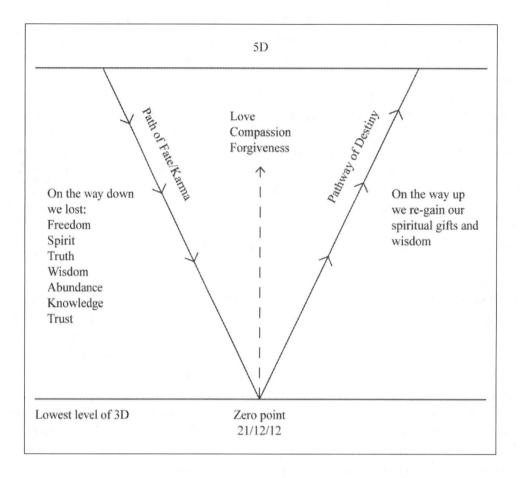

Ascension is a journey, not a destination. It is an individual journey of the soul. We are always on a journey of ascension because we are always seeking the truth, seeking that which we feel we have lost.

To live life in the lower realms of 3D demands that we lose our connection with God in order to experience duality, both sides of the opposing energies of our world. Our ascension journey is about traversing the frequencies of the lower realms, garnering the truth that we are beings of light, and then transcending the 3D vibrational frequencies of duality. This is a journey to find our truth, our light and our divine essence, that "We Are God Also".

Only when you have this belief well and truly imbedded into your heart can you reach up to the upper realms and begin the ascension home, taking your physical vessel with you.

In the journey of ascension into the higher dimensions of self, the Higher Self begins to meld with the biological body. Slowly the physical body takes on more and more of the Divine Intelligence, the Divine Wisdom, the Divine Creativity of the Higher Self, evolving into a manifested Lightbody form living on Earth.

This lightbody form is multi-dimensional and acknowledges its higher aspects of Self which have not been available to it for eons of time in the lower dimensions.

Challenging as it is, we need to proceed through the journey of ascension, moving into the higher frequencies of Self, while still living and working within the realms of 3D as seen and believed by the mass of humanity at this time. This process can be extremely difficult while trying to retain some sense of 3D normality with other people. It will however become easier as time goes on. This process is often called "walking between worlds" and is an apt description. We often feel like we have a foot in both worlds and it can be extremely uncomfortable.

At this pivotal point in earth history we have two choices: 1) to complete our karma and unfinished business and evolve, or 2) to die and perhaps reincarnate on another third-dimensional planet to experience a continuation of pain and suffering for perhaps another 26,000 year cycle, when collective consciousness may be given another opportunity of ascension.

## LIGHTWORKERS

Many people are incarnated on earth at this time to assist humanity to understand and return to their divine essence, to connect to God once again.

These people are usually called Lightworkers, or Warriors of Light, Wayshowers, or Pathfinders. They are also known as the Star Seeds. They are the ones who have taken on the arduous task of paving the way, of walking through the layers of duality and transcending 3D in order to show the way to those that follow. It has not been easy. The world has ridiculed the new age beliefs, the visionaries, and the new prophets of the new world. They have had to endure much, but their efforts have now been rewarded as the world and humanity commences in earnest to take upon themselves the journey to the higher realms.

Lightworkers began incarnating on the planet during the war, but many in the Lightworker movement were born in the years immediately after the war. They started their job of changing the planet even at that point, as babies. In a world torn and ravaged by war they brought Love to their families, a light that would erase the pain of war and loss. These ones are the Baby Boomers and were born in large numbers throughout the world.

They were the hipppie people, the flower people of the sixties, who told the world "make love not war". They practised "peace to all men". Some mistakenly used marijuana to achieve that peace in their hearts, but their intentions were always for the betterment of mankind. Perhaps they needed the drug because the world at that time was a difficult place to find or to create peace. It was the era of "think big" where global corporations started their raid on the dignity of the planet and as well as creating wars for soldiers, they created wars within industry, commerce and banking.

These Baby Boomers continued their mission by marching in protest against the Vietnam war. "We don't want war" they said. "Stop taking our sons". They have continued ever since trying to halt wars and bring peace to the world. They have often been involved in environmental issues and animal rights issues. They have worked hard to stall the tide of pollution and the decimation of animal species.

This Baby Boomer generation became the early healers and teachers, starting in earnest after the Harmonic Convergence of 1987. This was the beginning of our 25 year window of opportunity to cleanse and prepare for Ascension. These people have done huge service over many years to help humanity. Many

Lightworkers are only now taking their place as the teachers of new consciousness, teachers of new healing methods, teachers of metaphysics and spirituality.

It is time for the mass of humanity to wake up and understand their heritage, where they originate from, and the lies that have been told by our controllers. Time to take a stance for freedom, for peace, and for the future as we wish it to be.

One of the main roles of the Baby Boomer generation was to give birth to the Indigo children.


## THE INDIGO CHILDREN

Following on from the Lightworker/Baby Boomer generation came the Indigos. These children started to incarnate from the early 1970s and birthed in large numbers during the 1980s. These ones are called Warriors of Peace as their mission is to help create peace on earth. Psychic readers could see that their auras showed a lot of indigo/purple colour and so they were called Indigo children. All children born since are Indigos but with higher quotients of crystalline frequencies.

The Indigo Crystal children started incarnating in the late 80s and through the 90s. They carry the frequency of the Indigo vibration, but also carry a portion of the higher crystalline frequencies. These young ones are called Warriors of Change. Their very vibrations are helping to change the frequencies here on earth, causing change to be implemented in many different ways.

The Crystal children started incarnating in the late 90s and through the years following the new millenium. Many children born today are Crystal children, but not all children are necessarily Crystals. It depends on the vibrational frequency they were born with and their choices and requirements for this incarnation. These children are known as Warriors of Consciousness, and it is their job to assist in changing the consciousness of all those people around them and in the wider community and world. They are often seen to be different, highly intelligent and very creative. They will help to change societal patterns and structures of how humans live. They have trouble fitting into the world unless they are nurtured and loved by their family.

Recently children started coming in as Star children embodying much more of their stellar consciousness. It will be very hard for parents to act falsely in front of these children because they will look right through the parent and see the truth.

These children all come in with higher quotients of light than we have as parents and grandparents. We have to achieve these higher vibrations by clearing old karma, beliefs and emotions. They already have it in their DNA.

Children do come in with their own karma to clear. However ancestral karma and beliefs they have inherited can be cleared through us, as parent or grandparent, clearing those same issues from our system.

Many of today's children are taking on Lemurian attributes. They are tall, much taller than their parents or grandparents. Over six foot tall is not uncommon any more. Our Lemurian ancestors and our Pleiadian parents were all much taller and slimmer than we are now.

2008 brought in the first of the Sun Children. These children are born with a pure consciousness. They are angelic beings that have never incarnated on earth before, therefore they have no past, no karma to clear. They represent the pure love and light of God.

# THE FIFTH DIMENSION

The cells of our present biological body contain about 70% carbon. These cells are changing in order to hold more light and as they do this they become more crystalline based. Crystalline energy is "light", or what we would know as diamond light. As this process continues we become "Crystal Adults".

Our blood will change. It will, perhaps, become thinner with more light and more blue in colour.

The physical body will become "lighter", but not meaning weight. The physical "lightbody" will be lighter because it will vibrate faster and appear somewhat shimmery.

The body will be able to heal and regenerate itself, become younger, stronger, fitter and more flexible. There will be no illness and disease, no viruses, and no pain and suffering.

We will live longer. The original templates of life were up to perhaps 1,000 or more years old. Our original lives in Lemuria were long, but as we fell into lower and denser frequencies so we lost our ability to live long healthy lives. We will increase our lifespan, but in this current life we will possibly add only about 50 years to our lifespan. Our current physical bodies will not be able to rejuvenate to last 1,000 years. That will come in some future lifetime.

Our present 2-strand DNA will expand to once again operate on our original template of 12-strand DNA: 2 biological strands and 10 interdimensional strands will be reactivated.

Our bodies are presently being "rewired", so to speak. This rewiring is continually underway as we progress forward, and is necessary so the body can withstand the higher frequencies of electrical energy being received. Every cell, organ and system will be rewired. The two hemispheres of the brain are presently separated by synaptic pathways that allow a very slow transmission of information from one side to the other. These hemispheres are being rewired and melded together with what we could call fibre optic cables that will transfer information very fast. The left hemisphere is currently understood as using the intellect, what we call left brain logic. The right hemisphere represents our intuition and creativity. People were seen to be more dominant in one or the other, but in time these two hemispheres will operate more as one brain.

Our Chakra system presently operates on seven primary biological chakras. These are all being upgraded to receive and transmit higher frequencies. Many new chakras will be activated.

Our need for food and sleep will eventually decline. We will manage on about four hours rest for the physical body. Food will need to be the lighter fruit and vegetables, but will not eliminate the enjoyment we get from eating a wide variety of foods.

We will learn to communicate differently. The Indigo Children are presently working towards a global language in their texting and a common language will become the norm. We will eventually not need words as we will feel what another is transmitting to us: thought transference or mental telepathy as we would know it.

We will learn to live from the heart. The mind will be excused from its exhaustive job of protecting us from everything and everyone. The heart and soul will direct our choices.

As we gradually let go of our old ways we will go through a grieving process. It is always difficult to see change in our lives, and to a certain extent we can find this painful.

## LIVING IN THE FIFTH DIMENSION

Linear time will gradually cease and we will return to the universal cycles and spirals of experience. The planet will be healed. Pure water, pure air, and pure food once again—no pollution. New technologies will be found to clean up the planet, to detoxify waste products, to provide better food production, and to provide alternative methods of energy production.

Political, governmental, banking and corporate structures will change. The old ways of control will be changed. Wealth will be more evenly spread. We will learn to live once again in peace and harmony, joy and bliss, fun and laughter, with no more fears.

Jobs will change. We will work at things we love to do. No more having to go to work for someone else at a job we hate just to make enough money to pay the bills. Jobs will become more community, global or planetary oriented. We will use our skills and abilities to achieve, and we will find this work to be our passion. We will be more creative because we will have time to do what we wish. We will create the life we want, and the dreams we wish to manifest, but these will be heart based and not ego based.

We will manifest what we need when we want it. There will be no need for materialism.

Relationships will be balanced loving relationships based on unconditional love with a soul mate of similar vibrational frequency. Children will be valued and cherished by their parents and nurtured within the community.

The rewiring of our eyes and the return of our psychic ability to see into the other dimensions will mean that we will live side by side with those beings of different dimensions, enjoying friendships and family that we have long forgotten about.

The colour spectrum will expand to a wider range of vivid, luminescent, shimmering colours.

Money will eventually cease as we will have no need for it. We will learn to manifest what we want and it will be only what we need at that time. We will share what we have with people by going back to a barter system. However, money will be around for a long time yet, as it is only energy and a symbol of our giving and receiving.

New abilities to teleport around the world and the universe will evolve over a longer period of time.

Remember, we are not going anywhere—we are staying here on earth and creating the higher vibrations of the fifth dimension within. We are creating Heaven on Earth: not going up to Heaven in some other realm.

These changes will take time. Evolution doesn't happen overnight, but we are on the starting block to develop and implement some of these changes.


## PHYSICAL SIGNS AND SYMPTOMS OF ASCENSION

Sleep is one of the main problems of ascension. During our sleep or meditation state the non-physical beings are working on the rewiring and other cellular changes in our body. While we travel to the higher realms in our sleep state the physical body gets worked on and then rests. As we return to the body so we wake up, often at 3am or 4am. This is commonly known as the 3am Club. We all do it, often frustrating us when we fall asleep again as dawn breaks and we have to get up for work. If you stay in bed just try to relax and not allow your thoughts to get on top of you. Just accept that you are awake and be happy about it. That state of mind is much more conducive to falling asleep than tossing and turning and getting angry. Otherwise get out of bed and do something for a while, then try to sleep again. Sometimes this waking at 3am is the result of an excess of energy, too much of the higher vibrations overloading your nervous system. It will go, but take time out in nature during the day which is a good healer of excess energy.

Tiredness, fatigue and exhaustion are also prominent signs of ascension. There is a lot happening to our body, to our mental and emotional systems, there are a lot of changes we are making to our spiritual beliefs and truths, and all this is exhausting. Try to rest when your body wants it. Don't feel guilty about resting in the middle of the day if you are able to. It is part of the process and goes on for a long time. Look after yourself and don't beat yourself up because you can't do everything you want to. Simplify your life and just do the priorities.

Body aches and pains come and go from various parts of the body. All the systems are being upgraded and there are always aches and pains somewhere, particularly in the muscular system. Quite often we have cold or flu like symptoms and these may persist or might come and go quite often. These are symptoms of the clearing of chakras, and the rewiring of the body in general.

Headaches are common, particularly around the base of the skull. This area, known as the cerebellum, is where the ancient brain is and that is being re-activated so you can remember your true heritage.

Doctors will diagnose ringing in the ears as Tinnitus, but usually it is just a symptom of the ascension process. It is actually the workings of the universe, a sort of behind the scenes sound, or racket as I have called it. It usually goes away as you match up to the vibrations of the universe.

The body often feels like it is vibrating, a slight shimmering of the body, a slight extra beating of the pulses or heart, or a feeling of electrical currents moving through arms and legs. It usually doesn't last long, but some people may feel this more than others. This is an opening up of the electrical system to receive higher vibrations of energy. The spine can also feel a tingling sensation moving up and down the spinal column which is to do with the chakra system activating.

Digestive upsets can happen as the system gets overhauled. Just watch what you eat and eliminate anything that seems to upset you. The body will tell you what food it needs if you take note of what it is telling you, or what you are feeling like you need. These digestive problems can lead to either diarrhea or constipation as old energies are released. This can be a good thing.

Putting on weight. The obesity epidemic has its own separate reasons, but on the ascension journey we tend to put on more weight to hold more photons of light as they are being downloaded. This will pass, and doesn't always affect everyone. Eating light natural food can help eliminate this weight problem.

Short term memory loss or confusion is usually a symptom further along the journey. It gets to the point you can hardly remember what you did yesterday, or last week, and really hard to remember what you did last month or last year. It is about letting go of the past, of past beliefs, and of past memories or experiences that no longer serve.

Emotional reactions will happen in the most unexpected situations. We feel angry or depressed, or just burst into tears for no apparent reason. The emotional system is the one that needs the most work, and the soul is doing its best to bring to your awareness anything that needs sorting in relation to the way you react to people and situations around you.

Detaching from family and friends is part of this journey. As we increase our vibrational frequencies and start to access the higher dimensions, we become rather intolerant of the people around us who are still in the throes of drama, stress and chaos of daily lives. As we move into the higher frequencies we find a peace of mind, a quietness of the heart, and a need to be in our own space without the continual interruption of outside negative influences. Sometimes these family members and friends will come back to you at a later time when they have started their journey, and start to understand where you were coming from. Sometimes they don't come back to you at all, but have found the need to move on to new company and new teachers. It doesn't matter, all is as it is in the Divine Plan of our upliftment to the higher realms.

## HOW LONG DOES THIS PROCESS TAKE

*When you are flying to your destination it does not make you get there any faster when you run up and down the aisles of the plane!*

The journey of ascension can take several years. It is not an easy quick fix to our problems. It entails work and dedication to the clearing and re-programming of our beliefs and learning to place a new trust in the Love of God and the Divine Plan for our world.

So there is no "time period". It will take as long as it takes you to work through each step and stage. However, when you learn to just go with the flow and cease to have emotional reactions and panic attacks about the future, then you will help your body to ease into its new model with ease and grace.

## HELPING YOURSELF THROUGH THIS PROCESS

Get as much rest and relaxation as you can. When your body feels tired, let it rest. Sometimes you may feel on top of the world, and then the next day you are tired and lethargic. Just remember it is part of the process.

Make sure you have a good diet. Eat wholesome foods and avoid processed foods. Supplements are often required as the body needs a large supply of nutrients for the rewiring and regeneration of the cells.

Flower essences are excellent natural supplements to take for emotional reactions. Rescue Remedy is good for the trauma sometimes experienced during this journey. Fear is a natural reaction that we are trying to overcome so Bach Flowers Mimulus or Aspen are often required and depression can be helped by Gorse or Mustard. Of course there are many brands of flower essences and it doesn't matter which you take. Just know that what you take will help.

*There is a path open for each of you to follow, no matter at what station or circumstances you find yourselves, a golden opportunity waiting to enable you to assume your power, tap into your creativity, bring to the fore those many latent abilities you have stored deep within your memory banks. We are always close by, observing, waiting to assist and to encourage, to create the miracles, smooth the way and assist you in moving onward and upward.*

*. . . . The Ascended Masters*

Cell Salts/Tissue Salts are also valuable in helping the cells of the body to cope, to heal and to regenerate. These are natural bio-chemical remedies for the cells. A spray containing the 12 tissue salts is the best to use, but individual or combination cell salts can be used for various problems.

Drink plenty of clean pure water. This process is an electrical process, so the water provides the conduit for the extra energy pouring into your body. It will also help your body to remain hydrated during this process. The kidneys are an important part of the rewiring process and they need plenty of water.

Avoid coffee and other caffeine products as they dehydrate the body, raise the blood pressure, and stimulate the body when it should be resting.

## BIRTHING THE "NEW EARTH" HUMAN: HOMO CHRISTOS

*Ascension is happening right now, not in some far off distant future. Every moment, every day is another step on your ascension journey and holds the blessings of moving into your divinity and experiencing its joy. When you focus on each present moment, you experience your ascension. You must leave the past behind if you wish to create a new future.*

When you have cleared your third-dimensional karma and negativities, you are then ready to be birthed into the "new you", the "new life", and to become one of the founder members of the "new earth".

Having passed the initiations and learnt and embodied the cosmic laws, and having taken time out for the integration and fine tuning of this new divine human form, you will find yourself going through a challenging period called the re-birth into 5D. It is very much like being in a birth canal. It feels rather like being in the void of "nothingness", the emptiness. This is quite real as you are being emptied of all that does not resonate with the new 5D living.

You need to rest and allow this fine tuning to happen. You will probably feel very tired, fatigued and fed up with the whole journey. You will feel so close yet so far. When you look around at the people and the world, everything seems just the same and this creates confusion and conflicting thoughts which of course just makes you more fatigued.

You will become even more intolerant of the pain, suffering, fear and restrictions of the old world which is all around you. You will still be able to feel the fear of the collective consciousness. This period of time is about fine tuning the ability to remain balanced and centred in the heart without wobbling and falling into the old patterns of negativity.

During this period you will develop very strong self-love, self-acceptance and self-belief. You will give up worrying about what others think of you.

## MOVING INTO HIGHER LEVELS OF CONSCIOUSNESS

Throughout our ascension journey Higher Beings of the Universe, Gods and Goddesses, Ascended Masters and Archangels are sending information packets of knowledge pertinent to the next steps of our journey. These are pulsed into our auric field as pin points of light, and we can see these with our physical eyes. Sometimes they are white light, sometimes different colours; they can be tiny or large. Often in bed when your eyes are partially shut, getting ready for sleep, you will see little bursts of light. This is what they are: light packets of information.

These pulsations of light contain coded information: wisdom of higher knowledge. Our DNA is encoded and the various codes respond to the corresponding light packets.

Our Oversoul decides what needs to be downloaded into our physical body, and that is always relevant to the light quotient of our cells. No information is downloaded until you are ready to integrate that level of awareness, or consciousness. Our Oversoul/Monad, is always encouraging us on our path to our higher awareness and highest potential.

## THE OVERSOUL, OR MONAD

The Monad is our Oversoul from our Galactic lives. It has a record of our experiences and wisdoms gained from many worlds, civilizations, and life forms we have existed as and within.

We can say that our Oversoul contains our divine origins. It is our divinity. It is the "I Am God Also". We come to understand that we are multidimensional aspects of God. We are God playing out all these different experiences.

This Oversoul is expanded consciousness. It is the Mind of God. The Oversoul consists of all known and unknown dimensions, including those above the ninth dimension. We are expanding our individual 3D consciousness into this expanded consciousness—the memory of All That Is that we are an integral part of.

## WE ARE A UNIVERSE UNTO OURSELVES

Each one of us is our own universe, containing the same levels and layers of dimensions as the vaster universe. These levels and layers contain the aspects of ourselves existing in different time/space continuums, or realities.

The centre of our individual toroid is our Oversoul, our True and Authentic Self. During our lives we walk around the toroid levels experiencing life on earth in a variety of ways. All the dramas of life exist in the walk around, and we call this the journey of life. Within these layers, or dimensions of Self, exist past life aspects, future aspects, emotional aspects, personality aspects, multidimensional aspects and our inner child aspects. Therefore the fears, traumas and negativities we are releasing exist within these layers. To access them we need to work from the centre of Self, in the "Now", to understand them, heal them, transmute them, and integrate the wisdom learned.

Each of these layers, or dimensions, is the Kingdom we have created for ourselves. When we return to the centre as ascended beings, we have created the Kingdom of Heaven for ourselves; we do not have to wait for Heaven to come to Earth. We can create our own Heaven within ourselves and this Heaven contains the Purity of Spirit, the Innocent and Divine Self.

The ascension journey is long and challenging if we insist on taking the long way around the toroid, our individual universe. We shorten our journey by walking through the boundary we think is there, into the next level. We must lift our vibrational frequencies to achieve this.

These layers are like the onion analogy and we peel off the layers one by one as we walk into the centre of Self. We have been existing at the outermost edge of ourselves—separate from our divinity. We are now contracting into the centre of Self: who we truly are, and have always been.

The ascension journey is therefore the walk into the centre of Self. When we achieve this, we have ascended into the higher dimensions of Self and from this point we expand into a new evolution.

## RETURNING TO YOUR DIVINE SELF

This is a spiritual journey: returning to the centre of who you really are. This centre we call our Divine Self, our God Self. This Self is termed "authentic" or "impeccable".

We have seen ourselves to be separate from God, but this is not so; never has been and is not now, or any time in the future. We are always connected to our Divinity, which is the God within us. It exists in the DNA of every cell in the body.

Your God Self exists as a Higher Dimensional Self in "now" time, or "no time". It exists in the consciousness of Now.

When we move into the centre of Self we exist in the stillness of "Now" time, or "no time". It is only from this point that we access all other dimensional aspects of Self: past lives, future lives, the inner child, multidimensional aspects and our Higher Self. As we lift our levels of awareness we become more aware of these other aspects of Self and begin to understand that all these are part of who we really are: the vastness of our "real Self".

We start to experience many of these aspects and lifetimes in different ways.

> *Zen saying: Before enlightenment, chop wood, carry water. After enlightenment chop wood, carry water.*

## THE CONSCIOUSNESS OF "NOW"

This centre of Self exists in "now" time or "no time" and operates within cycles and spirals of expansion and contraction, just like all else in the universe.

As we move along this journey we begin to have experiences of past lives, sometimes as brief visions, or during meditations, in dream time, or sometimes as a feeling of deja vu, that we have been in that place before. We access these past lives in order to complete karma and to clear old negative emotions and distortions of beliefs that we still carry in this life time. This is a necessary part of the journey because we cannot move forward dragging the old stuff with us. To begin with, these past lives are in more recent history, and then they can become further back in the distant past.

When we are clearing and healing these past negative experiences we do not have to fully experience them again. We have already experienced them, and now it is understanding why they happened. From that understanding we realise the lesson to be learnt and the wisdom to be gained from the experience. We cannot change what happened, but we can change our emotional reactions to what happened. It is these emotional reactions that have instilled in our DNA the various fears and distorted beliefs.

For instance, if you experienced a shipwreck and drowned, you would have felt the fears at that time. These fears become part of the DNA carried into this life. You may have a fear of water, traveling on ships, or of drowning. It is time to recognise that what happened in a past life does not need to affect this life or future lives. The energies of the fear just need to be recognised, released from the cells, and replaced with a belief that this will not occur again.

Perhaps in a distant past life you were thrown in a castle dungeon with hungry rats. You could then carry a fear of rats and dark gloomy basement areas, and perhaps never wish to visit castles. The feeling of claustrophobia can originate with an experience such as this.

To clear these fears, you may simply see a vision in meditation. Make the intent that you wish this to be cleared from cellular memory, released from the cells and replaced with the opposite energy: the positive emotion or belief. Once you have cleared this fear from the cells, you need never experience it again in any circumstance, unless you choose to do so. This can happen if you continually experience life through the eyes of fear.

We can also access these past lives to source knowledge, wisdom, skills and talents that are part of our vaster Self, but which have become buried under the heavy burdens of fear and negative beliefs.

For instance, I was a High Priestess in the Atlantean Temples and I can access the skills and wisdom that I learnt at that time. During the Atlantean period I was also a scientist in the laboratories and learnt a great deal, but at the same time there was a karmic misuse of energy. I also experienced being a victim in the laboratories. Both of these experiences carried distorted fears and beliefs that have needed to be released.

So we can go back in time to release negative fears or access positive skills and wisdom.

# INITIATIONS FOR ASCENSION

*Ascension is the expansion of consciousness into higher dimensions of reality.*

In order to rise to the fifth dimension we undergo many levels of initiations. Every challenge, and every time you learn wisdom from a situation, you have undergone an initiation. Therefore every step on the path is an initiation of some sort, each one moving us forward. These initiations initially feel like enormous challenges because they can be traumatic. However the further down this path we travel the easier it is to surmount the difficulties that these challenges offer.

People and situations are placed before us by our guides, teachers and mentors in the non-physical realms. These situations will usually carry within them a belief, barrier or negative emotion that we need to address in order to move forward. Of course so many people just respond with knee-jerk reactions that result in anger, bitterness, retaliation, or perhaps envy, guilt, or depression. All of these feelings that we experience lead us to be a victim of the situation, instead of working through it and gaining the learning, understanding and wisdom that it was placed in front of us for.

Until people wake up and realise that what is before us is simply our lesson, our next step of initiation, then they will deal with it as an emotional reaction, instead of pro-actively working through the lesson.

In order to ascend, there are 7 series of initiations that we must complete in order to move forward. In various cultures, countries or religions these are given various names, such as 7 steps to Heaven, 7 levels of experience, 7 levels of initiation, 7 keys, 7 gifts, 7 sacred flames, 7 laws of God, 7 steps of ascension, 7 planes of existence, 7 doors to freedom, 7 levels of consciousness, 7 gateways to heaven, and probably many more. It doesn't matter what the labels are. It matters only that we complete them to move into the fifth dimension alongside our beloved Gaia, our planetary sentient being.

All the ascended masters have traveled this way. It is a requirement of ascension.

## THE SEVEN RAYS OF INITIATION

Although other paths and cultures will have their own similar orders of initiation, those of us who follow in the footsteps of the Ascended Masters understand the path as working through the initiations of the Seven Rays.

Each Ray has specific criteria that must be met before an initiate can move on. Each ray is looked after by an Ascended Master, an Archangel and their complement, and a member of the Elohim Council and their complement. Each Ray embodies the qualities that we need to strive for in order to become ascended masters, and to reside as fifth-dimensional humans on earth.

We are born under one of these Rays and embody the qualities and teachings of that particular Ray, and this becomes part of the lessons and ultimately the work we do here on Earth. Regardless of what Ray we are born under we must still do the ascension work of all the Rays.

Sometimes we are born embodying two rays, one primary ray and one secondary ray, and because all is connected we of course do touch on all of the seven rays when living and working here on earth.

We have a Monadic Ray, which is our primary ray, but we do incarnate under the various rays in order to complete the ascension initiations. We may have started this work back in earlier incarnations.

The first three rays reflect the three attributes of the Creator that represent the foundation of the Universe: Unconditional Love, Divine Will and Power, and Creative Intelligence. Rays four through to seven are sub-rays of the third ray, but all are equally important on the path of ascension.

## FIRST RAY OF DIVINE WILL AND POWER

This is the Ray of Ascended Master El Morya, Archangel Michael and Lady Faith. It is known as the Blue Ray, and many people working alongside Archangel Michel have incarnated under this Ray. If you have always loved the colour blue, if you have always felt an affinity to Archangel Michael, then perhaps this is the Ray you were born under, and you will carry the energies of Divine Will and Power.

The first ray is connected to the throat chakra, and the blue gems particularly of lapis and sapphire hold the qualities of this Ray.

The key point you are asked to embody under the First Ray is "surrender".

El Morya asks that you become willing to detach from your old outmoded way of living and embrace the new Golden Age. To do this he asks that you release fears and accept the path of love.

This Ray incorporates the "Will of God", and this requires that you surrender to the Will of God and allow your Higher Self and your Monad to guide you forward. The "Will of God" is not outside of you: it does not simply belong to some God up there. Within your DNA are the powers of God through which you seek in human form the expression of enlightenment and spiritual freedom. You as the embodied human will benefit from this God within. You will transcend the human ego, the limitations, pain and suffering of your old life. However you must be prepared to put aside all your old beliefs, your old paradigms of behaviour and attitude, and surrender to the pathway of your soul. If you struggle with this Ray, then your ego is putting up the barriers.

You must also understand that there is a Spiritual Hierarchy of the Universe who oversees the ascension of life in the universe, and a Spiritual Hierarchy of both our galaxy and our planet. They will ensure that the planet ascends as she is destined to do at this time, and you must surrender to this authority. Humans have become so incensed with authority figures that they often do not want to accept **any** higher authority, including that of the Spiritual Hierarchy. However this is mandatory for ascension. This is the way that allows the Universe to move in synchronicity. If all life just did what they wanted, there would indeed be chaos throughout the universe.

To surrender to the pathway of your Soul/Higher Self is to trust. Trust that you are being divinely lead, trust that all is well, and trust that what you are being led to is better than what you have ever experienced before.

You cannot simply wish ascension to happen. It is work. You are not going to be rescued by someone lifting you from the planet: "beam me up Scotty" won't happen. You must do the work, and I cannot stress this enough. Nobody else can do it for you. Nobody else can "save" you. You don't need to be saved, you just need to do the necessary work for ascension. It takes courage and commitment to complete this Ray, and El Morya will be with you every step of the way once you make that commitment. He is known to be stern, but that is for your benefit. His nature as an Ascended Master is one of love and compassion for your journey.

He also demands you release all your old obsessions such as tobacco, alcohol, and drugs. (This does not of course refer to your essential medications).

We have come to earth to experience a so-called separation from God. Through the Ray of Divine Will and Power you are to reclaim that God Self once more, and know that you were never disconnected from Source, that it lives within you. Understand that you cannot complete any of the other Rays until you have successfully completed the First Ray of Divine Will and Power.

**THE SECOND RAY OF ILLUMINATION AND WISDOM**

Representing the second attribute of the Creator, that of Creative Intelligence, this Ray is looked after by Ascended Master Lord Lanto and Archangels Jophiel and Christine.

This ray is connected to the crown chakra, and is the colour yellow. The yellow or golden stones hold the energies of this second ray.

The qualities you are seeking under this ray are wisdom, true knowledge, enlightenment and discernment. It is a specific ray of learning. The key point of the second ray is "wisdom".

This ray is about understanding the limitations, the pain, suffering and ignorance that you have been living under. The human ego is imprinted with fears, limitations and erroneous beliefs about Self which have resulted in a separation consciousness. You must surrender all these old limitations, these old inhibiting beliefs and fears, and integrate the knowledge of your Higher Self and your Monad.

This ray is about merging your human brain with the Mind of God, the Consciousness of God, and also attuning to your Sacred Heart, the Divine Aspect of your being.

## THE THIRD RAY OF COSMIC LOVE

This Ray represents the Unconditional Love of Creator and comes under the auspices of Ascended Master Paul the Venetian and Archangels Chamuel and Charity. This ray is connected to the Heart Chakra and therefore embodies love, compassion and brotherhood. In order to embody love we must let go of all judgments and criticisms.

The colour is Pink, which of course we are familiar with as being the colour associated with love. The pinks run from the palest of pinks to the dark pinks and the magentas.

## THE FOURTH RAY OF PURIFICATION

The fourth ray is the ray of Ascended Master Lord Serapis Bey and Archangels Gabriel and Lady Hope. This white ray is associated with the base chakra, and of the white gem stones.

The fourth ray is known as the Ascension Ray and is a very important ray for the initiate. The lesson you will need to embody under this ray is that of purity, whereby you clear all past negative human creations, transforming them into light. Ask Serapis Bey for help with this ray.

## THE FIFTH RAY OF HEALING AND MANIFESTATION

This ray comes under the auspices of Ascended Master Hilarion and Archangel Raphael and his Divine Complement Mother Mary. This ray concerns the Third Eye/Brow chakra and the colour it represents is green, the gem stones emerald and jade. This ray is used for healing at all levels.

Most health problems are caused by imbalances and unresolved issues in any of the four lower bodies: physical, mental, emotional and spiritual. As all of these bodies are interconnected, any one out of balance will then affect the others, causing chaos and illness in the physical body. In order to heal the body you must heal the deep-seated emotions and beliefs that have been imprinted into your DNA during this life, all your past lives, and also your ancestors' lives. External pain and difficulties are always mirrors of inner pains and fears. Most people just want the medical establishment to give them a magic pill or potion to make them better. All that can do is band-aid the problems occurring within your physical body without actually addressing the actual core issues, which are usually emotional blockages and fears.

At this time of transition to the fifth dimension, all these emotional blockages and fears are coming to the surface of your conscious awareness so that you can give them your focus for clearing and releasing. True and permanent healing can only occur in this way, and this is an absolute essential for ascension.

Master Hilarion and Mother Mary will support your healing process through the actions of the emerald ray.

## THE SIXTH RAY OF RESURRECTION

This ray comes under the overlighting leadership of Ascended Masters Lord Sananda and Lady Nada. These two beautiful beings are those we would recognise as the embodiments of Jesus and Mary Magdalen.

Their chakra is the solar plexus, and this ray resonates to the colours of purple and gold. Assisting this ray are Archangels Uriel and Aurora. The qualities this ray asks you to embody are those of spiritual devotion and Christ-like service. It is the ray of peace and true brotherhood.

The teachings of this ray is to know your Divine and True Self and to create a divine union between your human Self and this higher aspect of Self. This is the resurrection: to completely embody your Christ Self while in human form on earth. Resurrection means to restore to its normal or original condition, returning to wholeness, and so it is that we are required to achieve this for our ascension into the fifth dimension.

Jesus said "I AM the Resurrection and the Life" and this could become your daily mantra while you endeavour to process and embody this ray of resurrection. You embody the Christ essence and the consciousness of God in your DNA. It is time to remember and become one with the divine authentic Self you really are.

## THE SEVENTH RAY OF TRANSMUTATION

The well known and beloved Ascended Master St Germain oversees the seventh ray, incorporating the violet flame of transmutation. The assisting Archangels are Zadkiel and Amethyst.

This ray of course embodies the energies of the colour violet, the gem stone amethyst, and represents change, alchemy and freedom.

St Germain's role as alchemist of the violet ray is an extremely important one for our transition into the higher realms. Many people use the violet ray for clearing negative distortions and healing without truly understanding the magnificence of this violet flame and the work it does both for the planet and mankind.

When you begin your ascension journey you may be drawn to amethyst crystals and indeed may work with them in many ways. However the true benefits of using the violet flame will not become apparent until further down the ascension path. You must make the commitment to do the early work on clearing and healing the emotional blockages and fears before the power of the violet flame of transmutation can be utilised at its most powerful and formidable force.

> **ST GERMAIN:**
>
> *This Ascended Master is well known and loved by many and plays an important role in our ascension. He walked the earth many lifetimes embodied as those we know as the Prophet Samuel, Merlin, St Joseph (father of Yeshua), as Roger Bacon, Christopher Columbus and Francis Bacon. He is perhaps most well known as le Comte de Saint Germain, apparently having a life spanning 300-400 years and able to materialize and de-materialize his body at will, miraculously appearing hundreds of kilometres away a few minutes later.*
>
> *He is a Master of Alchemy and was known to produce pebbles from his pocket and turn them into gold.*
>
> *He teaches that the highest alchemy is the transformation of one's human consciousness into the divinity of the Higher Self, and he stands ready to assist souls at all times.*
>
> *Jesus was Avatar of the Age of Pisces, St Germain takes over as Avatar for the Age of Aquarius.*
>
> *He is Chohan of the Violet Ray of Transmutation and Freedom leading the way into our Alchemy of Consciousness and the new Golden Age of the future.*

## THE FIVE FURTHER RAYS OF INITIATION

You must pass through all the seven rays of initiation at which time your vibrational frequencies will be at the level of the lower fifth dimension. In other words, you would have achieved "ascension": the ascension into the higher realms of living.

People ask when they will know they have passed these initiations. Sorry, but there is no degree, diploma, or any certificate as such. Each step along the pathway of clearing and ascending offers you a greater and greater degree of peace, serenity, a detachment from drama, manifestations of goals and dreams and, without doubt, life flows with ease and grace. This is when you will know you have reached the fifth dimension.

Passing the first seven rays gets you into the fifth dimensional band of frequencies, and you may choose to stop at that point without continuing, even if only for the remainder of this life incarnation. However, to continue working towards self-mastery, ascended master status, and to become one with your vaster multi-dimensional Self, requires more work and more levels of initiation.

These levels are not revealed to us until we are ready to move through them. These higher levels of initiation are to do with embodying our higher wisdom, higher intelligence, higher levels of unconditional love, undertaking higher levels of spiritual work, and embodying once more our Monad, our divinity in the vaster realms.

*There are a number of channels and various teachings presenting the seven levels of initiation. Much of what I have referenced is taken from the book "The Seven Sacred Flames" by Aurelia Louise Jones and Mount Shasta Light Publishing, ©Victoria Lee, published in 2007.*

*For further information I recommend you read the book or visit her websites at [www.lemurianconnection.com](www.lemurianconnection.com) and www.mslpublishing.com*

# BIRTH, DEATH AND LIVING

*It is an honour and a privilege to be granted the opportunity of physical life on earth. Millions of angels line up waiting for the chance. Do not waste this life on trivial matters and materialistic possessions. The only real thing that matters is the journey of your soul back to the spiritual realms.*

## BIRTHING OUR PHYSICAL BODY

There is a lot of speculation, even controversy, over when life actually starts. Is it at conception, sometime during fetal development, or maybe it doesn't start until we are born? It really depends on your level of awareness of the divine nature of life.

At point of conception half of the father's DNA and half of the mother's DNA is absorbed into the fertilization process. At this point life begins. During the fetal development of the baby it has a "spirit", the spirit and consciousness of being human. If the conception happens in a mutually loving environment by two people wishing to give birth to a new life, the joining of egg and sperm will be strong and healthy. If the two parents have no wish for a child a weak fertilization may occur, or there may be a malfunction of the genes received and the baby may not be well when first born. The baby will then make the decision whether to continue growing or not.

At any time during pregnancy a fetus can choose to continue or to depart, particularly if it realises there is a malfunction of the cells. Coming from the realms of higher vibrations it is difficult for them, and of course has been for us as well, to adapt to the lower heavier vibrations of earth life, even if this life is still within the womb. The soul of the fetus can decide it doesn't want to come to earth after all, and the same applies after birth. The heavy and noisy atmosphere that suddenly impacts on the baby can result in the soul deciding to leave very quickly. We can only imagine how traumatic this is to an incoming soul.

If the pregnancy is the result of rape, an unloving sexual act, or perhaps a random "one-night-stand" sexual act, it matters not, as the contract is between the incoming soul and the parents, but most particularly the mother who will give birth. However this conception can have a lower vibrational frequency and the fetus a decreased vitality. What is important is the environment the child is brought up in, which will ultimately affect the child in the future.

The gender is chosen before conception and will be appropriate to the lessons and experiences required in the new incarnation. We all must experience both genders during different lifetimes on earth, although we often have a preference for one or the other. Sometimes gay people have chosen to experience the gender that is not their preferred one, and this can cause them to be confused as to which gender they are or which gender they are attracted to. Often gender choice will be a karmic issue.

Sometimes the "soul" will enter the fetus during pregnancy if there is a need by the soul to experience pregnancy and fetal development. However, most times the "soul" enters the baby at birth, or shortly after. The "soul" is the divine angelic essence, the part of God which is never lost during the entire human life. Most often only a small portion of the soul enters the baby at birth, because it would be too much to enter the complete soul consciousness. The complete soul will gradually enter the child as it grows and has until the child is twelve to fully embody into the human form.

The first breath of life sets in place the divine blueprint for the life of the child. The astrological signs of the heavens are what will influence this child throughout its life, and if these effects are negative, it is the lesson and journey of the soul to learn to transcend these negative archetypes to the positive archetypes. Natal charts are powerful tools giving us the blueprint of why and how we do things.

Most religions and cultures on earth believe that there is some form of afterlife, some place that we go to after death. However, most people do not give any credence to the fact that life has happened before birth. We all come from the higher dimensions, from the angelic realms. We have all had life within the universe.

We also have had life here on Earth before. Some angels come in as new souls, meaning they are completely new to the human experience on Earth. Most Lightworkers have lived on Earth many many times and are known as old souls. An angel enters into an incarnational cycle of Earth to experience what Earth and duality has to offer, and therefore gain wisdom to be used as part of Universal knowledge. We reincarnate over and over again, until we have learned the lessons our soul wishes to know, or until we have completed our karmic cycle and transcended third-dimensional duality, to rise once again to the higher dimensions of the angelic realms.

We have always been angels, we are human angels here on Earth, and will return to the higher dimensions as angels once again, with the benefit of life on Earth and wisdom gained.

## DO WE CHOOSE OUR PARENTS?

There is a lot of speculation about our parents. Do we choose them? Do they choose us? Many of us feel alienated within our family, different from our parents, so most people cannot conceive of the concept that we indeed choose our parents.

Our parents are chosen long before we are born, perhaps even hundreds of years before. In the higher dimensions we see the big picture, the divine plan. We see potentials of life on earth, of what we may incarnate to do, and what may be the potentials for us as individuals and for humanity. In the higher dimensions our Higher Self works in tandem with our soul family, most of whom incarnate and play roles within our life. Our parents are no different. They are usually members of our soul family, and we all agreed to be the parents or the child within a certain lifetime. We choose parents to help foster the lessons we need to learn, perhaps to complete a karmic debt, perhaps we chose parents who work with dark energy so that we could come to realise that we needed to work toward the light. All of these things come into play in an interdimensional way long before we are actually born. So all is as it should be.

We choose a primary parent, the one we will be most closely connected to in life. This may be mother or father. Sometimes we may choose both parents, but usually we choose the primary parent and then allow them to marry whoever they wish.

The incoming soul is carried in the energy field of the mother before birth. This gives the soul time to learn and adapt to the parental relationship and the family environment before birth. It is not such a complete shock to the baby when it arrives as it is already aware of the family dynamics. We ask "why does a soul choose to incarnate into an abusive family?" This may be chosen for many reasons, perhaps a karmic debt, perhaps simply an attempt to bring love into an unloving environment.

The length of life of the baby or child is also known before birth.

There may be occasions when accidents happen at conception and a soul finds itself in the womb of the wrong mother. The Higher Self of the fetus can decide whether to continue with that pregnancy and birth, or whether the pregnancy will be terminated.

Sometimes, as has happened in recent decades, souls choose the time they wish to be on earth to do their work for humanity and the planet in this time of transition, and occasionally the chosen parents do not create a pregnancy at the right time, so another set of parents within the family is chosen to allow the birth to proceed and place the baby on earth in the correct time/space.

In recent times there has been an increase of premature babies. Usually these are incoming souls who just can't wait to be here on earth, can't wait to get going with this ascension process that they have come to both experience and to assist the collective consciousness of humanity.

The baby develops its biological body in accordance with the DNA given to it by the parents. It thinks, feels, and knows within the womb, and consequently anything that happens within its environment, within the womb or to the mother, or in the mother's surrounding environment, is known and felt by the baby. If the mother is loving, nurturing, and looking forward to the birth of this baby, the baby will grow strong and healthy and also look forward to becoming part of its parents' lives.

If the baby is unwanted, if the mother is unhappy, abused, or living within much negativity of life, then this will impact on the baby and it will not thrive so well.

If a pregnant mother takes alcohol or drugs, particularly to excess, she can be setting herself up for a karmic misuse of energies. Conception, pregnancy and birth are acts of creation, and must be honoured. Often such mothers are young, single, lonely and vulnerable, but the misuse of alcohol, drugs and tobacco can seriously affect the growing fetus, both in the womb and through its life. There are many cases these days of babies being born already addicted to hard drugs. However, I believe the mother can exorcise her karma by becoming a good mother and making a worthwhile contribution to the life of her child and to society.

*"Shortly after conception, the mother downloads much unresolved pain, conflict, traumatic experiences and unconscious longings into her unborn child through a process called "imprinting". Later in childhood the unresolved issues from the father also appear in the field of the child. The imprint determines the physical and psychological development of the child and plays a large part in the tendency to suffer illnesses such as autism, learning disorders, immune dysfunction, inability to detoxify, seizure disorders and*

*brain cancer. Later in life the "downloads" from both parents play an important role in the development of physical illness, psychological problems, ineffective life strategies, relationships, job and financial problems, in seemingly random occurring traumatic events, and more. The unresolved issues transferred into the field of the child can stem from the life of the parents or from ancestors much further back and can be unraveled, understood and healed with work, even generations later".*

> . . . *Dr Dietrich Klinghardt MD, PhD*

## GUARDIAN ANGELS

We have a Guardian Angel that walks with us through our entire life from the moment of conception till the moment our soul leaves this planet. It is important that you connect with these beautiful angelic entities because they love you and care for you. They can help during times of challenge and offer guidance on potential directions. They can't live your life for you—they can only guide you on your journey. They never leave your side so you need never say you are alone. They will surround you with their loving energy when you are distressed. You can ask their name and speak to them as a friend.

We also have hundreds, maybe even thousands of angels surrounding us every day. They are here to help us with life and our journey, and they do the running around making synchronicities work for us. Ever heard of the "P" angel . . . the parking angel? When you leave home and ask for a parking place outside the desired destination, do you realise how much work these angels are involved in to make the synchronicities happen to ensure that the park is there just as you arrive?

We also have other guides, teachers and mentors throughout our life, and never more so than right now walking this journey of ascension. Archangels, the Ascended Masters, the Gods and Goddesses, Lords and Ladies of the Light, and many others are with us at all times. Although guides and angels don't change through your life, your teachers do, just as your teachers change when you move from primary school through to college and beyond.

## REINCARNATION

Reincarnation was always accepted as part of life and death, both before and during the times of Jesus. The early Bible accepted reincarnation, or re-embodiment, and it was never challenged. So why, 2000 years later, does the majority of the western world and western religions disbelieve in reincarnation? It is well understood and accepted by most indigenous tribes around the world and most eastern religions.

If the early Bible mentioned reincarnation, then what happened to change it? It goes back to the time of the Roman Emperor Justinian and his "Empress", or mistress, Theodora.

At the Fourth Ecumenical Council (known as The Council of Chalcedon) in 451[AD] attended by over 500 bishops or their representatives, re-embodiment was re-affirmed as a church doctrine, a so-called natural law. Justinian and Theodora wished to overturn this for personal reasons concerning Theodora, who was a prostitute and lowly born, and after many years of persistence the Fifth Ecumenical Council of 553[AD], attended by only 165 bishops or representatives, voted to abolish reincarnation from all religious texts and teachings. This was achieved by Theodora removing the Pope of the time and establishing a Pontiff of her own choice.

Today reincarnation is still not believed due to rigorous religious dogma. As far as power and control games went this certainly served the interests of the church, who instead instilled the fear of God and the notion that we were all born sinners into the minds of the people, thus creating a fear of death and retribution by an avenging and wrathful God.

Imagine if, for the last 2000 years, we had believed in reincarnation. We would have understood that what we do to our world will affect not only our children and grandchildren and onwards through our descendents, but that we would be coming back to also experience what we had created. Perhaps this would have stopped the raping and pillaging of Mother Earth, the total disregard for the consequences of pollution, the disinterest in eco-friendly agriculture, and so many other ways we have abused our planet.

We can say, therefore, that the stupid and ignorant interests of Justinian and Theodora, supported by the Roman church, has led inadvertently to the gross neglect we see in our world today.

Regardless of whether or not reincarnation was, or is a church doctrine or not, it is still a natural law of the universe, and we do reincarnate. Perhaps Justinian and Theodora have already reincarnated to experience the effects of what they chose to manifest in 553[AD].

# FATE AND DESTINY

We believe we are fated to live the life we have. If we have no money, if we have pain and suffering, illness, a mundane life, or bad relationships, these are the cards God has dealt us and we have to learn to put up with it. Not so!

We are the creators of our reality. Fate is based on our beliefs, which we could call karma. We are fated to experience our karma so that we can complete it. This often makes people feel they are not in control of their lives, and they submit to being a victim of life, a victim of their fate. When we complete and release the karma we transcend it. It will not affect us again unless we choose to allow it to.

Our destiny on the other hand represents the highest potentials of our human life. Once the karma and fate are completed, we can then move on to new things more in line with the embodiment of a divine human living on earth.

You can be anyone you choose. You can do anything you choose. You can live anywhere you choose. All is available to us on our path of destiny. This path of destiny is what we are on for this journey: the journey home to the higher realms. That is our true destiny!

Even our divine blueprint at birth can be transcended which can allow us to live longer and healthier lives.

# THE LAW OF CAUSE AND EFFECT: KARMA

*The creator must experience his/her creation.*

When we enter cycles of Earth life we usually enter for a period of 26,000 years as that gives us the experience of living through all the zodiacal cycles. We come to earth to experience both the "light" side and the "shadow" side of human life. By living the shadow side we become the dark energies of control, manipulation, greed, power, abuse, violence and destruction. This area that we move into is what we term the negative side of human emotions, the negative ego personality. Do not be fooled . . . we have all done this. It is pointless judging others currently experiencing that side of life. See them as being perhaps where you have been in the past. The difference is you have completed many of those negative experiences and are now on your Path of Light.

When we have learnt what we need to, we move to considering the light side, the positive qualities of human life. This is the journey of transformation into the Divine Human.

One of the major universal laws we live by is "The Law of Cause and Effect". This means that we must always experience that which we have caused or created. If we murder someone then we must experience being the victim at a later date or in a later life. This is duality at work, experiencing the effects of both sides, and it applies to everything in life.

This murder creates what is known as karma. Negative karma does not exist in the rest of the universe, it is unique to our human life on earth. In fact as earth humans sank to the density of 3D and the misuse of energies, so much karma was created that the Spiritual Hierarchy of the Universe had to set up a Karmic Board to watch over human karma, and to ensure that in some lifetime we would be exposed to the opposite. There are seven members of the Karmic Board, known as the Lords and Ladies of Karma. The ones we would recognise are Lady Quan Yin, Lady Nada, Pallas Athena and Lady Portia. In between your incarnations, you will find yourself before this Board to examine which karmic issues you need to include and complete in your next incarnation. These Karmic Masters do not judge, but dispense justice to this world and work with compassion and mercy for all souls who appear before them.

In the past karma was often not experienced in the same life time. The experience, or the karmic contract, was often carried out in a future lifetime where we have had to experience the opposite in some way. Perhaps this is an undermining resentment we currently have that the wheels of justice turn slowly. Ultimately we must all face up to and complete our karmic contracts, and this is why we have had to reincarnate so many times.

There is no need for us to take individual revenge upon another in this lifetime. Know that the perpetrator of the accident, crime or abuse will face the opposite at some time. However, individual criminals can most certainly find themselves in court for their abuse or misdeeds, and this is appropriate. So too those who commit crimes against humanity, whether of a political, military or economical nature can and will increasingly find themselves in court facing the wrath of the public eye. When we enact the justice system to right the wrongs, we must do it out of love and compassion for the journey of the perpetrator. Jesus said "Forgive them Father for they know not what they do". If you dispense justice from a point of anger or revenge you simply create karma for yourself. Those negative vibrations will come back to you.

In this lifetime we have been given special dispensation from the Creator to work through multiple karmic issues with ease and grace, allowing us to move rapidly towards ascension if we so choose. This means that now we can complete karma in other ways. For example, if I had previously murdered someone and needed to complete that karma in this life, I could ultimately perhaps be on the jury of a murder trial. I would hear both sides of the story, I would feel the emotions, the pain and suffering of all involved, and by utilising my higher intelligence and wisdom I could assist the jury to come to a fair decision. After this trial,

I would have experienced the karma (albeit someone else's), but would have learnt from it and gained the necessary wisdom, thereby completing my karmic contract.

Experiencing both sides, being perpetrator and victim, gives us the opportunity to learn and gain wisdom. Once we have experienced this we will never wish to do it again. The wisdom takes over.

Of course, there is also positive karma. All the good things we do and have done bring rewards: rewards of abundance and the positive attributes of life.

## LIFE LESSONS

Karma is about our emotional reactions from this life, past lives and ancestors lives, and has to do with our interactions with events, situations and people.

Life lessons on the other hand are only about us. It is what we came to learn in this lifetime, lessons such as Trust, Compassion, Integrity, Love, Patience, Communication, Acceptance, Happiness, Discernment, Surrender, Humility, Gratitude and others. As you can see it is all about our individual Self.

Many people have incarnated with a life lesson regarding relationships, or perhaps poverty, and these lessons are about looking at themselves, not other people or outside causes.

The most important life lesson is of course Love. Most people need to learn to love themselves. How can we move into a realm of Unconditional Love of All That Is without loving Self? This love of Self is very difficult for most people to achieve because of low self-esteem and low self-worth.

The second most important lesson is to Trust. We must trust Self, believe in Self, trust in our own power, wisdom and truth. This then extends out to trust God, the universe, and the divine flow in our lives.

## LINEAR TIME

The Universe operates on what we term "no-time", or "now time", meaning everything is in the present moment.

In order to understand human life to its fullest we created linear time. This means that we go through life slowly. We take the point of birth and stretch it out in front of us, allowing us the time to experience and understand things in "slow motion".

So in living our lives we walk this linear path, creating a past behind us and a future in front of us. We stand in the present moment, but never appreciate it. We are always too busy looking at the past, at our failures and the mistakes we have made, and allowing those aspects to colour any thoughts and dreams we may have for the future.

Because of this linear time, from the moment we are old enough to understand, we know we are heading towards death. This alone can prevent us from enjoying life, living life to the full. We start to notice the years going by, we get older, the body starts deteriorating, the inevitable death comes closer month by month, year by year . . . and the present moment of living slips through our fingers.

Who convinced us that we grow old and die? Who told us to keep adding a year to each birthday we have? I haven't been adding on years for a long time, rather taking them off and moving backwards in regards to my age.

Illness usually results from uncompleted cycles, from the disillusionment of living, from the acceptance of death, and mostly because it is just expected. As we get older we expect illness and death. However, in the future we will be able to choose when we wish to leave the earth plane, and the method by which we wish to leave. Illness, pain and suffering are not meant to be part of our life here, and will not be a part of the New Earth.

However, death is not the end. Death is only a transition back to the higher realms. It is merely a death of the biological body. Our soul gathers its experiences and wisdom and reunites with the Higher Self, becoming its angelic essence once again. We are energy, and energy is infinite. We never die, but live eternally in the higher realms when we are not incarnating into worlds throughout the galaxy.

If we draw a line and put birth at the beginning, living in the middle, and death at the end of the line, we have our linear life. If we take both ends of this line and bring them together, then we have created a circle. We now have a circle, or spiral of time. Looking at this circle, you will see that birth and death meet, there is no separation. Death is merely a transition into the spiritual realm and re-birth into the next cycle of life.


## THE JOURNEY OF DEATH

*When you die, God is always present. He welcomes you back home and comforts you during your transition. He does not judge or condemn, rather offers you the love that perhaps was missing from your life as a human on earth. He knows that you and your life have been just perfect for the experiences and lessons that your soul desired. There is no such thing in God's Kingdom as the fires of hell. You simply get to enjoy the freedom of heaven.*

Many people, and particularly the elderly amongst us, do not like to talk of death and dying. It frightens them. So many people have been put in a state of fear about death, and this misleading and corrupt influence stems from many religions. They might talk of God, and even mention an afterlife in heaven, but from many religions comes the talk of hell, the devil or Satan, and the day of judgment. God sits in heaven waiting to judge us on our life. Are we allowed into heaven, or consigned to the fires of hell forever? These are terrible burdens to place on people.

God is a God of Love: Unconditional Love. God loves us regardless of what we do, right or wrong. He loves us whether we have done good on earth or evil on earth. We are all sparks of God, loved by him regardless.

However, many churches do not preach this. They are too concerned with the sinner and taking it upon themselves to exorcise the so-called devil from our soul. Our soul can never be the devil. The soul is angelic of origin. The devil, or Satan, is a man-made illusion to create fear so that we are easily controlled and manipulated. Churches have a lot to answer for in this regard.

Whatever beliefs you have of God, heaven, Satan, hell, etc. are carried with you to the other side when you die. If you believe so strongly in these man-made beliefs, then you will re-create them on the other side. We are told there is a level in the fourth dimension where millions of souls wait to be judged. Despite the best efforts of the masters, the angels, the archangels, and even humans who travel there interdimensionally, these souls will not budge from their belief that they must wait until God arrives and judges them. What a sad waste of a soul. This is perhaps what we could call "hell" and it is man-made. These ones will, of course, eventually wake up and decide to change their belief and understanding, but if the fear hadn't been forced upon them, they could have enjoyed a pleasant transition to a state of love in the higher dimensions.

So let us examine what happens when someone dies, or is in the process of dying.

First, understand that often the soul has already left the body before the physical vessel dies. In the case of a traumatic death such as an accident or perhaps murder, the angels lift the soul out of the body immediately prior to the event, and it hovers over the scene of tragedy. This prevents long term damage to the soul, which would ultimately need repairing in some future human lifetime. The soul is given a choice: does it wish to return to the traumatized body, or does it wish to continue on to the other side. Each of us always has a choice whether to remain or continue the journey home. Many parents with young children choose to return. The minute your soul chooses to return you are instantly transported back into the body, and will then continue with the experience. This concept can help people who hate the thought of their loved one experiencing the pain and trauma of a violent death. They are always looked after by the angels. There is always someone with them. They do not die a lonely agonized death, as we believe.

In the case of a body slipping into a coma, whether it be a few days or years, the soul of that person often exits the body, but remains alongside it until the physical vessel either dies or recovers. The soul has a lifetime contract with the physical body and will never leave it until the last breath is taken.

When people are in the last stages of dying and perhaps sleeping or in a drug induced sleep/coma, they are still capable of hearing the talk and emotional reactions going on around them. Unfortunately they are not able to respond to what is happening, but we need to be careful what we say when sitting with dying people. We need to continue to talk to them, to reassure them that all is well, that God is with them, or that the angels and loved ones will be visiting soon to take them home. All of these things at an unconscious level will help that person transition peacefully to the other side. When there are family arguments and flare-ups going on, the person feels that they must not die because they need to sort out the family, but of course they are no longer in a position to do so. It is vitally important that support, love and encouragement is given to the person in a transition stage of dying. Put the family problems aside till later.

Often family members need to give permission to the person to die. That may sound strange, but often, particularly with elderly parents, they worry that we won't cope when they are gone. We need to reassure them that we are quite okay and will be able to cope. That permission often allows them to transition peacefully quite quickly thereafter.

Some people in transition tell of being able to feel the presence of angels or loved ones. Sometimes they even see them and this can give them a wonderful feeling of peace. This is why we so often see a peaceful countenance and a smile when they are taking their last breaths. When they die, angels are said to come down and lift the soul aspect of the person up into the higher realms, and many psychic people report actually seeing this happen. In the case of babies or young children dying this must be a great comfort to the parents and extended family.

Many people ask why babies or young children have to suffer and die. We need to remember it is a choice made by their soul/Higher Self. Maybe they learnt all they needed to in that short time frame, or maybe they experienced the other side of their karmic debt and that was all that was required. Sometimes they do it as a gift to the parent or family, to allow them to open up to love and compassion that may have been missing in their lives. Many people having lost a child turn around and help others in the same situation. So it is often a gift of love from the child.

Sometimes a child may allow itself to be born to absorb some of the karma or the pain and suffering of the parents.

Sometimes they come willingly to sacrifice their life that the world may wake up to the terrible abuse or poverty that exists.

Suicide often happens without warning and can be extremely traumatic for family and friends. This situation often happens when the person reaches the lowest point of despair and loneliness, and can't see any other way out. There is no judgment from God on suicide, and the family must eventually come to accept and honour the choice their loved one made. We always have a choice whether to stay in the physical body or to leave. The choices to leave may vary, and of course very often it is through accident or illness. The suicide person has elected a quick route out of his/her pain. This soul probably did not complete whatever experiences and lessons it came to earth for and will have to incarnate again at a later time. This soul will need extra special care from the angels and guides to help move him/her through whatever caused the depression here on earth.

I don't really wish to enter into the abortion debate, however, I believe this has also been contracted between mother and the incoming soul. In that case there is no judgment. Perhaps it is something the soul wished to experience, and the mother had something to learn from it as well.

Our soul is usually ready to die when everything that was meant to be experienced and learnt in this lifetime has been completed. We usually have no idea what that may be while we are living, but it will all become clear on the other side.

There are so many reasons for birth and death that we should never presume anything or make judgments on what has happened. Acceptance and forgiveness are part of becoming a higher dimensional being.

After death the soul has three earth days to complete its earthly life. The soul has the opportunity to visit loved ones to say goodbye, perhaps visit someone to apologise for something they did. They can use that time to visit a special place or take a last look at where they lived, played and worked. People often report seeing these souls just before or just after they die when they come to say goodbye. At the end of the three days the soul attends their own funeral. This is the last act and completes their physical incarnation. They then move on to the other realms.

At the funeral they are fully aware of everything happening and what is being said, even thought, by everyone present. This actually helps them in their life review with their guides. What people said and thought about them gives them some idea of how they acted in their life and what they need to improve on next time. The life review is not a judgment from God. It is the individual soul looking at what they learnt during the recent incarnation.

An imprint of the soul always stays with close family members and friends. This soul fragment will stay with you in your auric field until you die. It is this imprint which enables you to easily communicate with loved ones. All you need do is to acknowledge them and that gives them permission to communicate.

Talk to them just as you would if they were still alive. Many people can feel their love surrounding them and this brings a quiet peace.

Just a word here about grieving. It is perfectly natural to grieve. In fact it is required because it is the way we process the death of loved ones. However, when we grieve over an extended period of time it prevents the soul moving on in the other realms. They are held by the strong emotions of your grief and cannot move on with whatever they need to do on the other side. So please grieve; it is right, but do not carry that grief with you for years and years. We do miss our loved ones, but remember they are always with us and we can communicate with them at any time.

Long term grieving is caused by a lack of understanding of the process of dying and the afterlife. When we understand we can let loved ones go. Long term grieving will also cause illness in the physical body. It is a blocked and distorted emotion, in other words stagnant energy, that affects the functioning of the cells.

Grieving the loss of a loved one from something as traumatic as murder is a difficult lesson. Family and friends usually cannot see any reason for what and why the murder happened. They usually blame the accused and often continue through life carrying that blame, resentment, anger and unforgiveness. Unfortunately this does not make for a happy life and will ultimately cause illness in the physical body. It also upsets the loved one in Spirit because they see and feel the heavy emotions of family left behind, but are unable to do anything to help.

Many people then question whether God exists. How could God let this happen to their loved one? How could he allow evil to happen? Did he just watch and do nothing? These are questions that naturally arise in the grief that follows such cases.

God did not do these acts of evil. God allowed it to happen because we as humans live in a free will universe where all actions are honoured. Yes, it has caused harm to an innocent person, yet we do not know, and will never know in this life, whether a karmic contract was enacted.

Usually we grieve because we do not understand the circular nature of embodiment. We often conceive of our life as being the "only life". This is a false misconception as each life is but a short stay here on earth in a physical body. The angelic essence of our soul continues to live and will reincarnate back into a physical body in due course. Often that loved one will incarnate back into the family, so watch out for a baby or young child that feels very familiar.

## TRAUMATIC DEATHS

I do believe that we choose when we die according to our divine blueprint, but some deaths are so horrific and traumatic that what I have stated sounds too glib, too easy. For many families and friends who have lost loved ones in traumatic ways, it is not so easy to understand why. Why must they die in such circumstances? How can that happen? How can God or the angels allow that to happen to such a lovely person, perhaps a young and innocent child? How can that happen? Suddenly there seems no meaning to life if such an event can happen.

I cannot offer much in the way of explanations.

The feelings of the family and friends is real: too real to pass off with glib statements.

However let me try and offer the following.

We have a finite time of life, in other words we will all eventually die. Sometimes that is a short life, sometimes a very long life, which is set in place before incarnation. When that finite time is due, the soul/ Higher Self determines whether indeed that potential of death will happen.

I believe the human has free will as to "how" they die. The human can choose to experience death quickly or slowly, by illness or accident. This is of course at a subconscious or unconscious level, not known as a conscious awareness.

However, I do believe that humans, in ignorance, make bad choices about how they die. This can be where random traumatic deaths can perhaps be viewed. These bad choices can also be seen as part of the densities of 3D human life we have been living under for over 3000 years. We have been oppressed and controlled, making us victims over and over and over again through hundreds, perhaps thousands of life times. This belief in being a victim brings situations to us that continue to make us a victim, even in death.

If we were to choose to die using our Higher Intelligence and Higher Wisdom we would choose simple relatively painless deaths but without this Higher judgment we make bad choices. As humans we take unnecessary risks, we carry out silly actions, and in our ignorance and without the Higher Wisdom, we do not see the potential consequences of our actions.

In the case of horrific car crashes and the deaths of loved ones, again I can say that these were choices, perhaps bad choices. However, if the crash occurred through the use of alcohol or drugs, and particularly if innocent people were killed, the driver will have created serious karma for themselves. The addiction to alcohol and drugs is a serious misuse of energy, but in human terms, simply a bad choice as a way to live and die. These people will have the opportunity to come back and learn to live life in a better way.

Writing this section came to me early one morning. I woke up with such a sad feeling for the loss in recent days of a 10 year old boy in horrific and traumatic circumstance. The family, friends and all those who were there will have this death forever on their minds.

This 10 year old boy apparently moved through the safety barriers and fell into one of the boiling mud pools at Rotorua, a geothermal area here in New Zealand. He was pulled from the pool, and died the next day in hospital as a result of burns to 100% of his young body.

I say this not to create more pain for the family, but because I believe this young boy came to me and asked me to write the words that would help explain these types of tragedies.

Not that I can.

Maybe there are some things we never understand.

This young boy came with this gift for my book.

He now understands what we don't understand.


**THE CAVE OF CREATION**

The Cave of Creation is an actual physical cave deep beneath the earth that will never be discovered. It has an energetic force around it that cannot be penetrated by humans. This cave is interdimensional and contains billions of crystals, one crystal for each soul. This means there is one crystal there for each one of us . . . not one for each life, but one for each soul. When we die we pass through this cave and leave all our experiences imprinted on our crystal. Perhaps we could see it as placing the palm of our hand on the crystal and all our experiences are instantly downloaded into it.

Remember . . . crystals are receivers and transmitters of energy, and are capable of storing vast amounts of information. They are indeed wonderful storage libraries.

When you are in the process of reincarnating on earth, before you enter the birth canal, you pass once more through this Cave of Creation, whereby you place your palm on your crystal once more and all the required information for the new incarnation is transmitted into your DNA.

We can say this cave contains the Akashic Records of human life on earth. The energy of remembrance never goes away, but becomes part of the consciousness of earth.

## THE AFTER LIFE

So what is this mythical afterlife that we know so little about?

During all our reincarnation cycles we've died many times, it is actually nothing new to us. Religious teachings have created fear. We are told, if we are good we go to heaven to sit at the right hand of God, or we are sent to the pits of hell for eternity. Hell doesn't sound like a great place to be dispatched to, so we can understand the reluctance of many people to actually pass from this life to the next.

As for sitting at the right hand of God, either there are not many of us who make it there, or he must be really overwhelmed by the souls at his right side.

In neither case does it make any sense.

Although we have died and moved on many times, we can't remember what happens, and this is apparently for good reason. If we remembered how wonderful the higher realms are, the peace and harmony, and the joy and bliss, then we would want to be there . . . to heck with life on earth, it's too hard! So not remembering actually allows us to live a full life here on earth, and to remember only the peace during the transition stage of dying.

You can also forget about the picture of sitting in a rocking chair and doing nothing, perhaps chatting with God or the angels all day. All of that stems from ignorance and a refusal to believe what the Ascended Masters and Archangels tell us. They say "life continues after death". Death is simply a transition to another dimension where you have no physical body.

Most people who have had near-death-experiences report that they travel through a tunnel towards a light and when they enter this light they feel completely enveloped in the Love of God. There is a tremendous amount of peace and no questions are needed: everything is known. They say that this is the most exquisite experience, and if they choose to return to their physical body most of them are changed forever by this incredible journey into the afterlife. They become spiritual, loving, compassionate people, often quite the reverse of their prior personality. They have no fear of death because they know there is nothing to fear. There is only Love.

After dying and transitioning to the other side, the soul goes through several stages. Firstly they realise that they have no body, that they have died. They then realise that they are still living, but with no physical body. This can be confusing for a time, but the angels and soul family members are there to help them work through this confusion.

Secondly, they experience whatever they believed in their life incarnation. Whatever beliefs you take with you to the other side will be experienced. If you do not believe in the afterlife, then you will experience emptiness—nothingness. If you believe there is no God, then you will experience no God. If you believe in hell then that is what you will create and experience. If you believe that you just get to sit in a rocking chair and do nothing, then that is what you experience. If you think you are going to tend the gardens of heaven then that is what you experience.

If you believe in God, then you will meet him. If you believe in Jesus, you will meet him. Do you believe you will meet your loved ones when you die? If you believe that, indeed you will meet them again. If you do not, then you won't meet them. The experience is individual to everyone according to their earthly beliefs. You get to create all the things you believed.

However, any negative experience that you create is void of emotional attachment. You are more observing the experience, therefore you will eventually work out that you don't want to believe in that anymore, and consequently you will let go that belief and move forward.

The important point here is you experience whatever you believed in your earthly life.

So, what do you believe?

As I have stated previously, thoughts create your beliefs, and your thoughts today are setting in motion what you will experience in the afterlife.

Once you have moved on from these created experiences, with the help of the angels and guides, you then move into the essence of your Higher Self, and once more feel the true and authentic Divine Self that you are.

You will move on to studying, learning, experiencing, meeting with your guides and teachers, deciding on your next incarnation and preparing for that ahead of time. Depending on your level of awareness, or your vibrational signature, you may travel around the galaxy visiting other worlds, civilizations, and perhaps family and friends.

You may choose to incarnate into another world instead of earth. However, if you have karmic contracts with earth you must eventually reincarnate on earth to complete them.


## PAST PRESENT AND FUTURE

These coincide with our birth, living and death.

The past is behind us on the linear track: we live in the present, and the future is ahead of us, with death of the biological body at the end.

If we take both ends again and join them up, we note there is no past, present and future separation. If you walk into the future, or forwards around the circle, you meet up with your past which then becomes your future. So there is no separation, there is only the eternal NOW moment. As long as we are in a reincarnational cycle we continue to go round and round in a circle until we have reached a point of completion. When we complete a cycle we then move upwards in a spiral motion to a higher level—a higher level of consciousness and awareness, attaining a higher level of living.

The universe works on cycles and spirals of time, which is everlasting expansion and evolution.

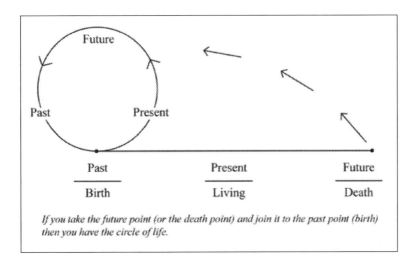

| Past | Present | Future |
|------|---------|--------|
| Birth | Living | Death |

*If you take the future point (or the death point) and join it to the past point (birth) then you have the circle of life.*

If you imagine a straight line behind you, consisting of your past lives, and a line in front of you which is the future, imagine yourself standing in the middle, the present NOW time. Your left brain records all the events of your past and the emotional reactions experienced. These it files neatly into a filing cabinet. That is the job of the left brain/ego personality.

Whenever you go to do something new in your life, the left brain opens the filing cabinet and brings out a file that has a comparable experience, and then says to you, "No, don't do that, look at what happened last time. It didn't work, so it won't work this time either." "No, you failed then, and you will fail again". "No, look at how upset you were last time you tried something like that. It's just not worth trying again".

And so on and so on. Over and over again the left brain and the ego will look to the past and find all the negative experiences to tell you never to try again. This leaves you stuck, stagnating, with no forward movement in your life. Rather than allowing this to make you angry, understand that the ego has been protecting you. It doesn't want to see you get hurt again. It was only doing its job but it is now time to let the ego know it must step aside and let your Higher Self guide your future. The ego is still required, but it must work in tandem with your heart choices.

Instead of standing looking at your past, turn around and look towards the future. There is a blank slate in front of you. No experience of the past needs to influence it. You can do anything you want. You can be anyone you wish to be. You can have all your dreams manifest. You can create the life you desire.

The past can only influence your future if you allow it to. Instead of using the negative past, use the positive attributes of the past.

## THE "NOW" TIME

*Time exists in sequences of experiences.*

It is said that the universe exists in "now" time, which is the nature of a hologramic universe. There are no linear time lines as we have here on Earth. It is difficult for us to understand that all happens at the same moment in time, but we do need to come to grips with this difficult concept.

All events happen in the universe in either cycles or spirals of time. It can be said they happen at once, but in effect they are all happening separately on different space/time continuums, in different realities, parallel worlds, and parallel universes. Although we get confused about them all happening at the same time, this is because we are thinking from 3D linear perceptions. During this journey we start to understand the interdimensionality of all life within the Oneness of Now.

From this perspective we have future lives playing out at the same time as our current linear life time, as well as our past lives. If this confuses you, don't be too concerned. It will make more sense further down your journey. Our future earthly lives were planned a long time ago, and we can say that prior to this incarnation we established future potentials that we may wish to experience during this incarnation. This potential energy is stored in our cellular memory.

If I wished to become a landscape artist, I could access past lives to ascertain if I had ever been a landscape artist where the skills and knowledge would already be present in cellular memory. It I hadn't had a past life as a landscape artist I could then access the future lives to see if it was stored as a potential energy. As future lives are playing out in some other time/space continuum I can access the skills just as easily. If I hadn't experienced past or future lives as a landscape artist then I would have to start from scratch and learn in this lifetime. The knowledge and skills learnt would then be with me forever.

All that I am talking about is termed your "consciousness", that which is imprinted in your cellular memory.

The potential futures you have instilled in your DNA prior to this incarnation are those you will most likely wish to use. These are only potentials. You may have placed in these potentials that you wanted to marry, have three children, live in Spain, anything. These are only potentials and you can choose them or not. You can change them or not. You will have potentials in place to have no children, 1 child or 5 children, perhaps to live in Japan, South America, or Ireland. You may have placed potentials to be an opera singer, a life coach, a florist, an architect. You have so many potentials placed in your cellular memory and you can access them whenever you wish, or choose not to at all.

You will also have placed in those future potentials the ascension journey you will carry out and complete in this time frame if you so choose.

You may have already lived this time of ascension and returned from that spiral of ascension and evolution to experience a physical life on earth doing the journey slowly. In this way you have time to see the results of your actions, and time to see what could be termed "good" and "bad" choices. Of course there are no good or bad choices, no right or wrongs, all is simply experience in which to gain knowledge, skills and wisdom.

# MULTI-DIMENSIONAL ASPECTS OF SELF

*You have the computer programs in you for all of the experiences of anything you can imagine. You can call it up seemingly as imagination, and yet if you can imagine it, you have already lived it. Your science fiction, as it is called, is a most wonderful doorway to remembering what you have done as you would measure the linear time, what you have done in the past, and what you may want to move into in the future, or not.*

*. . . . Mother Mary*

Multidimensions and multidimensionality are often referred to during this journey of ascension. What are they? What does it mean? This concept is confusing to our human brain and I am not sure I can find the words to adequately explain it.

We have an Oversoul in the higher realms which represents the 'all of you' that is God as an angelic essence. Then we each have a Higher Self, the larger part of us that continues to exist in the fifth dimension. This Higher Self is our expanded soul: our larger existence as God within the lives of its aspects.

When we are born into a human body, we are only a small part of this Higher Self. The Higher Self is so large and vast, meaning it contains so much experience, knowledge, wisdom, love and compassion that it could never fit into the lower density third-dimensional body that we are when we are born. We are always connected to our Higher Self which is there as our guide and mentor through life. However, because we have never been taught this we are not usually aware of it until we wake up and start our journey to the Light. The Higher Self contains the memories of all our past lives throughout the galaxy, and all the skills and talents we have learnt through many lifetimes.

This Higher Self is an energy field of higher vibration with the attributes of God. It is inter-dimensional and multi-dimensional.

The human DNA also has multidimensional aspects which you are born with: the God and Goddess energies, the Triple Goddess known as the maiden, mother and crone, and the Triple God known as the warrior, father and king. There are also personality aspects you were born with and the personas you have taken on for this incarnation or have adopted through life, those such as quiet and shy or loud and boisterous, confident or nervous and hesitant, lazy or energetic, demanding or unassuming, organised or disorganised, victim or persecutor, business person or healer.

We have positive aspects of love, compassion, integrity, honesty and many skills and talents but these are often buried under layers of negative aspects.

These negative emotional aspects we often refer to as the wounded inner child. These aspects carry our anger, our fears, sadness, distrust, jealousy, hatred and the many other emotions that inhibit us throughout our life. As well as our own, these aspects also come from past lives and our ancestors. The inner child is the part of us that feels wounded, traumatized and abandoned. When we are young we do not have the ability and maturity to deal with such wounds so we suppress them and bury them in our cellular memory. As we encounter similar hurts and wounds through life these add to those of the inner child, causing many levels of trauma that need to be healed. When we reach maturity and are wise enough to deal with them, these wounded aspects emerge for healing.

As well, we receive imprints from people we are with during life, particularly receiving DNA imprints from those we have sexual interactions with, when we take on board their emotions as imprints into our DNA. We then have to clear these from our cells. We are not clearing their emotions for them, but we do have to clear what has been received into our own cells.

As we judge people, perhaps abuse people, the emotions incurred by both parties is transmitted into our cellular memory and is held there until we accept what we have done and transcend the emotions by forgiveness.

Our biological brain uses only 5%-10% of its functional ability. The other 90-95% is inter-dimensional. This is the part of the brain that functions within the higher dimensions of the universe. As we take on the journey of light, or ascension, we are able to download more of our Higher Self which gives us access to our higher intelligence, higher wisdom and higher levels of love and compassion. The amount of our Higher Self that we are able to carry is in direct relation to the level of consciousness, or awareness, that we have. As we gain higher levels of consciousness, so more of the higher attributes are downloaded into our system.

The Higher Self not only allows us to exist on earth as one facet of it, but it also creates multiple beings. You are not the only "You" in existence. When you are born the Higher Self creates 11 other aspects of "you". To experience the variety of life on earth it would take us many more lifetimes to even experience some of them and so the Higher Self creates 11 other fractal pieces of itself, as "you", to have alternate experiences, sometimes on earth, sometimes in the non-physical realms or more usually in alternate or parallel realities. It is the same Soul/Higher Self creating and experiencing these many aspects of different lives. These aspects may often experience a choice that we didn't make. If we have to choose between say, three varieties of experience, our physical body can only choose one, and so two other aspects take on those other two experiences. When you return to your Higher Self following death, you actually have the experience of all three choices.

This is hard for humans to comprehend and it is very hard to explain in words, but we exist in multiples although we may never know them until after we have died and passed into the higher realms.

We also have multidimensional aspects of us scattered around many dimensions of space and time. We have lowered our expression into third-dimensional density, but we also have aspects both in the higher dimensions and lower dimensions. Understand there is more to you than what you actually see in the mirror.

This is the multi-dimensional experience and knowledge that is part and parcel of moving to the fifth dimension and higher. It is normal and natural in the higher realms to work with many of our own aspects in other dimensions and realities.

Many people experience multidimensionality in dream time, where they remember going to unknown places, seeing unknown people or other beings, experiencing some form of life or situation that seems vaguely familiar but upon awakening in the morning they cannot remember much about the experience. Most of our sleep time is taken up with cruising the other dimensions of time/space. The physical body gets left behind to rest and the inter-dimensional part of us, the soul aspect, journeys elsewhere. Sometimes this is to try and work out a solution to a human problem. Sometimes it is about meeting our Higher Self or other guides and teachers to discuss the next stage of our journey. Often it is about receiving teachings and information that is required in our human life. It is not unusual to wake up in the morning with a brilliant idea that you immediately want to put into practice. It is what you accomplished during your nightly travel.

Day dreaming is much the same, allowing your mind the freedom to wander off into other dimensions.

Meditation does the same thing but often in a more controlled way. You are guided as to where you go and what you do. This is an important way of receiving information that you need for your life. If you sit in meditation without being guided, and without having any thoughts about what you want or where you wish to go, then the soul will take advantage of the silenced mind to lead you to something that is relevant for you at the time.

Imagination is the creative mind wandering in other dimensions of space/time. These creations can be made manifest if you understand how manifestation and creating your reality occurs. When you envision something it sits in the ethers awaiting your manifestation of it into physical reality. As so many people doubt they can do this, the creation never materializes.

# PAST, PRESENT AND FUTURE
# OF PLANETARY CONSCIOUSNESS

Again, the nature of the hologramic universe also affects our planet. Gaia, our planetary sentient being, holds the consciousness of all earthly events. Within this planetary consciousness exists every thought, word, action, reaction, and every event and life form that has existed within and upon her throughout time. These are interdimensional aspects of our planetary history. They exist in "Now" time and are therefore accessible to anyone, including us.

The Earth has a past history, which we know the more recent of, as well as present situations and future potentials. We read about history in our books, but you can access it directly through higher consciousness, or your Higher Self. We can understand this more when we visit a sacred site and feel the energetic vibrations of what happened there, how it was, who lived there, what they did and thought. We can access any one of the people who lived there and request information.

In meditation we can also access any of these times of the past, perhaps receive visions of what life was like there and talk to the people who lived there.

Future potentials of earth are just the same. Earth has potentials of a future of darkness, a potential for a future of light, the very "Heaven on Earth" we envisage and are working towards. Future potentials for the earth to return to her pristine state, where deserts are returned to forest, air and waterways become clear.

Which future do you wish to particpate in? One continuing the darkness and fear, or one that encompasses love and compassion, living in peace and harmony? It is the consciousness, the thoughts and actions of each of us as individuals that create the world we wish to live in. The collective consciousness of humanity is what will change the planet and our world. We need to think, believe and live the higher vibrations of peace and harmony.

## INCARNATIONS INTO PAST TIME LINES

Many people say they have had past lives as Jesus, Mother Mary, Mary Magdalen, Apostle Peter, King Arthur, Ghandi, Leonardo da Vinci, King Solomon, Cleopatra, and many more.

How can so many of us all have been these people in past life times?

To explain it simply: there is always an original person that created that persona and life and the circumstances that surrounded that life time.

However, in a hologramic world, these all exist in the "Now" time of planetary consciousness and are therefore accessible.

When we are contemplating our next reincarnation to earth, we may decide that we never experienced the time of Jesus, or perhaps King Arthur, or King Solomon's time. We feel that we missed out on a very important time of history, a very important set of circumstances that perhaps altered history. Because of the hologramic "Now" time, we can choose to incarnate into and act out any of these individual lives. I can incarnate as King Arthur and live that life as if it were just my own. I don't believe we can alter that life because it has already been lived and established, but I could live it and experience all the things that befell King Arthur.

I could choose to experience life as Leonardo da Vinci and experience painting the Mona Lisa or the Sistine Chapel. What would it feel like? The only way I would know is to physically experience it as an incarnation.

Not only people are accessible, but also the events and time frames. We can incarnate into the ages of Avalon, Camelot, the Knights of the Round Table, the time of the crucifixion, Atlantean or Lemurian ages—all are filed in the cellular memory of our planetary consciousness.

# WHO AM I?
# WHY AM I HERE?
# WHAT AM I SUPPOSED TO BE DOING?

*The Masters had a phrase: "It is well with me, it is well with my soul". They would say it even in times before death, in times that were frustrating, and in times of difficulty. It is because they were focused on one thing and one reality—that the love of God inside them creates love of Self. Get to the place where you are content with that which is in you, which is God, and let all of the other things around you slowly develop in appropriateness as you learn what to do with your life. Do not decide in advance where you are going to go or what you are going to do.*

The suppression of ancient wisdom has led us to believe that we are small insignificant humans bound to a single life of pain and suffering. When we start asking ourselves these questions, it is an indication that we are ready to move on to a path of knowledge: a path of higher wisdom that is not readily available in mainstream literature and education.

We are vast beings of the universe. There is nothing small and insignificant about us. We are creator gods from the higher realms and we lowered our vibrational frequencies into this third-dimensional reality in order to experience life on earth. We could not fit the vastness of Self into this body and so we left parts of ourselves in higher dimensions.

Parts of you exist within all bands of frequencies, in other words, you exist in many dimensions of time/space continuums. You exist within many parallel worlds, parallel galaxies, and parallel universes.

We are a fragmentation of the higher God/Goddess that we formerly existed as. In order to experience the vastness of creation our God/Goddess Self fragmented as it moved into lower dimensions, into the various worlds, and various life forms.

We will exist in our fragmented earthly state until we complete our earth incarnations and then rejoin our Higher Self, which will then rejoin our Monad in the higher realms.

Each of us contains the vastness of the whole. We are both individual and part of the collective of universal consciousness.

Does this make sense to you?

Perhaps not now, but it will gradually become accepted as you move into the higher frequencies of Self. We all have an inkling, an idea, that all is not what it seems. We have an innate feeling that we are more than we appear to be, that life is more than what we see around us. It is now time to start integrating this knowledge of higher wisdom because it will need to be understood in the years immediately ahead of us.

When we wonder why we are here, it is because again there is an innate feeling that we must be here for a reason. If we are more than who we think we are, then why are we here on earth?

The answer is simple, but humans don't like simplicity. We are simply here to experience life on earth, life in a dense third-dimensional reality, and to pretend we are separate from God and from others around us.

Many of us have, however, incarnated with a special purpose. That purpose is to complete our own individual human ascension on planet earth, and to also assist the collective of humanity to raise their vibrations enough to move into the fifth dimension alongside our planet and all her kingdoms. We are helping clear toxic energies from earth, from countries and cities, and from sacred sites. Many Lightworkers are called to assist in re-activating portals or sacred sites around the world. Many Lightworkers assist in anchoring the higher energies into earth and into the collective consciousness. Some Lightworkers assist in transistioning millions of souls or energetic imprints that have become earthbound.

We committed to this ascension work before we incarnated. We knew it would be challenging and difficult with the dark energies fighting for their very survival. We knew we could help and so here we are, doing it. In order to take on this work and manage it with ease and grace, it is essential that we clear our own negative energies first.

Having cleared our negativities and distorted beliefs, what do we have to do? In actual fact, you don't really need to do anything. It is as important to "just be". This way you are holding the higher vibrations of love and light, keeping it grounded wherever you live and work, and radiating out those higher vibrations to all around you. This is assisting in the ascension process for humanity and the world, without the need to be actively doing "lightworker" work.

You are here for a reason.

You are here to be the Light.

We are all here as part of the tapestry of creation.

We are here to create "Heaven on Earth", the peace on earth that we have prayed for, begged for help with, and fervently hoped would happen in our lifetime.

Well, here it is.

We are in the middle of it.

So buckle up and enjoy the wild ride!

It is an adventure that may never come again in the history of the planet.

---

*A starseed of Light: that is who and what you are. You have come from many other constellations, many other planetary bodies, a long, long time ago, so long ago that you can barely remember it, and yet it is true. You, as a small one, have said to the parents, "Where is home?" And the parents have said, "Well, right here; you're home." "No, that's not what I mean. Where is home? I want to go Home."*

*Truly, anywhere you are, you are home, because you* **are** *Home. You carry it within you. You seek outside of yourself that which you carry within you all the time. You seek in the books and the teachers, the gurus, the friends, "Teach me, tell me who I am." And all the while you carry it within you, the Christ that you are, the power that you are.*

*. . . Mother Mary*

# THE ENERGIES OF NATURE

*We must realise that we cannot live without nature. It supplies our food, water and air. To pollute it is to our disadvantage, maybe even fatal to our species if we don't take heed now.*

Many humans have disconnected themselves from the worlds of nature, encouraged once again by the Illuminati. This has allowed the rape and pillage of Mother Earth, the mining of her resources, and the polluting of her waterways and airways.

The earth has consciousness and at present is feeling very abused, neglected and unloved. The land of each country has its own consciousness as well as being connected globally. The consciousness of the land is affected by the consciousness of the people who live on the land. The countries that have abused their lands for eons of time have karma which needs to be cleared. This abuse also refers to widespread intensive farming methods that have depleted the soil of its precious nutrients. The agro-chemical industry has played a large part in this pollution of our lands.

The waterways, rivers, lakes and oceans also have consciousness. These are being regularly polluted by chemicals, turning them into barren wastes of water without the essential elements for regenerating the water quality. All waters of the earth carry global information, the electrical nature of water. When they become so polluted, then perhaps the information also becomes polluted. Water relates to the emotional nature of the elements and is therefore connected to the collective emotional consciousness of humanity.

Within nature are many dimensions of spirituality. We are one with nature and must urgently find this reconnection once more. Each element of nature contains wisdom and this is accessible when we become one with the plants, the trees and the animals once more. Most indigenous cultures have had shamans who work with the elements of nature to ask for guidance. I am sure that many people do not even realize why they find it so important to rescue the whales and dolphins, but these ancient stellar beings have been holding the vibrations of light for earth for eons of time. Once the collective consciousness of humanity has moved into the higher realms, guardianship of the land and waters will be handed over to humans once again and the whales and dolphins will be free to stay or depart. They have done their job well against adverse conditions.

There was a time in ancient history when flowers were sometimes six foot tall and very wise, and humans could seek their advice. We are starting to return to that concept, beginning with communicating with the trees. Tree hugging is a positive trend towards the future. When entering forest, bush or park we must greet the trees, those ancient guardians of the area, and ask for permission and protection to walk the land. Give them blessings and receive their love back, and you will enjoy your time in the bush so much more.

The birds of the air, the creatures of the earth and waterways, the animals of the land, all are creations holding a spiritual consciousness. They do not have a soul but they are still Spirit beings. All species of insects, birds and animals hold consciousness and wisdom, and these are often reflected in such things as tarot cards.

All creatures would be happy to live side by side. However the pollution, the hunting of the species and the toxic thoughts of humans have created animals that carry anger, and this is often directed back to humans. Even our pet animals can turn on their human owners due to neglect and despair. Very often angry dogs that attack are simply a reflection of an angry owner. Animals pick up emotional energies from people and their environment just as we do. We should not blame the dogs for their violent actions but look to the owners who are the direct cause, whether consciously or unconsciously.

We farm animals as if they have no Spirit, no consciousness, and many owners convince themselves that these animals do not feel pain. The intensive farming of animals such as dairy cows, pigs and poultry as if they are merely machines, is animal abuse. We leap to the defense of pets when they are abused, but we conveniently overlook the abuse of these factory farmed animals. The farmer-owners, without realizing it, are creating karma for themselves. The food from such animals is depleted of higher vibrational nutrients and may well contain toxic emotions that will be received by the cells of people who eat the food.

These animals are in service to humans but deserve our respect and love. When this is given, the produce then generated is full of higher vibrational nutrients beneficial to humans.

The hunting of wild animals for necessary food should also be with respect and appreciation of their sacrifice. The indigenous races have always asked permission for the kill and never killed mothers with young. They were killed only when there was a need, not the indiscriminate killing of animals for fun that pervades modern thinking.

The same applies to creatures of the sea. The slaughter of whales for so-called scientific research is abominable, and I presume really reflects a desire to eliminate these stellar beings from our world.

Karma is created through all of these selfish acts.

## The Benefits of Hugging a Tree

*I have benefited on many occasions from "Hugging a Tree." When I am in pain, feel tired, out of balance, have a headache or feel low in energy, I go to my garden, find a suitable tree; a flowering Cherry, Copper Beech, Claret Ash, any tree that has a strong established trunk or thick branches within my reach. I first ask the tree if I may please receive some of its beautiful energy.*

*I remove my shoes, stand facing the tree with my arms around the trunk, or place my hands on the thick branches. Closing my eyes, I feel the energy flowing. Sometimes I feel it pulsating strongly through my hands and into my body. Usually my body will sway in a rhythmical way, often moving in a clockwise direction. With knees relaxed and a firm hold on the tree, I feel as if I am being drawn down into the earth's centre. At times I feel a tingling sensation that moves through my hands, down my arms and on through my body, out the soles of my feet. I spend between 5 to 20 minutes - depending on the problem that needs clearing at the time. I always thank the tree before leaving.*

*Afterwards I feel more relaxed, clearer in my head, free of tension and pain and my energy levels rise considerably.*

*I have also used this form of healing when my lower back was out of alignment. After about 15 minutes of receiving the tree's energy, my body suddenly shifted, physically lifting me off my feet, as an obvious adjustment took place. When my feet returned to the earth, I was standing pain-free and in a balanced position again.*

*Just being amongst trees can have a healing effect on the mind, body and soul. Walking along a bush track, sitting under trees beside a stream, breathing in their clear healing energy is so beneficial.*

*Submitted by Trisha*

## ANIMALS AS PETS

Our pets are here for one reason, to love us, and to bring us joy, happiness and company during their relatively short lives. They have consciousness and they have Spirit because they are all part of God's creations, as is everything that exists. However, they do not have divinity: they are not an aspect of God as humans are. They do not usually reincarnate, but can do so at the express wish of their owner, and they often do. It is their choice as to whether they reincarnate or not depending on the love and respect they received from their owner.

However, they are not immortal, cannot ascend as we are doing, and have no control over the energies and the future of the planet.

## THE MYTHICAL CREATURES

In ancient times the mythical unicorns and dragons lived with the people of earth. They hold higher vibrational frequencies and a great depth of ancient wisdom. When the earth sank deeper into density and these beautiful creatures were hunted and often killed, they either departed or moved into higher dimensions of earth where they await the time they can return and be with the people once more.

The dragons are returning. Their energies are being felt by many people and retail shops are filled with dragon ornaments, posters and dragon tarot cards. Humans feel that dragons are just part of fairy tales, but we must then ask the question: Why do they appear in so many fairy tales, why are they part of so many legends, why are references found to them in many cultures around the world, why do the Chinese people celebrate Dragon festivals? The answer is because they are real, they were part of our ancient world, and somewhere in our cellular memory we remember this. There is much more to fairy tales than just a story. Many of these contain realities that are awakening our dormant memories.

Lightworkers around the world celebrate the return of these mythical ones and many find themselves working alongside dragon energy to lift the consciousness of humanity.

## THE ELEMENTAL KINGDOM

The Elemental Kingdom comprises the devic people, the elves, fairies, gnomes, leprechauns, all those "little people", the fey folk. The ones with form are visible to many people, and children often see and play with these magical beings in their garden. Some of the elementals are non-physical, just energy beings.

These magnificent energies have always assisted in keeping the earth clear and healthy. However, with so much pollution and toxicity entering the earth, some of these elemental energies have become toxic themselves and not very friendly towards humans.

As we move into the higher vibrations of the new earth, so these devic beings will make themselves known to us more often. Don't be surprised if you look out your window and see them dancing on your lawn. They are inviting you out to play!

## THE MINERAL KINGDOM

Our human body is made from the mineral elements of earth. The density of our third-dimensional cells contain 70% carbon, plus a range of major, minor and trace elements. The earth element of silica is important and is of crystalline vibration, and the iron element gives us our gravitational pull to earth by connecting us with the iron core of the planet.

We are made from the elements of earth and are therefore connected to the very natures of the energies of earth. To pollute and destroy the earth is to destroy and plunder our own human body resources. The earth replenishes us with the food and water we need and it makes no sense to destroy our very life sustaining resources.

The rocks and stones of our planet are ancient and also have consciousness. Pick up a pebble from the beach and you can have a very intelligent conversation with it. Try it sometime and you may be very surprised by the amount of wisdom you will be offered.

## THE CRYSTAL KINGDOM

We are very familiar with the qualities of crystals. They appeal to our senses, and we often intuitively feel we need to purchase a particular crystal when we are browsing through their vast range. All pure crystals carry higher vibrations of knowledge and wisdom.

The colours of the crystals, the purity, the number of facets and the areas they come from influence the qualities they carry. Healers have used them for a long time to assist in directing healing vibrations. Some crystals have a stronger effect on the physical body: these are the darker coloured earth crystals. Many of them are lighter in colour and vibration with more of the qualities of the stars, sun and moon. These can often help spiritual seekers in clearing and raising their consciousness.

## THE ELEMENTS OF AIR, FIRE, EARTH & WATER

The elements of air, fire, earth and water are profound energies that affect everything on earth, including us and our lives. Humans have sought to control the elements, to make them abide by our wishes, and many a curse has been uttered when the floods and the tornadoes come, the earth rattles and quakes, and the fires of volcanoes erupt. It is time to understand that these are the aspects of nature which Gaia, Mother Earth, uses to keep the planet in balance and to clear toxins from her body. These elements represent the many cycles of nature here on our planet.

All matter in the universe, including earth and humans, contain these elements. Our bodies are just as much made up of these elements as we are formed from the minerals of the earth. When we incarnate on earth we manifest a body that incorporates all the natures of the spirit elements.

Instead of fighting nature we must learn to work alongside it, to work with the elements, appreciate their natures and what they do for us.

## THE DESTRUCTIVE NATURE OF THE ELEMENTS

*We hear your questions regarding the violence of the Earth and the death of many in the wake of Gaia's rage and we wish to tell you this:*

*However difficult it is for you to accept what appears to be meaningless death and destruction, never forget that those who take themselves to the moment of Gaia's rage, the innocent who swim in the waters; the not-so-innocent who commit to the killing fields of war and violence . . . all have an appointment and are aware, at the soul level, that they are fulfilling a soul pattern when they elect to leave the Earth School of Karma. Even the children.*

*The age of the soul has no direct reflection in the age of the physical being and many of those who are washed away in the tide or buried in the rubble are old souls who came in for just a moment, serving a higher purpose or completing a contract that is not clear to those who remain, suffering the loss.*

*All is divinely in order in the Cosmos of the Soul.*

*Know that the true Mother would not abandon her young nor obstruct the destiny of the one and the many.*

*. . . The Sirian High Council*

*channeled by Patricia Cori 2010*

Nothing happens by accident. Everything happens for a reason, albeit a bigger picture that we can't see. Mother Earth uses her elements of nature to keep her body in balance, and considering the pollution we have caused and the toxic waste we have dumped within her, our current natural disasters are major events rather than smaller events, and can be catastrophic to humans. If we lived healthy and harmonious lives with nature, she would not need to have these so-called major disasters.

Some places in the world have very ancient, very dense karma and negative energies to release, and this includes the energies of the bodies that have died under traumatic conditions and the imprints of the souls who have died in fear, many perhaps on the battlefields of war. These toxic energies and fears are held within the earth and must be released. The energies of those who have been abused, and the energies of the abusers themselves, are imprinted into the earth at the scene of the abuse.

The way Mother Earth releases these toxic energies is through her elements and so we have earthquakes, volcanic eruptions, floods and tsunamis, tornados and hurricanes. Mother Earth does not wish to harm us, but she must release these energies in order to achieve her own ascension into the fifth dimension.

The lands that receive the most devastation are those with the most ancient of energies that need releasing.

We must allow Mother Earth to clear these toxins and we can help by refusing to enter into fear, no matter what happens. To have understanding, acceptance and allowance, and to remain centred in light and love will help Mother Earth to keep the disasters at a lower level. If people become fearful they only contribute to the strength of the disaster and its consequences.

An example would be if a tsunami is reported out at sea off the coast of land, people go into fear. They panic. Their fears and their negative responses actually magnetically attract the tsunami to the land, whereas maybe the tsunami would have safely blown itself out at sea where no-one would get hurt. It is time to understand just what and how our thoughts and actions affect! Thoughts do create reality, whether good or bad.

There is always a positive side to whatever happens. The land, water or air gets cleared. It also brings out the higher vibrations of love and compassion of the people of the wider world, and this helps increase the love/light quotient of consciousness. Compassion is a wonderful human quality and we must always be in compassion for the journey of others.

Most people want to send their prayers to those in need. The survivors need humanitarian aid, medical help, food, clothing, etc. for their immediate needs until they can get back on their feet and rebuild their lives. What they need is LOVE in its purest state.

When you send prayers or healing energy, remember it is not your right to heal anyone, it is not your right to change anybody. You do not know what their journey is, what the bigger picture is, what lessons they need to learn within this survival. Perhaps it is to awaken them to their spirituality, their belief in the Divine.

In sending healing, you are judging them as needing your help . . . that they cannot do it without you. Perhaps it is their journey to learn how to transcend this.

The only thing you have any right to send to these people, and the land, is Love. They can receive it or not, their choice.

Understand that these people knew before they incarnated that they would experience some type of natural disaster. They chose this for whatever reason it was needed in their lives.

As we move down our journey and release our karma, the Ascended Masters tell us we need never experience such a natural disaster unless we choose to. Some of us may have contracts that require us to be involved and to help, whereas others will receive guidance not to be in the area at the time of the disaster. It really means listening to your guidance and intuition.

We will see more of these natural disasters over the years to come. All I can say is, do not go into fear. Transcend the lower negative emotions and know all is well.

## THE CYCLES OF NATURE

We are familiar with the cycles of plants and trees when they lose their leaves or the flowers die. This cycle is nature at its best, and we ultimately see the leaves return, the flower seeds produce a new plant that in turn flowers its beauty to us. The growth, the blooming, the re-seeding into the earth, the dying and then the new growth arriving in the spring: this is the way of life, and we can look at our own lives in the same way.

The seasons come and go, beginning and completing their cycles in tune with Mother Nature and her kingdoms. The abundance of spring leads to the dormancy of winter, before starting the cycle again.

The animals have their seasons, the spring for procreating their young, for nurturing and growth, and then the maturing of the young in the summer months. The winter, often a time of hibernating and resting. Perhaps it is time that humans learnt the cycle of retreat and hibernation after a busy spring, summer and autumn.

The sun and moon rise and set each day and night, offering us their warmth and then their coolness, the sun showing us that its cycle always brings a new dawn.

In not recognizing our connection to nature we neglect our own cyclic needs.

> *Imagine being a bird and free to fly over any country. Free to land anywhere, no boundaries, no visas, no passports required. No rules and regulations, no dictators preventing entry. Feeling the freedom to cruise the skies, eating from land or sea, sleeping where it takes your fancy.*
> *What freedom!*

## THE FOUR DIRECTIONS

The Medicine Wheel is the Wheel of Life, celebrated by many indigenous cultures of the past, and many still today. Different cultures, tribes and clans had slightly different rituals and interpretations of the four directions, but there are still close generalizations. We are perhaps more familiar with the North American Indians and the South American Indians, and the interpretations of their Medicine Wheels.

The Medicine Wheel was used particularly by shamans to gather information that the tribe needed to know or be aware of, or to help the chief or one of the tribe with a personal situation. The Wheel is closely allied to all systems of nature, and plants and animals were closely associated with their rituals.

The Medicine Wheel is seen as the Universe, and we a part of the complexity and the interconnectedness of all things. This is represented by the connecting paths between the four directions and the 12 stones the shamans placed around the circle, placing the first stone in the south as the beginning of physical life, and the last stone in the east, closing the Wheel. We would say now that the 12 stones represent the 12 pathways of life: the 12 paths of karma and then the 12 paths of destiny. Inside the Wheel the shaman was connected to the earth, the cosmos, the four directions and to the plant and animal kingdoms. This represented the "above, below, and within". He would often place sacred objects in the centre of the Wheel to strengthen the connection to the forms of nature he required.

The ancients told of the walk through earthly life as being from South to North. When the earthly life was finished the Spirit walked the road from East to West before being incarnated back into another form.

We can use the Medicine Wheel in our lives today by understanding the meaning of these elements of Nature. Each direction, north, south, east and west, shows us our shadow side and helps us to move into our inner nature to identify the problem and the solution. The ultimate goal is to be balanced in all directions so that life flows harmoniously, like a wheel turning effortlessly.

**The South** is where physical life begins at birth. The South is the Spirit of Wind, the element of Air. It is connected to our breathing, how we take in the Sacred Breath of Life. Do we allow the Winds of Change to move through our bodies and energy field? The Air Element embodies our Mental Body, so this direction is how our minds and lower egos are manifesting themselves in our lives. People with allergies such as hay fever and sinus, anything to do with breathing, need to focus on this direction. The colour of the South is red: the colour of our base chakra, where anger, resentment and fears are often held. We gain freedom when we release ourselves from these limitations. The totem animals most often used are the snake or lizard in South American tribes, and the coyote in the North American tribes.

**The North** is the Water Element, the Spirit of the Waterways, and relates to the fluidity and flow of life. It is particularly connected to the Spirit of the Moon cycles, and the movement of tides and the water content of our bodies. The North has much to do with our glands and immunity. When there are blockages that prevent the flow of the hormones from the pineal and pituitary to the thyroid and thymus the body is unbalanced and the immune system is compromised. The Water element represents our Emotional body, and the psychic abilities of our Brow Chakra. When transcending the fears, sorrows and stress of this direction we learn Gratitude, Truth and Wisdom, reflections of the colour white. Totem animals most used are owls, dragons, turtles and dolphins by the South American Indians, and buffalo and wolves by the North American Indians. The North is the home of the ancestors and it is from this direction they will come to greet us.

**The East** is the direction from where the sun rises, giving birth to a new day. This is the Earth Element and so it relates to the Physical body and the rebirth into a new day, a new life free of limitation. The East focuses on the physical healing of imbalances and illnesses. We need to release the negative emotions and beliefs that cause disease. We need to detoxify the body and reconnect to Mother Earth once more to regain balance in our lives. The East is the home of the Eagle who symbolizes freedom and who guards the

Golden Door to higher levels of awareness and understanding. The colour of the East is Yellow, the colour of illumination and clarity.

**The West** is the home of the Fire Element, the Spiritual body, and represents death and rebirth. It is the fear of death that prevents illumination and this direction assists humans to develop a healthy respect of death, the afterlife and reincarnation. This direction is also associated with the Sun, the connection between the physical life and the world of Spirit. It is the place of sunset, the time of relaxation and inner contemplation. The totem animals are usually jaguars, lions or bears. The colour of the West is black, the dark cave of bear, the place of introspection, the Void.

## HEALING WITH THE FOUR DIRECTIONS
## AND THE FOUR ELEMENTS

When we are healing and transcending our lower ego and the negative patterns of our lives, we must understand that these elements are embodied within our cells and chakras. The Earth Element is our physical body, the Air Element relates to our Mental body, the Water Element is our Emotional body and the Fire Element is our Spiritual body. We must address all these areas to effect permanent healing.

We can effect healing by meditating and sensing these four directions around us. We would normally sit facing north, or alternatively facing the direction we know we are needing to work with. Ask for the energies of Mother Earth and the Spirits of the Four Directions to help you source the problem or the fear you are needing to deal with. You should sense from which direction you are being led. Focus your attention on that direction and ask for assistance from the Spirit of that direction, or for the totem animals to come into your awareness and offer advice.

This connection is between the human, the earth, the cosmos, the Spirits or Guardians of the directions, and the totem animals that are responsible for holding these energies.

## THE MANDALA AND LABRYNTH

Eastern spirituality encompasses the mandala which represents the circle of life. It is often described as a microcosm of the universe. They are very intricate and amazingly beautiful.

A mandala is created with pure intent and used as a spiritual tool to focus attention and to aid meditation. Accordingly it can help one to access progressively deeper levels of the unconscious, ultimately assisting the meditator to experience a mystical sense of oneness with the cosmos. Carl Jung saw the mandala as a representation of the unconscious self.

Labyrinths are presumed to have dated back to ancient Egypt. A walk is created from an outside point and spiraling into the centre. The energies of the spiral are connected to the earth upon which it is created, then moves into its epicentre as a connection with the cosmos, the connection between heaven and earth. The energies will build in intensity from the outside point to the centre. Once in the centre a meditation can be done, offering an intense connection between heaven and earth, and between the higher realms of the universe and the human Self.

The individual walking a Labyrinth will start as the lower ego 3D human, moving around the spiral reviewing their life, recognizing the challenges and the wisdom gained. This walk must be made slowly, and upon reaching the inner circle the individual will have reached the highest point of self-realization that they are presently capable of: in other words their Divine Self or God Self. Moving through this spiral can move the consciousness of the individual to the next level of self-awareness.

## GAIA, OUR PLANETARY SPIRIT

Gaia is our Planetary Spirit, our Earth Mother. Gaia is a sentient being, meaning that she holds the energy and consciousness in a stationary place for the planet and all kingdoms upon and within her. She is an intelligent consciousness and is here in support of humanity.

Gaia as a consciousness holds all memories and records of who has lived here and what has happened here on earth. Her energy is therefore a huge memory bank called the Akash, or the Akashic Records of Earth. This is deemed the "life force" of our planet of which we are a part.

---

*As the planet progresses on its path, it too will take initiations and move into the higher realms. Your earth will eventually become a bright and shining star, as she takes her place among the stars of the higher realms. She too is experiencing great growth, and the most difficult of the birthing process is soon to be complete. As your earth transitions into the fifth dimension, her initiations will no longer be taken with great distress and physical upheaval. Her initiations will be taken in the love and joy which is her divine birthright, just as it is yours. All life forms on your earth will eventually return to this state and live in peaceful co-existence with each other, side by side.*

*. . . . The Spiritual Hierarchy*

---

## THE ENERGIES OF SPIRIT

When we are speaking of Spirit, we are generally referring to the energies of the higher realms, perhaps the energies of the higher Beings of Light.

The energies of Spirit are actually the energies of Mother/Father God, being expressed through the energies of Christ Consciousness.

The energies of Christ Consciousness are then expressed by our seven major planets working through us in human form.

These Planetary Spirits express through the 12 signs of the zodiac, and together the planets and the zodiac represent the Christ Consciousness which we individually experience according to the archetypes that were present at the time of our birth. These archetypes are shown on our natal charts, the templates for our life on earth.

These Spirits have both a dark malefic side and a lighter benefic side. They are expressed through us according to our natal chart, that which we call karma. The work of this journey is about transcending these dark energies and connecting to the beneficial Planetary Spirits who will then support us in creating the life of our dreams.

Christ is not Jesus. Christ is the collective energy of all the natures of these Spirits. Jesus was a physical embodiment of these energies.

The energies of the Spirits represent the essence of what we call "divine timing". It is the lower ego, the lower physical, mental, emotional and spiritual bodies that demand instant gratification. We must learn patience, to trust in the energies of Spirit and in the divine timing of all that takes place in our lives. If we allow Spirit to lead us and guide us, all will happen for our highest good and the highest potential of our human self.

When we receive the energies of Spirit, we could liken it to the way in which Mother Earth/Mother Nature communicates to animals, triggering their natural instincts to move, to stay, or to be still. We need to reconnect to Mother Earth so we can be forewarned as are the animals. We also need to reconnect with the divine energies of the Planetary Spirits which will guide us on our spiritual journey through life.

The Law of Spirit is about the flow of divine energy. The lesson with this Law is about letting go, letting go of control, letting go of expectations, and letting go of the need for things or possessions to happen, which we often don't really need anyway. Let go and let Spirit do the work. This is when synchronicities occur and when manifestations and miracles happen.

## THE PLANETARY ENERGIES

The planet Saturn is a large cold planet, the furthermost from the sun. It is dark and heavy and has no moisture. In its density, its heaviness, its darkness and coldness, the Spirit of Saturn represents our fears. We can therefore say that the Planetary Spirit energies of Saturn working through us represent our darkness, our shadow side, our fears, or in other words our karma. These can relate to this life time, our past lifetimes, and our ancestor's fears lurking in our DNA. As we clear these fears from our cells so we transcend the dark archetypal energies of Saturn and take on the opposite, the lighter side of patience, wisdom and trust. This allows us to move on our path of destiny, instead of being controlled by our fate and karma.

Jupiter is a large gaseous planet, sixth from the sun. It is light filled and considered by the ancients to have benefic energy. The energies of Jupiter bring abundance into your life. It shows us our dreams, visions and the bigger picture of life. The dark side of this Planetary Spirit is about guilt and judgment. Transcending our dark side of guilt and judgment, both of ourselves and others, allows us to move into abundance.

Mars is a small, hot, dry planet. The Planetary Spirit of Mars is associated with war and aggression, the dark side. When we learn to transcend the contentious fighting nature of ourselves, the lighter side of Mars will show us how to move into enthusiasm and courage, and to fight the good fight for the highest good of the collective. The misuse of energies can be destructive, but the fight for a higher cause is justified, and is supported by the energies of Mars.

The Planetary Spirit of Mercury represents the dark energies of dishonesty, untruths, deception and corruption. It is these energies which have dominated our world for thousands of years. Mercury rules business, commerce and the academic world and will assist in exposing these lies and corruption. We all have a dark side expressing these negative energies and we need to transcend them into truth, integrity, and honesty. The lesson of Mercury is to use discernment in all situations and people in our lives.

The Planetary Spirit of Venus embodies all the levels of love. The dark side of Venus is lust and the misuse of the energies of love and sacred union. This lust entraps people in the dark side of Self. The Spirit of Venus will assist in transcending the abuse and lack of true love in our life, the lack of love of Self, instead finding freedom within the magnificence of Self and the presence of Divine Love.

The Spirit of the Sun is the masculine energy and the source of our light which gives us life. The Spirit of the Sun sheds light on the pathway before us, illuminating the answers we seek. This Spirit will support us by showing us greater visions and greater perspectives of ourselves, illuminating a new pathway to our destiny. The light of a new day always dawns, and so it is with us.

The Spirit of the Moon is a feminine energy and brings growth, nurturing and nourishment. Her dark side is one of decay, the decay of old endings, replaced by the lighter energies of new beginnings. She speaks to us intuitively through our sacral and throat chakras. The mystical nature of the Moon requires us to surrender to our hidden mystical nature, those creative aspects of our life. Many people have become stuck in the old book of their life and it is time to write a new chapter, a new book. The Moon energies will support and nurture you through this process.

> *These planetary energies have been referenced from the work of Masters Kuthumi-Agrippa and Mary Magdalen channeled by Michelle Manders of www.palaceofpeace.net*

## ORBS

So many people are now capturing images of orbs on digital cameras. The old cameras couldn't capture these energies but now the higher resolution of digital photography can. Some people even see them with physical eyes, and we will all be doing this as our vibrational frequencies rise.

They create excitement! What are they? What do they mean?

Orbs are spiritual energies and they could be one of many kinds of beings. They might be an angel, a fairy, a spirit animal, a nature deva, the spirit of an ancestor, or a guide. They can indicate the presence of a protector. Perhaps the orb carries information to be downloaded into your physical form.

The true crop circles have been created by orbs.

There are so many varieties of beings in the universe helping us that these orbs can be one of many. They can have a form, but more often they are just energy entities. We usually see them as a ball of light because that is what our physical senses and brain are capable of comprehending. You will need to use your intuition to assess why this orb is presenting itself to you.

In digital photographs these orbs are often guides, teachers, protectors and ancestors. They may be around particularly when you are giving or receiving healing.

These orbs operate at the higher dimensional frequencies of the crystalline grid, and prove to us that the planet and ourselves are indeed transforming into crystalline matrix. We can take from this therefore that they are a wonderful sign of our ascension progress.

# AURAS AND CHAKRAS

**THE AURIC FIELD**

The aura is an energy field that surrounds our physical body. It is our 'non-physical' body. This energy field has the same electrons and atoms spinning throughout, except they are spinning faster as they are higher dimensional energy.

Our aura and chakras are constantly connecting with nature and people around us. This draws in information or energy from other people, which is why we need to surround ourselves with happy, healthy and emotionally balanced people.

The auric field contains what we know as our mental, emotional and spiritual bodies. The first layer is blue, called the etheric layer and is very close to the physical body. Outside this we have the Emotional layer, the Mental layer and the Spiritual layer. There are no boundaries between these, they merge into one another, and their vibrations are higher than the physical body, which is of course why we can't see them.

We also have a Body Elemental in the auric field.

The physical, mental, emotional and spiritual bodies are our four "lower" bodies, the result of our third-dimensional way of living and being. As we clear these four lower bodies we then access our four higher bodies.

The chakra vortexes spin out through this non-physical auric field and are affected by the energies carried therein. Blockages and distortions of energy are seen in these energy fields before they manifest in the physical body, so attention to the health of your mental attitudes, your emotional feelings and your spiritual beliefs will assist in maintaining a healthy auric field and consequently a healthy physical body. When a person is stressed, ill or living with a lot of fear, then the auric field is contracted very close to the body. When a person is healthy and spiritually confident then this auric field expands out a long way from the body, and in this state cosmic energy flows in and out easily, which in turn causes life to flow easily and effortlessly.

The auric field vibrates at higher vibrational frequencies which in turn create the colours of your aura. When you are mentally and emotionally happy and physically healthy, the colours are bright and clear. The negativities and illnesses create dark colours of browns, greys and blacks.

We are limited by our 3D perceptions and see only a very little of the colours of the aura. As we clear this auric field the colours will be beautiful, glowing and luminescent, radiating out from our body.

## HEALTH OF THE AURIC FIELD

When we are sick, stressed, depressed, angry and so on, our auric field is contracted close to our physical body. When the auric field is clear and we are healthy, our aura extends way out from the physical body. This distance will vary for different people, and will constantly expand and contract according to daily situations. An expanded healthy aura allows the maximum of life force energy to be drawn in through the chakras.

It is important that we take care of this auric field. When you are going into dark and challenging situations, or will be with very negative people, you need to place a protection of light around your auric field to protect both it and your physical body from harm. This protection prevents you from taking on the dense and negative energies of other people. When you start your journey of clearing negativities, it is a requisite that you place protection around yourself each and every day.

Psychic attacks from both the physical and non-physical realms create tears in the auric field and allow your energies to leach out. This results in a constant feeling of low spirits and continual fatigue. Emotional stress within the aura results in a similar tearing and leaching of energy.

As we reach the fifth dimension, this auric field will evolve to a higher light quotient to become your 5D light body form. In other words, our transport system to other worlds.

## THE BODY ELEMENTAL

This is a non-physical you . . . perhaps we could say it is a copy of our original template. The Body Elemental exists with us as long as we remain in human form and stays with us through all our earthly incarnations.

My understanding is that it is about 3-4' tall, stands around shoulder level in the auric field and looks just like you, with all your perceived perfections and imperfections. It is the Body Elemental's role to keep your physical body in perfect health, to keep your heart beating and the various organs and systems of your body functioning harmoniously. With a fall into fear, stress and illness, this Body Elemental has to work extremely hard to repair the physical problems, but these can get beyond its capabilities when the human is determined to stay within the negative realms.

It is contracted to work alongside you through your life and it would much prefer to be working with positive healthy spiritual energies, because that is what it is after all, rather than being forced to work with stress and fear. It can't change you or your choices, so it must assist in carrying out the choices you make, even if they are to the detriment of the physical body.

## THE MENTAL BODY

This non-physical mental body contains all our thoughts that are both part of, and beyond, our brain capacity. When this mental body in the aura is overloaded with negative thoughts of fear it can create many of the mental and physical illnesses within the physical body. This mental body contains the higher intelligence of the Divine Self, but this higher spiritual knowledge gets buried under so many layers of negativities that we constantly make bad intellectual decisions.

## THE EMOTIONAL BODY

This non-physical emotional body contains all our emotions that are part of both the physical and non-physical bodies. When this emotional body in the aura is filled with negative emotions and fears, negative beliefs, attitudes and patterns, then it creates emotional imbalances in the body that result in physical illnesses. As this emotional body is cleared of negative energies the physical body can heal. The by-product of emotional stress is a tearing of the auric field, creating a constant draining of energy and the feelings of depression through not being in control of our lives.

## THE SPIRITUAL BODY

You may wonder what is meant by a spiritual body. This contains all your spiritual understandings, your spiritual beliefs, your connection to your Higher Self, your Monad, to God, to the higher dimensions and the higher Beings of Light. If this spiritual body is filled with negativities and disbeliefs of the non-physical realms, and of God, this has the effect of lowering the life force energies coming through the auric field, resulting in a lowered immune system and physical illness. These attitudes and beliefs in relation to the non-physical realms come from the conditioning imprinted on us by religious teachings. We can therefore say that these spiritual beliefs are based on old 3D programming and it's time to change them. The Ascended Masters tell us that many people no longer believe in God because he seems not to have ever answered their prayers. He certainly listens and knows what we are going through, but it is a free will universe and it is our choice as to how we live our life. He can only support what we believe because that is our truth at the time. It is time to make better choices.

## OUR HIGHER SELF AND MONAD

When we incarnate into a third-dimensional body, there simply is not enough room in our cells to incorporate all the experience, memories, knowledge and wisdom that we have gained over many hundreds, perhaps thousands, of incarnations. It is necessary to leave much of ourselves in the higher realms during our sojourns to earth.

What we leave in the fifth dimension, referred to as our Higher Self, is all the information that we decided was not immediately pertinent to this third-dimensional incarnation. We are always connected to our Higher Self, and without realising it, we work with our Higher Self every moment of every day. Whenever you need information it is available by accessing your Higher Self, often done during meditation.

The Higher Self retains the information relevant to our Earthly incarnations. Higher than that is our Monad, or Oversoul, containing our Divine Blueprint or Template for life here on earth and within the galaxy. This becomes more and more accessible as we move further through the ascension journey. Your Monad contains the information and memories relevant to your life in this Galaxy and is working very closely with you, the human form, as you diligently work towards ascension.

Our Monad, the Oversoul, is expanded consciousness. It is the "Mind of God" and we are expanding into this.

Beyond these two higher selves, we have a multitude of Higher Selves relative to other activity we have undertaken within this Galaxy and Universe.

You need to understand that your Higher Self, your Monad, and other Higher Selves are actually "you" existing in the higher realms in different time/space continuums.

I realise this is a little hard to understand but you are not just the "you" here on earth. You are multidimensional and exist through all dimensions of time/space.

# THE SEVEN PRIMARY CHAKRAS

We have been aware through energy healers and people with psychic vision that we have seven primary chakras: Base or Root, Sacral, Solar Plexus, Heart, Throat, Third Eye or Brow, and the Crown Chakra. These chakras are spinning vortexes of energy that draw in your life force energy through your auric field from the Cosmos and from Source.

The chakric system should be balanced in all seven chakras, none being superior or inferior to any other. They are simply a system that works cohesively. We also have minor chakras on many points of the body, the most important of which are the chakras on the palms of the hands, used by healers, and the soles of the feet, your direct contact with Mother Earth.

All chakras work individually, but also with inter-connectedness and harmony with each other, allowing the energy from Source above and Earth below to flow unrestricted by blockages anywhere in the system.

The seven major chakras extend from the body far out into the auric field as spinning vortexes of energy. If the aura is burdened with negative thoughts, emotions and beliefs, the chakras become constricted, deformed, blocked and shortened. This does not allow the health giving life force energy to flow in, and the chakras themselves lose a great deal of their connection with each other.

These chakras spin clockwise and outward from both the front and the back of the body like funnels. They meet in the pranic tube which runs down the spine. It is said that the chakras in front represent our future, and the ones at the back represent the past. The bottom three chakras are known as our survival chakras and can send out vibrations of fear. The top four chakras represent our higher divine self and emit vibrations of love.

These chakras meet in the spine where the spinal cord of the central nervous system sends the life force energy to all cells of the body. We can say this energy is electrical, and the nervous system as the conduit of energy is our electrical system. When people are out of balance we can see how the nervous system will be emitting erratic and distorted electrical connections resulting in pain.

Most people do not have strong healthy chakras that spin harmoniously in a clockwise direction. They are instead very short, twisted, blocked and often nearly closed off. In this state they can become quite dense and carry dark colours representing the darker energies contained in them. They can also spin in reverse causing imbalances and illness.

We all know that we breathe in air that provides the body with oxygen which we need to live. At the same time cosmic energy is drawn in through the chakras, which provides us with life force energy. This is the interdimensional energy, or life force energy, that is the foundation of every cell in our body. You can understand that if the chakras are blocked, shortened or twisted, there is going to be a lesser amount of life force energy entering the body. Without this essential energy in your cells the immune system gets run down, and you will get tired, depressed and ultimately sick.

People with closed or partially closed higher chakras, particularly the heart, can seriously hurt or kill someone without a second thought because they do not feel love and compassion, either for themselves or others, because their heart chakra is not functioning.

If you live your life constantly in fear and negative emotions you are surviving in the lower three chakras. The top four chakras will be closed or severely curtailed. You are then radiating out the vibrations of fear from the lower chakras.

I have talked about the Illuminati feeding off fear. These people have closed higher chakras and have difficulty drawing in cosmic energy to feed their systems. To survive they must draw the energy of fear from people. So the system of creating fear not only keeps people under control, it also feeds the Illuminati. The more you live in the fear category the more you are supporting them.

It behoves us all to release fear from our physical and non-physical bodies so that we can take our control back and starve the Illuminati of their life force.

Individual chakras contain hundreds of smaller chakras which are activated as you move along the journey of ascension. Within each chakra are also what we term black holes and white holes. When you release negative emotions such as fear, the energy moves through the black hole to be transmuted into light. This re-formed energy is then reabsorbed through the white holes back into the chakra and the cells of your body.

## BASE/ROOT CHAKRA

This chakra represents the earth element and sits level with the tail bone, extending out from both front and back of body and also down towards earth, grounding us and connecting us with Mother Earth. It is known as the survival chakra. It is a masculine chakra, which of course also aligns with the male reproductive organs, and represents the action principle of the Divine Masculine energy, the God.

The atoms of this bottom chakra spin more slowly, allowing the experience of human life on earth. The colour of this chakra is red, and if you are into harmonics it resonates to the key of C.

It is in the area of the base chakra that our Kundulini energy is held in the tailbone.

## SACRAL CHAKRA

This chakra represents the water element and is the second chakra situated between the base chakra and the navel, extending out front and back of body. It is a feminine chakra, and aligns itself with the female reproductive organs. It is this chakra that represents the sacred creation energy of the Divine Feminine, the

Goddess. Held within this area is the womb, the Holy Grail. For centuries men have searched for the Holy Grail. Here it is in all its beauty . . . the womb of creation in the Divine Feminine, the Goddess.

The colour of this second chakra is orange.

## SOLAR PLEXUS CHAKRA

This chakra is centred just above the navel, extending out front and back of the body. It is a masculine chakra and is the seat of our power. This power centre reflects our self-worth, self-confidence and self-respect, all of which are very affected by the fears and negative emotions of the base and sacral chakras. This is the area where you can delve deep within to find your inner courage and strength to tackle the situations in your life. So often, however, the negative emotions affecting self-worth make it difficult to find the strength of will and power to tend to the daily chores and routine.

This chakra represents the fire element and within this chakra are some of our vital organs: the liver, the stomach and the pancreas. It is easy to see why these organs can be so affected by the power of intense negative emotions. Chinese medicine tells us that the liver is the seat of fire.

## THE HEART CHAKRA

The Heart chakra is the centre of our spirit and soul and is a feminine energy chakra extending out around the heart area of the body. It is the connecting point between our three lower chakras, which represent our connection to Mother Earth, and our three higher chakras, which represent our connection to Spirit, our Higher Self and the wider universe and Beings of Light. This is the chakra of balance and harmony, and all decisions and choices we make must be made from this point of balance. It is where we hold the energies of self-love and love of others.

The soul resides in the body in a space just behind the physical heart, sometimes referred to as the high heart chakra or soul chakra. The colour of the heart chakra is green representing healing, harmony and balance. Any problems with the heart indicate a lack of joy and abundance in one's life. Problems with the lungs, also contained in this area, indicate an inability to breathe in life, love and joy.

## THE THROAT CHAKRA

The throat chakra is our communication chakra, in other words how we communicate to others. If you are burdened with negative emotions and thoughts then your words will communicate negatively. Also extending front and back of body, the colour of this chakra is blue, and is one of the most important of the chakras needing work during our ascension journey. For many lifetimes our throat chakra has been closed down because we have not been able to express ourselves for fear of reprisal, reprimand, retribution, and often death. This inability to speak has impacted on our feelings of self-worth and self-confidence.

Within our throat chakra is the neck area. People with neck problems may have a tendency to be inflexible, stubborn or resistant to change. These people can be very single-minded and not able to see other people's point of view, and certainly won't be slow to voice their opinions.

The throat chakra represents masculine energy and actions the choices of the heart chakra and the visions received from the brow chakra.

## THE BROW OR THIRD EYE CHAKRA

The sixth chakra holds the indigo colour and psychic vision. This is the gateway to viewing other dimensions used by psychic visionaries and mediums. We all have this psychic ability but it is stronger in some people than others. It is a skill we will all master as we move into the higher realms.

This chakra represents feminine energy and it is interesting to note that many psychic readers and mediums are women.

This chakra aligns with the Pineal Gland. This Master Gland of the endocrine system is the first of the glandular system to change to crystalline frequencies. Science has recorded that the Pineal in many people is experiencing a build up of crystals—the crystalline cells of the fifth dimension. As crystals are receivers and transmitters of information this will enable those people to have stronger connections with other realms and dimensions. The Indigo children that have progressively been born since the 1970s and 1980s and the more recent Indigo/Crystal children have enhanced crystalline pineal glands, hence they are living proof of the evolution of mankind into crystalline energy. This pineal crystallization in children has been noticed by medical science.

## THE CROWN CHAKRA

Centred at the top of the head, this is the connection point with our Higher Self, our Monad, the higher realms and God/Source. It spreads out wide from the top of the head, radiating out the beautiful colours of white, gold, silver and platinum in a fine spidery web of interconnected threads of energy.

## HIGHER SOUL CHAKRA

The previous seven chakras are attached to and work with and through the biological body. Above the body is one called the Higher Soul chakra and this is your connection to your Higher Self, to your Guardian Angel, and through this chakra together with your Heart chakra you will access the higher realms of guidance. It is often called the Star Chakra and exists in the auric field about ten inches above the head. When the physical body is severely traumatised or stressed, the soul often leaves the physical body and takes up residence in this chakra above the head. As the body is cleared and re-balanced, the soul will choose to enter into the physical body once again, but may need encouragement to do so. This can be done through meditation or a healing modality.

## FUTURE CHAKRA ACTIVATIONS

As you journey there are many more chakras to be re-activated, some attached to the physical body, some in the auric field and many within the seven primary chakras. These will happen naturally as you lift your vibrational frequencies.

## THE LIMBIC BRAIN

This ancient brain, also referred to as the reptilian brain, contains our past wisdoms, knowledge and experiences. This brain has been relatively dormant for a long time but is gradually reactivating as we move through our ascension journey. This enables us to access much information from our recent past and ancient past. This limbic brain exists at the base of the skull, interestingly between the brow chakra and the throat chakra. As this part of our brain wakes up we will remember our galactic origins and strengthen communication visually and orally, both receiving and transmitting higher truths.

# OUR BIOLOGY OF FEARS

*Imprints from our childhood are surfacing so that we can understand our repetitive behavioral patterns. Clear these negative patterns and instead become passionate about standing in your own truth and power. Do not be isolated, but paradoxically learn to stand alone. Be complete without needing someone to take care of you.*

## THE ATOMS OF OUR BIOLOGY

The basic anatomy and physiology of our body comprises 11 Systems: muscular, skeletal, digestive, nervous, lymphatic, cardiovascular, respiratory, reproductive, and so on. Within these systems are our organs such as liver, kidneys, heart, lungs, etc. These organs are made up of tissues, which consist of cells.

Cells are made up of atoms, and groups of atoms are classed as molecules. Atoms comprise of sub-atomic particles: the electrons that spin around their nucleus. This is called the electron haze and it is within this haze of "light" that interdimensional information is carried, both receiving and transmitting.

The sub-atomic particles spin around the nucleus and create the vibrational frequencies emitted by the cells. The atoms and sub-atomic particles are the "light" of the cells.

Within the biology of each cell is what is called interdimensional energy, or what we would refer to as our life force energy, chi, or prana. The definition I have received for interdimensional energy, is "energy that weaves light through all dimensions of space and time".

This interdimensional energy is our life force. We could not live without it. It is quantum energy, and is the consciousness of our cells. Quantum means "oneness", so this quantum energy is our connectedness with the quantum universe, the All That Is. All things are interconnected and are one with each other, including humans with each other, with nature, and with the wider galactic and universal worlds.

We have over 200 trillion cells in our body, and they have been in a state of separation consciousness. We are beginning a shift into quantum consciousness as we move into a higher light quotient in the cells.

## OUR SPINNING ATOMS

As I stated earlier, our planetary cycles of time are coming to a close. The atoms of our planet have been spinning in a clockwise direction forming dense matter.

With the shift in consciousness occurring after 21$^{st}$ December 2012, the planetary cycle will commence spinning in reverse, anti-clockwise, becoming "lighter" in density.

The atoms of our cells will do likewise. Our clockwise atoms will reverse their spin, making the cells "lighter".

This spinning of the atoms is probably a very basic conceptual understanding, and I am sure the universe, and even our scientists, have a more comprehensive explanation of matter and anti-matter. However this serves my purpose in helping you understand some very important information about these spinning atoms.

## DIVINE TEMPLATE OF LOVE

The template, or blueprint of our body is created from the Divine Template of Creation, which is Love. Within each cell the atoms of light spin to the Divine Blueprint of Love, that which is the true essence of each of us. These atoms spinning to the Divine Template carry out the functions of the cell. If the body is in a state of love, joy and happiness, then these atoms are spinning according to the Divine Template, and we experience health, wellness and abundance.

If the atoms are debilitated by illness, stress and negative emotions and beliefs they do not resonate with the Divine Template, then the body is unbalanced. Negative beliefs are the biggest disruptor of the atoms of cells.

Underpinning all these negativities is always a fear. There are actually only two emotions in our duality system: love and fear. If we are not in a state of love, then we are in a state of fear. When we are looking at clearing negative emotions and beliefs we therefore need to identify the fear associated with them.

When cells are in fear they begin to spin slowly and at lower vibrational frequencies. This lowers the immune system, causes illness and triggers DNA pre-disposition factors, perhaps even cancer.

## QUANTUM CELLS WITH AWARENESS

A single celled bacterium is microscopic and used in most biological experiments to understand how a cell functions. This cell is a blob of jelly-like cytoplasm with a membrane barrier holding it together. This cell absorbs, digests, and excretes waste products. When put into a petri dish in the laboratory it will move away from toxic substances placed in the petri dish, but will move towards nutrients.

This movement shows us that a single cell displays "Intelligence, Consciousness and Awareness". It has intelligence because it recognises the difference between toxins and nutrients. It has a consciousness because all life has consciousness, and the cell is self-aware of itself and what it needs.

Our body is made up of over 200 trillion multi-cellular cells. No longer single-celled cytoplasm, but groups of them that have joined together in communities and evolved to do specific jobs, such as our liver cells, our muscle cells, our skin cells and so forth. Whereas unicellular cells have to do everything themselves, now organelles do these jobs within the variety of multi-cellular cells that make up our body. Organelles are like miniature organs.

In a petri dish these multi-cellular cells will move away from toxic substances and move towards nutrients. They also absorb, digest, and excrete. They also have a membrane barrier that controls the movement in and out of the cell.

Evolution has engineered these cells to have "Intelligence, Consciousness and Awareness" on a superior scale to the single-celled bacterium.

## ENTRY INTO THE CELL

On the surface of each cell are thousands of tiny phospholipids. These little receptors line up on the outside of the cell to let things in, and line the inside of the cell to let things out. They operate on a type of key and lock system, or gates that open and shut. Substances have to travel around the cell to find a lock that their key fits into and once this happens, entry is granted. There is a key and lock for all the elements and nutrients in our system and many of them allow the entry of more than one type of substance. Nutrients are absorbed into the cell and by the same means waste products are excreted from the cell. These receptors respond to all the nutrients, medications, hormones and neurotransmitters that travel in our bloodstream.

All our cells are stimulated by environmental signals: i.e. from the surrounding environment of the cell. The biological signals mainly come from toxins (viruses, bacteria, heavy metals, drugs, etc.), from nutrients (carbohydrates, proteins/amino acids, and lipids), and from hormones.

Then we have non-physical vibrational frequency signals such as stress, emotions and beliefs.

## THE BIOLOGICAL SIGNALS

### NUTRIENTS

All the healthy food we digest consists of a range of vitamins, minerals and trace elements that the body requires for efficient functioning of the cells. The food is processed through the digestive system and transmuted into the nutrients that the cells need. Each nutrient has its own unique vibrational frequency.

We need a variety of protein, carbohydrate and lipid (fats and oils) foods.

We can have too much of some foods which then make cells unhealthy. If we eat a kilo of bananas every day for months at a time, then perhaps we could have absorbed too much potassium into our system.

Much of our diets are now deficient in certain nutrients, causing imbalances in our systems. In New Zealand selenium is well known to be deficient in our soils. If a nutrient is deficient in our soils, then plants, vegetables and even meat and milk, will be deficient in that mineral.

In nature all foods can have a good effect or a bad effect. Many beneficial herbs also have a toxic quality if taken in too high doses. Digitalis can cure heart problems, but can also kill if taken in large quantities. There is always a fine balance in the nutrients our body needs.

In today's society of fast foods, takeaways and processed staples, our bodies are receiving too much in the way of additives and food that contains no nutrient value. It is now being said in some medical quarters that although obesity is epidemic, many patients are nutritionally starving.

## TOXIC SUBSTANCES

As well as vitamins and minerals, our body requires tiny levels of trace elements, such as copper, silver, gold, aluminum, fluoride etc. There are dozens of these elements in our systems. However today our bodies are over-burdened with these elements and they then become toxic. As an example, mercury is perhaps seen as the worst of the elements which have become toxic. These toxic elements are referred to as heavy metals. Mercury is widely used in dental amalgam, vaccinations, and as a binder in many food and medical products. Mercury is not readily flushed out of the body and will accumulate mainly in the brain and fat cells, causing toxicity. Mercury may sit within the body and do no harm at all, but for many people it causes serious health problems.

Even essential minerals such as iron and calcium can become toxic. Too often the medical establishment keeps telling us to take in more and more calcium to prevent bone fractures. However calcium must be taken in balance with magnesium, boron and selenium. Too much calcium and not enough magnesium will give you problems, just as much as having too little calcium.

*Personal care products are a $50 billion industry in the United States, yet the U.S. government doesn't require any mandatory testing for these products before they hit the shelves.*

Drugs, whether prescription drugs, hard drugs or social drugs, all have a toxic effect on the body and can result in long term damage that cannot be repaired. Very often drugs and alcohol travel immediately to the brain, where they seem able to by-pass the blood-brain barrier for direct entry into the brain cells, from where they affect our memory and our reasoning abilities.

Pharmaceutical drugs also have toxic effects on the body. Many medications of course do help to cure us, but most drugs are not specific to the illness in the body. Therefore when you ingest a medicine it goes into the bloodstream and travels all round the body and will affect sites other than the ones you wish to target. This is why there are so many side effects listed for medical drugs.

These pharmaceutical drugs do not always have a key and lock system to enter the cell, so the pharmaceutical industry hides the drug within a natural substance that has free entry into the cells.

Cigarettes and alcohol have toxic effects on the body when consumed in large quantities. We are all very aware of lung cancer caused by toxins (nicotine) in cigarettes, and alcohol can have severe inhibiting effects in our brain along with seriously affecting our liver and kidneys.

*Mercury enters the body and quickly becomes bound in the nervous system: the brain, spinal cord and nerves. Mercury impairs the immune system making the body susceptible to infections, chronic sickness and fungal infections. High levels of accumulation can cause thyroid problems, learning disabilities, neurological problems, hormonal imbalances and can damage the heart, brain, lungs, kidneys, pituitary, adrenal and thyroid glands. Mercury conveys immunity to antibiotics so they may no longer be able to control certain bacteria. Mercury can also transfer from mother to fetus, and to the baby via breast milk, affecting the baby's central nervous system. Mercury is most often found in body powders, thermometers, cosmetics, amalgam dental fillings, diuretics, fungicides, vaccinations, laxatives, paints, seafood, adhesives, fabric softeners, and industrial wastes.*

## HORMONES

Our endocrine system is one of the main functioning systems of the body. In most cases our hormones have become so unbalanced as to cause a variety of problems.

Tumours associated with the thyroid, thymus and adrenal glands are becoming more common. No doubt these can be attributed to an over-burden of hormones such as adrenaline and cortisol due to stress, causing a constant "fight or flight" response and putting the glands into a serious state of imbalance. During ongoing stress the adrenal hormones shut down the immune system by causing constriction to the blood vessels of the brain's pre-frontal cortex which then diminishes conscious awareness and intelligence.

The reproductive organs suffer from an imbalance of estrogen, received from immunizations, food and air and water borne pollutants.

Imbalances in the pineal and pituitary glands which should be receiving the higher Source energy are compromised, and fear, confusion and other mental imbalances can occur.

## THE INVISIBLE TRIGGERS

### STRESS

In today's world, stress is a major player in illness and disease. It affects our work, home, relationships, family, and almost any situation that involves interacting with other people.

Stress causes an immune response, called the "fight or flight" response. If you are faced with let's say a hungry dinosaur, the body responds in that way, caused by the release of hormones, and prepares for fight or flight by temporarily shutting down unnecessary systems such as digestion and reproduction. Hormones such as adrenaline pour into the blood and circulate throughout the body, sharpening brain function and getting the muscles ready for the pending fight or flight. This fight or flight response causes high levels of cortisol in the body. In ancient times, after a fight or flight situation, the human would probably have collapsed under a tree and fallen asleep to recover, allowing the body to return to normal function by decreasing the levels of cortisol.

Nowadays when people are continually stressed, their body is in fight or flight response all the time. The body systems do not see any difference between a dinosaur and stress. They both activate the hormonal response of fight or flight. This means that the body is continually operating on high levels of cortisol in the bloodstream, which again is an imbalance and not our normal state of being.

When stress is continual it results in cessation of growth and the breakdown of cells. Almost every major illness that people acquire has been linked to chronic stress, including heart disease, diabetes, high blood pressure, hormonal imbalances, back pain, headaches, digestive problems, sleep loss, fatigue, skin problems, irritability, tooth grinding, and much more.

Medical science is now beginning to understand there is a strong link between stress and depression. Stress alters brain wave functions triggering fears which then predominate a person's thoughts and actions. The chemical imbalance in the brain holds on to the stress, causing it to become long term depression.

Because our body systems are therefore not functioning effectively, the vibrational frequencies of stress affect the health of all of our cells.

**COUNTERACTING STRESS:**

Meditation is one of the most effective methods of counteracting stress in our everyday lives. Quiet time, even without meditation, is helpful—just letting go of worries and anxieties that keep the mind in a constant loop of stressful thoughts.

Massage is good for the soul. Be willing to let go and relax.

Visit friends, family or counselor to talk about your issues. Talking gets the thoughts out into the open, reducing stress in the mind. "A problem shared is a problem halved" is an old adage that actually carries a lot of weight. Don't bottle up your problems and don't isolate yourself.

Take time out in nature. Visit the park or rest by a river, lake or beach. Nature is particularly soothing to the nervous system. Visit a zoo or wildlife sanctuary, because animals and birds are very receptive and are an integral part of nature. Take time to smell the roses . . . remember their beauty and exquisite scent.

Embrace a good nutritional plan and exercise regularly.

Shout yourself and a friend or partner an evening out, or a few days holiday. Change is always good for us . . . often puts our life in a better perspective.

Check on whether your problems are major ones that need dealing with, or just minor issues that really aren't that important. In other words, don't sweat the small stuff!

Learn to love yourself.

---

*Scientists have discovered that everyday emotional stress is a trigger for the growth of tumours. Any sort of trauma, emotional or physical, can act as a "pathway" between cancerous mutations, bringing them together in a potentially deadly mix. The findings seem to show for the first time that the conditions for developing the disease can be affected by the emotional environment, including everyday work and family stress.*

*From article 'Stress Linked to Cancer'*
*February 2010*
*www.mercola.com*

---

**EMOTIONS**

Emotions affect our cells and can have a positive or a negative effect on cellular health. If you exist mostly on the Love side of life then cells respond to the positive nature of your emotions and remain healthy.

If you exist much of the time in the lower negative vibrations of fear, anger, jealousy, depression, etc. then the cells become flooded with negative vibrations. This causes unhealthy cells which will trigger illness.

Fear inhibits all movement forward.

It halts us in our tracks.

It stagnates us in inactivity.

It takes away the experience of life.

Fear is an illusion, but a very powerful one. We can allow true healing to take place when we let go of the attachment to the belief in our fears.

Anger is one of the most prevalent negative emotions we have in collective consciousness. Anger festers, it boils, and eventually it must burst out and usually does this in the form of illness. Unresolved anger can manifest in excess weight, a variety of cancers, high levels of acidity in the body, joint pain, swelling and inflammation, bladder and kidney infections, boils and blisters. This is an emotion we really must release from the physical body if we wish to continue here on earth.

The best antidote to anger is forgiveness, forgiveness of Self for feeling the anger, forgiveness of Self for the anger directed at others, and forgiveness of others who have directed their anger at us. Unless we look at all these aspects and transcend them, we will continue to experience eruptions in the body.

> *Learn to use your emotions, your feelings to perceive reality.*

Depression is very prevalent in society today, causing the person to feel powerless as their life spins out of control. Depression inhibits the release of the happy hormone, serotonin, causing illness, which could be the body's response to feeling unloved and unwanted, and the ultimate process of leaving the planet through death. It is well accepted in medical circles that depression is a result of chronic stress.

Judgment also has serious implications. When we judge another, we are really judging ourselves, for we have all been in that same position, whether in this life or past lives. Judgment means one feels superior to another. Judgment causes wars, particularly racial wars and religious wars.

When you judge someone, that causes hurt and wounds in them, but be aware that the energy of judgment boomerangs back to you, and you feel the same pain. One more thing you will have to clear and release from your cells.

We are all one in the eyes of God and it's time we realised that.

*Disease comes from a state of unforgiveness. When we are ill, we must look at who we need to forgive. The person you find the hardest to forgive is the one you need to most work on the act of forgiveness. Let go of the past, whatever the cause. If you continue to carry the burden of abuse and always looking for revenge it ultimately takes its toll in creating physical illnesses. Allow the universe to take care of the perpetrator.*

## BELIEFS

Like stress and emotions, beliefs are an invisible force that have a profound effect on the health of our cells. Beliefs we are not even aware of having can sit in our subconscious causing harm and illness.

In past lives we have all taken vows of celibacy, vows of poverty, of silence, oaths to fight for king and country, and so many others. These are very powerful and stay in the subconscious, brought through each lifetime in the DNA. If we have a vow of poverty sitting quietly and unknown in the DNA, how can we ever hope to become wealthy? If we have oaths to fight for king and country, it is no wonder it is so easy to convince men to go to war.

We have been conditioned to feel unworthy, that we are a sinner, and that we will go to hell when we die if we haven't been good. We believe money is evil, that the rich get richer and the poor get poorer.

We have been subjected to so much abuse we no longer believe in our ability to feel. This has affected our self-worth, along with our self-confidence, our self-respect and our self-esteem.

We believe we are failures so how can we ever be successful? We believe that we grow old and die. We believe in illness. We believe in fate. All of these issues affect the health of the cell and the ability to live long and joyful lives.

We really don't know what sits in our cells inhibiting our life, but it is time to find out. This can happen during meditation or through various healing modalities.

## HEALTH OF THE CELL

*Thoughts, the mind's energy, directly influences how the physical brain controls the body's physiology. Thought energy can activate or inhibit the function of cells and is a more efficient means of affecting matter than chemicals.*

Cells are either positive and healthy—or become negative and toxic. Our cells are healthy if they resonate with the Divine Template of Love and Light.

Our cells are negatively affected by toxic elements, by stress, negative emotions, fears and beliefs. These affect our immune system by creating hormonal imbalances which lead to illness. In a positive state our immune system is healthy and we have an abundance of the happy hormones.

The health of our cells is affected by negative DNA modifications that sit in our subconscious that we are unaware of.

Any negative fears or beliefs will create blockages in the chakras and in our electromagnetic system, which means life force energy is not flowing.

These negative emotions or beliefs impact the vibrational frequencies of the cells. In other words, they affect the spinning of the atoms, causing slower spinning atoms and a denseness in the cells, which we call dark energy. These negative fears are ego based, which is a left brain activity.

*If positive thinking can heal you, then consider what negative thinking does to your biology and your life.*

The third dimension is the home of the ego: the lower ego and ego personality. Life is not about overcoming, destroying or dismantling the ego, as it serves an important purpose. It has always tried to protect us. Our challenge is to take the ego into higher dimensions by transforming its limited thinking into an unlimited spiritual partnership with our soul. When we try to destroy the ego we are trying to correct something that is not wrong. Transformation is not about destruction, it is about shifting energies, changing form and creating a new vibration.

Our cells are positively affected by good nutritional intake and by positive beliefs and emotions. Our chakras and electromagnetic systems then receive an abundance of life force energy, which is the interdimensional Love and Light of God.

## LIGHT AND DARK OF CELLS

It is the amount of love and light within cells which make it a healthy cell. The healthy cell is connected to God which brings joy and happiness in life. This results in abundance and a feeling of self-worth.

The shadow side of our cells should be a small proportion of our cells. We do have a shadow side, and always will, but we should always live with a greater amount of cellular light. We cannot beam darkness into a cell. It comes in the form of fears and negative beliefs. Humans can create darkness just the same as they can create light.

If the cells are full of dark vibrations, meaning the shadow side has taken over your life, it can be said that that person lives within his own man-made "hell". It is not of God's making, it is purely based on the darkness within the cell, and can be controlled by conscious thoughts, words and actions.

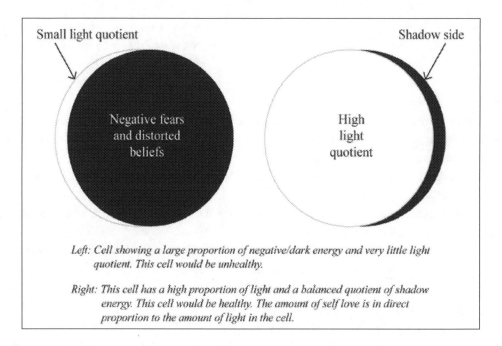

*Left: Cell showing a large proportion of negative/dark energy and very little light quotient. This cell would be unhealthy.*

*Right: This cell has a high proportion of light and a balanced quotient of shadow energy. This cell would be healthy. The amount of self love is in direct proportion to the amount of light in the cell.*

## WELLNESS vs ILLNESS

The Ascended Masters tell us that only about 5-8% of illnesses are genetic, caused in the main by faulty, missing or dysfunctional chromosomes in the protein strands. These can't be changed and are genuinely hereditary.

This leaves 90-95% that are caused by something else: that something else being external stimuli in the form of toxins, negative fears, emotions and beliefs. We can therefore say that the majority of illnesses are man-made, not genetic. We need to also understand that the fears, negative beliefs and negative emotions of our ancestors are passed on to us through the DNA, as are all the negativities from our past lives.

Negative emotions and fears are toxic to the body. If you want to live a long and fulfilling life you need to dump the toxic baggage. We continue to hang on to it because we are so used to dragging it around every day.

Imagine you are a dump truck and all this toxic baggage is the load. You carry it around on the back of the truck every day. However when you attempt to drive up a steep hill, the truck can only get so far before the heavy load causes the truck to stop. It simply can't take the load any further up the hill. What to do? Hoist the load up and dump it, and then the journey becomes easy.

You have the Divine Template of Health and Wellbeing within your DNA.

Why not use it?

# DNA MODIFICATIONS

## THE CELL NUCLEUS AND DNA

Within each cell is the nucleus which contains our 2-stranded biological DNA. DNA, short for deoxyribonucleic acid, is two strings of amino acids. These amino acids are our protein codes and combine to become our genes, containing our genetic inheritance from our parents and ancestors.

Scientists believed for a long time that the nucleus was the brains of the cell. It was therefore believed that all illnesses and diseases originated in the DNA, or the genes. We are still presented with that theory even though the attitude of scientists is changing.

Scientific experiments are showing that in fact when the nucleus (containing the DNA) is removed from a cell in a petri dish, that cell continues to function as normal. The only thing it is no longer capable of is reproducing itself.

So the conclusion is that the nucleus and genes are not the brains of the cell and therefore not necessarily responsible for all illnesses and diseases.

DNA modifications can however happen and cause problems to the functioning of the cell and the systems and organs in our body.

I have already used the example of the hungry dinosaur and the fight or flight response, where we would decide very quickly whether to stand and fight the dinosaur or run very fast to escape. In these circumstances the body systems would learn very quickly that strong legs, muscles and lungs were required for running or fighting and so these would develop as an evolutionary strategy to beat the dinosaurs. This would result in a DNA modification which would then be handed down in the DNA to all progeny (offspring), because they would also need the same attributes. In this day and age, perhaps that modification could be sitting in our cellular memory, but would not need to be triggered because we are no longer running from dinosaurs.

These DNA modifications are carried in our DNA/Cellular Memory. Our cells carry this memory until such time as we need to kick it back into action, or it is triggered by an outside stimulation, i.e. toxins, stress or negative fears and beliefs.

DNA modifications can happen in many circumstances but need a trigger to cause the sequence of amino acids to activate the modification.

As an example, in the case of the common flu, once having a strain of a flu virus our cellular biology creates memory cells that kick into action within our immune system when we come down at a later stage with the same or similar flu virus. This is beneficial as it assists us on the road to recovery.

In many instances, however, these triggers can be to the detriment of our health.

## DNA MODIFICATION EXAMPLE: BREAST CANCER

Doctors tell women if they have breast cancer in the family, then they will more than likely experience it also, as it is a hereditary condition. However, let us look at it from the point of a DNA modification.

If a woman has a mother, grandmother, auntie or any member of the family who has died from breast cancer, or had a serious battle with the illness, then their illness creates a DNA modification of fear, pain and suffering that is passed on to the progeny. These progeny then have a "pre-disposition" to breast cancer. This modification of fear of cancer sits in the DNA until it is triggered.

There appears no logical reason for a woman to get breast cancer if there is no signal to activate the DNA modification in the cellular memory.

Even if a woman is not a biological progeny of a family member who has had breast cancer, a close energetic link can also create the same fear factor that sits in the cells.

## SYNTHETIC ESTROGEN (HRT)

A woman's body needs a certain amount of estrogen, particularly during her reproductive years. But estrogen needs to be balanced with its complementary hormone, progesterone. Doctors ignore the progesterone requirements and have simply medicated women with synthetic estrogen, and called it Hormone Replacement Therapy. This can over-burden many women with estrogen that they do not require and therefore they become estrogen toxic.

It could be that this toxicity triggers a DNA modification which if activated could affect the reproductive system and organs.

Synthetic estrogen is manufactured from the urine of pregnant mares and was never approved by the Federal Drug Administration.

This synthetic estrogen is also not specific in its targeting, and will travel the body and affect any of the reproductive cells, as well as possibly other sites. It enters the cells under the same key/lock system as our natural hormone estrogen. Too much estrogen in reproductive cells can be the trigger that causes breast cancer, ovarian cancer and uterine cancer.

It has also been scientifically recorded that the waters of our world are vastly polluted with estrogens, partly stemming from contraceptive pills released into the water supplies, albeit unintentionally, but if pills are flushed down the toilet then the estrogen content can ultimately end up in the waterways or water tables. Urine will also contain amounts of estrogen that is passed from the body.

The sad pictures and stories we hear of deformed fish and frogs is an indication of hormones running amuck in our natural world.

## XENO-ESTROGENS

These are classed as chemical estrogens and are a by-product of the oil industry in products such as plastic containers and plastic wraps, and are also found in herbicides and insecticides, polluting our land, our crops and our waterways.

These chemicals have estrogenic qualities and when plastics, particularly plastic wraps, are heated, the xeno-estrogens are released from the plastic and absorbed into the food or drink contained therein, providing the body with much unwanted and unneeded estrogenic activity. This is the reason why we are told not to have water bottles sitting in the sun because the water can absorb a high level of xeno-estrogens.

We should never microwave food in plastic containers or covered with plastic wrap as the hot food will draw the xeno-estogens into the food.

Xeno-estrogens may be contributing to the high levels of reproductive cancers that women, young and old, are getting. It could be a sad contributing factor to the very early puberty that many young girls are going through. Do we believe it is normal for girls as young as 7, 8 and 9 years of age to start developing breasts and having periods?

Apparently in less than a decade the average bra size in Britain has increased from a 34B to a 36C and a quarter of all bras sold are a D cup or above. General obesity may be a factor, but it could also be attributable to the xeno-estrogens found in the many cosmetic products used by women. Xeno-estrogens are fat soluable and are stored in the body, perhaps in breast tissue. Could this be a major factor in the increasing levels of breast cancer in women?

Many men these days are getting breast cancer. Why? Their main hormone is testosterone, not the estrogen that would cause breast cancer in women. Xeno-estrogens are more than likely the answer. Not only are women overburdened with estrogen, but so too are men. These xeno-estrogens in men can affect their reproductive organs, possibly causing breast cancer, prostate cancer and testicular cancer.

# BIOLOGICAL CELL vs COMPUTER CHIP

No doubt you have heard suggestions that our body is like a biological computer, far more complex than any machine that could be designed. This is actually correct, but let us look at the comparisons between the two.

## COMPUTER PROGRAMMING

A programmer creates a programme, downloads it onto a computer chip and the computer will then do what it is programmed to do. At a later date, the programmer can re-programme the computer chip by making a modification to the original programme and downloading it on to the chip. The computer will then carry out the modification, or the modified programme, if required.

Because the computer chip controls the function of the computer according to its programming, it is known as a semi-conductor of information, because the chip has "gates" to prevent it operating outside of its programme.

In older computers and televisions the field of the screen was quite still, like solid energy. Nowadays, in plasma and digital screens of computers, televisions and watches, etc, the energy field is created as a liquid crystal field. This makes it a fluid field and is seen as wavering or shimmering.

This liquid crystal field means that a computer has a crystalline field of consciousness. It knows what it is, what it can do, and knows it is connected to the universe within its flow. There are already available computers that respond to voices, to thoughts, and can actually talk. This area will increase exponentially over the next few years.

Already computers are being programmed with brain cells from rats and it is scientifically noted that the computer responds to the programming of the rat.

## CELLULAR PROGRAMMING

The cell has a programmer—YOU.

We each programme our cells according to our attitudes, beliefs and emotions.

We can also programme in DNA modifications which are available to be used as required. Negative modifications have often triggered illness, but positive modifications will have a beneficial effect on the health of the cells and the body.

The membrane acts as a semi-conductor because it controls what goes in and out of the cell, and the phospholipids are the "gates" for entry or exit.

The cell consists of a Liquid Crystalline Field, which is fluid cosmic energy. This liquid crystalline field surrounds the 200 or more trillion cells of the body. This liquid crystalline field of our body is fluid and flows with quantum consciousness connecting each cell with everyone and everything in the universe. This fluid energy asks that we "go with the flow", because fluid energy wants to keep moving, changing, and evolving. Its natural state is fluid, not to stagnate and become solid. This is why we are continually advised by the higher realms to go with the flow of life. This flow of quantum consciousness connects you to the Divine Love of God and the Universe. It allows us to know we are part of the whole of God.

This is our difference to mechanical computers. Nothing can and will ever compare to the human biological computer.

It is Divine!


## RE-PROGRAMMING OUR CELLS

Each of us programmes our cells.

Remember . . . the cell's original template resonates to Love.

We create negative modifications by our negative beliefs about ourselves and our lives and what we can do or can't do. These beliefs have come from our own feelings about ourselves, and also from ancestors, parents, teachers, doctors, religions, work mates, peers, governments, groups, etc.

Consider some of the beliefs you have about yourself and where they have come from? If a teacher told you "you will never amount to anything", and then you absorb that belief about yourself, it will create a modification in your cells as a sub-conscious belief that you will then continue to believe in all your life until you re-programme it.

Parents can tell us we are "useless". They tell us we can't sing, dance, swim, do maths. So many beliefs are set in place when we are young. Up to the age of about 7 we are like a sponge, absorbing everything we are told. We take these statements as fact and the beliefs are set in place about who we are and what we are capable of.

However, we are able to create positive modifications by re-programming our beliefs.

To create new beliefs means looking at the beliefs you have, where they came from, who gave them to you and are they good for you or not. These old patterns of behaviour need to be released from the sub-conscious and replaced with new positive beliefs.

This is achieved by working step by step: releasing negative stress, emotions and beliefs, controlling our thoughts and words, and by changing old patterns of behaviour.

These will gradually start to create new modifications that will serve your highest good and move you forward into living within a state of love and light, your natural state. This in turn will create your dreams, which will bring you into states of joy and happiness. Then your body will return to its divine template of health and wellness.


## WHO CONTROLS OUR BIOLOGY?

Simple really . . . . OUR THOUGHTS DO !

If thoughts create our reality then our physical body, our biological creation, must therefore also be controlled by our thoughts.

Yes, the Illuminati attempt to control us by their control methods, their brainwashing and conditioning.

Yes, the food chain is polluted, the air we breathe is polluted, the water is polluted. Nature has become polluted.

BUT . . . . YOU ARE IN CONTROL OF YOUR BIOLOGY!

Your physical body will do what you tell it to. We know that we can tell the arm to pick up a ball from the floor. We can tell our legs to run fast, we can tell our eyes to see, we can tell wounds to heal.

So why on earth is it any different to tell our cells to be healthy?

The DNA in our cells is waiting for us to give the commands. Are you on auto-pilot, blindly allowing subconscious patternings to control you, or are you on conscious awareness alert, in charge of both your reality and your biology?

Yes, we can talk to our cells. Our body is our friend, so talk to the cells as a friend. Make the intent that they return to their Divine Template of perfection. You will have to do some work to make that happen. Instead of expecting a miracle, do the work. The cells do not respond to lip service, you must take action, such as eating better food. You must believe that you and your cells can work together to produce what your intent may be.

Feed the body the best nutrients and water you can. Exercise or be in nature as often as you can. Balance your work life with rest, relaxation and things you love doing. Above all, get to work on clearing those old negative emotions and beliefs that stop you moving forward. If the body realizes you are serious about health and wellness it will support you in every possible way.

Check your beliefs on illness. Do you believe you are sick, will get sick or that sickness is inevitable with age?

We believe in illness. We believe in pain and suffering.

Does that make any sense at all?

Stop feeling sorry for yourself and stop being the victim. Stop believing in illness. It doesn't matter how polluted the world is, how much control continues around us, how much chaos exists. None of it matters because each of us can create our own health, our own heaven for ourselves and our individual life that is free of outside control.

We are Divine Beings of God. Would we imagine for a moment God getting sick? No, of course not.

Then get with it, people, get yourself well and healthy. It is our divine birthright to be fit, healthy and abundant.

Miracles can happen if you allow them!

> *If you choose to see a world filled with love, your body will respond by becoming healthy. If you choose to see a world as full of fear, the health of your body will be compromised.*

# 12 STRAND DNA

*The quantum human is the one who will be able to activate the quantum portions of his DNA to work with greater efficiency. It is time to start thinking outside the paradigm you were born in.*

*. . . Kryon*

Our DNA exists in a quantum field of Oneness. Therefore it is our DNA that connects us with the vastness of the universe. Individual DNA is controlled by our consciousness. It is our intents and desires contained within the vastness of our individual consciousness that dictates how the biological body should operate.

We know we have two biological strands of DNA that contain our genetic code. The genes we inherit from our parents and grandparents give us our eye colour, our skin colour, our hair colour, big ears, stubby nose, etc. These are our biological sequences of amino acids, our own genetic make-up which we in turn pass on to our children and grandchildren.

It is the 2-strand DNA that was studied in the Human Genome Project, a combined work of many scientists to map the human genetic codes. They assumed, somewhat incorrectly, that there would be a coding in the 2-strand DNA for every illness and disease. This has been proved to be wrong as in fact they could only identify 22,000 genetic codes which nowhere near covers the number of labeled illnesses and diseases on the planet. To a major degree, to the lay person anyway, this coincides with the understanding that most illnesses and diseases are man-made, the result of incorrect living and distorted beliefs.

The other ten strands of DNA are interdimensional and therefore invisible to the eye, even under the best microscope. We can say that the atoms of the 2 strands spin slower than the atoms of the other 10 strands. In actual fact these 10 strands are what we would term 10 layers, each with 2 strands. So in fact we are really talking about 24-strand DNA.

Although our thinking conceptualizes these as layers, one following another in linear fashion, in fact they are not. To medical science our DNA is seen as a long strand, rather like a ladder. However all strands, physical and interdimensional, continually twist and intertwine and exist somewhat in the form of the circle. DNA is not static. DNA continually changes every day with our emotions, thoughts and experiences.

All 12 layers are interconnected and work together. No layer works separately to any of the others. You cannot make an intent to work with one of the layers. This does not happen. They all work together.

Layer 1 is the human biology. The other layers are our Divinity and in reawakening these dormant layers we are melding the human with its divine nature.

Each layer carries an aspect of interdimensional energy.

Layers 1, 2 and 3 are the Root Group and our self-worth is represented in these 3 layers:

Layer 1 is our human genetic coding. It is our bio-chemical layer and it is who we are in 3D. We have lived for thousands of years in 3D limitation because we have functioned mainly on the biological layer and not fully utilized the other 10 DNA layers: the spiritual or divine layers.

Layer 2 contains our Divine Blueprint which is the divine template of our individual human biology. It is an intuitive layer and contains the memory of our emotional reactions to past, present and future events.

Layer 3 is the Ascension and Activation layer. It is this layer that is assisting us on our return journey to the light. The pineal gland is connected with and communicates with this layer during our ascension journey.

Layers 4, 5 and 6 are the Divine grouping, or Angelic Group:

Layers 4 and 5 are the layers that represent our divine expression on earth.

Layer 6 is the communication layer and it is this level we access in our prayers and meditation. It is communicating with the Higher Self, with God, the higher Beings of Light and with the angels.

Layers 7, 8 and 9 is the Lemurian Grouping:

Layer 7 is the Master Lemurian layer containing the Star Seed codings and brings to us the potential of the original star seed biology. It is the creative layer and also known as the Dragon Layer. Layer 7 has been dormant as a time capsule and will remain dormant until we awaken our spiritual consciousness.

Layer 8 contains our Akashic Records, the records of all our lives, experiences, skills/talents, lessons and wisdom gained during our many earth incarnations.

Layer 9 is the layer of St Germain and his Violet Flame of Transmutation, the flame of expansion. It acts as the bridge between Layer 1 human biology and the other interdimensional divine layers. It is the layer that moves us forward to self-worth and self-mastery.

Layers 10, 11 and 12 is the God Grouping:

Layer 10 is about the Call to Divinity. It is The Divine Source of Existence and it represents new beginnings. It is this layer that is waking us up to our spiritual journey, the return pathway to Light, to Home.

Layer 11 is the layer of Divine Feminine Wisdom, the energy of pure compassion and creativity. This is the layer of balance between Divine Feminine and Divine Masculine energies.

Layer 12 is GOD.

So the energy of "God" is contained in every cell in the body, for every human on earth.
God is truly "within" us.
We are God also.

*Your DNA is a far larger system than any medical authority has ever believed it to be. It is an interdimensional system that has the ability to modify itself at any time. It explains spontaneous remission. Spontaneous remission is the human who decides they are done with the disease, and who then picks up the energy from a past life that never had the disease. Many humans rid themselves of the most virulent diseases known to man. They suddenly come up clean.*

*That is not a miracle from above . . . that's a miracle from within.*

*. . . . Kryon, channeled by Lee Carroll*

---

*These attributes of DNA have come from the teachings of Kryon® as channeled by Lee Carroll.*

*If you wish to learn and understand more of the workings of cellular DNA I highly recommend you read "Kryon Book 12: DNA" by Lee Carroll 2010, published in 2010 by Platinum Publishing House*

---

# WE DO CREATE OUR REALITY

*The time to live on "automatic pilot" is over. Humanity has lived this way for thousands upon thousands of years and it has caused you all untold sufferings, sorrows, poverty, sickness and all the social and economic problems that have been facing humanity for those thousands of years. The time of your deliverance is upon you now but you as a soul evolving on Earth can be "liberated" only if you consciously choose to do so and make it the most important priority in your life. It will not happen by continuing to live on an "automatic pilot" consciousness. It will happen only if you embrace now the Christ Consciousness and start thinking and acting with your Christ Mind and Christ Love.*

*. . . . High Priest Adama from the city of Telos.*

## RESONANCE

If we placed two violins, one at each end of a large hall then plucked a note on one of them, a resonance would instantaneously travel across the room to the other instrument which would then sound the same note. The second instrument has recognised the resonance and has responded by playing the same note.

When the two notes meet the sound is amplified and expanded.

When an opera singer sounds a high note and breaks a crystal glass, it is this amplification that is happening. Crystal stores high vibrational frequencies. When the sound hits the crystal glass, the vibration is amplified, until the glass can no longer contain the expanded note. It explodes.

A similar resonance can happen between two people. Soul mates are attracted to each other by this simple act of resonance.

Our biology functions within a band of frequencies. These frequencies are emitted from our cells, and reflect the state of our biology . . . healthy and positive, or negative and filled with fear.

If we meet someone that resonates to the same band of vibrational frequencies that we have then we will recognise the similarities of that person and we will get on very well, perhaps become good friends, perhaps we will create a partnership. However we all have had instances where we meet a person that we don't take to. In fact it often feels like we can't stay in their energy field or their space for long and we need to move away. This is because their band of frequencies is different to ours.

I am sure we have all walked into a room full of people and felt a thick, heavy atmosphere that hasn't felt good at all. We also want to move out of this situation as quickly as possible. We can also walk into a room of people where the energy feels light and happy and we will enjoy the gathering, simply because we subconsciously recognise a similar range of frequencies to our own.

If we are happy and we meet an angry person or a depressed person, for example, we won't feel compatible at all with their mood, their personality or their energy field. Happy people do not want to spend time with angry or depressed people. No doubt depressed people want to spend time with happy people because it may help them to lift their mood, albeit temporarily. They can't understand why people actually don't want to be with them.

If we need to be with these lower vibrational people we should do so only for short periods of time.

I read a story once that is a good example of high and low vibrational frequencies affecting the outcome of a situation. This man was in a crowded hall where the tension and mood amongst the people turned hostile. The man picked up on this energy and began to feel angry as well. He decided to leave and was walking home still carrying angry thoughts. Coming up the other side of the street, a few blocks away, were three thuggish looking guys. As they came closer he could see that they looked pretty nasty, two were swinging bats and one was thumping what looked like knuckle dusters into his other hand. They saw him and started to cross the road toward him. This man thought, "oh dear, I'm in trouble here. I am not going to get out of this in a healthy state". However, his knowledge of light and dark energies came to the fore and he realised that his anger was radiating out and being picked up by these men. He instantly dropped his angry mood and filled himself up with the love and light of God and radiated out that high frequency. Apparently these three threatening individuals suddenly crossed the street in front of him and walked off down a side street away from him. The outcome could have been very different.

In situations like this, where you are in the presence of lower vibrational frequencies, stay centred in your heart, in your integrity, and radiate love. This can quickly restore normality to a stressful situation.

If you are about to conduct a meeting, fill the room first with love and light, so lifting the energy quotient of the room. This will help to ensure the people attending the meeting will not become demonstratively difficult, as so often happens in meetings. They will be affected by the high energy vibrations of the room. This can help achieve a successful outcome for the meeting.

In the same way, if you are attending a meeting and someone gets angry, radiate love to that person for him to use if he so wishes. You cannot change anybody, but you can make available a loving energy field to help them overcome their arguments.

I was at a seminar many years ago sitting beside a lovely lady. Halfway through the lecture she started to get extremely fidgety, constantly moving, obviously very hot because she kept waving papers around her face to cool herself. She was obviously very uncomfortable and was causing some disruption to me and others around us. We could not concentrate on the speaker. I asked her Higher Self if I could send her cooling energy to settle her down. The answer was yes, so I directed a flow of cool energy down on her and after five minutes she had settled down and seemed normal again. I continued the flow of cool energy for another ten minutes just to make sure. This was using a benefic energy to settle her down without her knowledge, but only after asking my Higher Self/her Higher Self if it was okay to do this. We must always bear in mind we cannot change anyone but we are able to ask their Higher Self if it is appropriate, such as in this case. Of course, if someone asks you for help or healing, then do it . . . no need to question further. You have been asked, so respond.

If we are having a happy day, then we are putting out that resonance and our day will continue to be happy and satisfying.

If you wanted a successful meeting, for instance, then you need to put out the resonance of success and *feel* the emotions of a meeting that runs smoothly and achieves a successful outcome.

If you know that you have to handle a difficult person or situation at work, *see* peace in the situation, *feel* a successful outcome, *see* yourself knowing the right words and actions to take. In this way your resonance is helping to resolve a difficult situation. If the outcome is not as you had hoped, you have not failed because you have done everything you could to make it work. Sometimes that person has unresolved issues in their life. Do not take this on as your burden. Know you did your best.

The result that is wanted in any situation has to match the resonance. What we focus on is what we get.

At the lower end of vibrational frequencies are the people who are in states of anger, depression and poverty, which lead to them feeling a victim. These emotional states are then the frequencies they are emitting and they therefore attract to themselves similar people and situations.

A depressed person, an angry person or a judgmental person, cannot have a happy day because they are putting out the wrong resonance for a happy day.

A person who does not believe in themselves, or has low self esteem, will not attract successful and confident partners.

We often wonder why people in abusive relationships keep going back to the same partner, or another partner with the same abusive tendencies. Many times it is a dominant person, a bully in fact, over a weaker person. If someone feels like a victim then they are attracting another abusive relationship into their life, whether they know it or not, and whether they want it or not. Like attracts like. It is a case of magnetizing similar resonances to you.

Therefore to create the reality that we would like, we need to lift our vibrational frequencies to match what we desire. This takes time and practice, but in gradual steps we can move beyond the lower frequencies and into higher frequencies, which are more in line with our desires and dreams.

One of the ways to do this is to watch what we think and say. Thoughts are powerful. Are yours negative or positive? When we continually think negatively about ourselves, about people and situations in our lives and about the world we live in, then we create for ourselves a life of negativity: a life in the lower frequency vibrations.

To think positive happy thoughts and voice those in our words, then we move toward our desires that resonate with the higher frequencies.

Thoughts do create our reality.

When we are tired and constantly think to ourselves "I am tired of working" we manifest tiredness for ourselves. After all, that's what we are asking for.

We can be thinking "I don't like my job" and so maybe we will be made redundant.

What about "I wish I didn't have to go. I don't want to go". Well, how about falling and breaking your leg? Then you are unable to go. We get what we wish for but not always in the way we imagine.

In reality we are wanting the opposite, but because our thoughts and words are phrased in the negative we create a negative result. The universe simply gives us what we ask for.

## LOVE AND FEAR

*When you let go of resistance, life becomes easier. Surrender to the*
*guidance of your Higher Self and live with Grace.*

There are only two emotions in our duality state, those of Love and Fear. Under the heading of Love we have the emotional states of bliss, joy, happiness, peace of mind, integrity and truth, etc., which are the higher vibrating frequencies of emotions.

Under the heading of fear we have a loss of control . . . losing control of a situation, of the interaction with another person, perhaps feeling like we have lost control of our life. When we feel we have lost control over life or a particular situation, we become a victim, and from there the victim enters into the negative emotional states of anger, depression, resentment, guilt, jealousy and hate etc. These are very low vibrating frequencies, what we would call dark energy or negative energy. Underlying all these negative emotions is always a fear, and we need to search within to identify just what that fear is. At the most basic level, fear is always about a lack of love.

When we are in a state of anger, that is the resonance we are putting out, and we will draw angry people and angry situations to ourselves like a magnet. This is the Law of Attraction at work. We will attract to us the frequencies we are putting out.

These frequencies are way below the higher frequencies of joy and happiness etc. and "never the twain shall meet" until we do the work of clearing and releasing the negativities.

If you are counseling or healing these people you need to spend the shortest time with them and then let go any residual energies left with you, and return to your higher vibrating self. Do not take their problems on your shoulders. Their anger is not yours, you do not want it. Allow them to keep their anger, and solve their own problems. We can only be there to help as needed.

---

**There are only two emotions: Love and Fear.**

| LOVE AND LIGHT | DARK AND FEAR |
|---|---|
| Joy and Bliss | Loss of Control: |
| Happiness | ↓ |
| Creativity | Feeling a Victim: |
| Compassion | ↓ |
| Integrity | Anger/Rage |
| Trust | Hatred/Intolerance |
| Abundance | Envy/Jealousy |
| Health | Resentment |
| Fun and laughter | Guilt/Shame |
| Peace of mind | Blame |
| Wisdom | Depression |
| Empathy | Discontent/Frustration |
| Self-belief | Worry/Anxiety |
| Self-trust | Impatience |
| Confidence | Hopelessness |
| Intuition | Judgment |
| Patience | Sadness/Unhappiness |
| Gratitude | Grief/Sorrow |

**If you are not in a state of love you are in a state of fear.**

---

## WE DO CREATE OUR REALITY!

*You are the power source, and your thoughts, actions and intentions radiate forth from you in a loop of energy that connects with like energy. That energy magnifies and manifests in the world of cause and effect and then returns to you, reinforcing your picture of reality. Your body absorbs a portion of that energy, creating pain and suffering or joy and blessings, depending on the frequencies.*

Whether you believe it or not, we do create our reality. Whether you choose to believe it or not, we do create our reality. When things go wrong, or we don't get what we desire, it is so easy to blame everyone else. It's always someone else's fault. When we run out of people to blame, then God cops our anger. Thoughts are powerful. Thoughts create. Thoughts, words and actions create our reality every day.

Let's look at your life from a different angle—your life is a play running on Broadway.

You are the writer of this play.

You are the producer and the director.

You are the main actor on stage.

You are also the audience.

The other actors in your play are there at your request, playing the parts you have asked them to. Some will be nice people, some will be negative, some may be nasty, some may be part of your life to complete karmic contracts. Prior to this incarnation, you asked these people to come into your life and play these parts.

They are all members of your soul family.

Now, be an observer and watch yourself in this play. Are you pleased with how you play your part in your life? Are you happy? Are you angry? Are you depressed? Are you playing the role of a victim? What can you see in yourself that needs changing?

Now, be the audience. You are sitting in the auditorium watching. What do you think about your play? Are you happy with it, or would you say that it isn't a particularly enjoyable play? What is wrong with it? What needs changing?

Is your play focused on negativities? Or is it happy, positive and exciting?

You are also the editor of this play and you are therefore free to change or rewrite the script at anytime. Perhaps there are characters in this play that you would like to remove from the play. Perhaps you would like to introduce new actors into the play. You change the actors in your play by changing your own vibrational frequencies.

Whatever needs changing, you can do at any time. It is your play.

This gives you the understanding of how your life is playing out . . . to your satisfaction or not. Make the changes in your life so that you become happy with your play.

People get really cross when it is suggested that they create the things that happen in their life. All those really awful things that happen, the abuse, being made redundant from a job, losing money in a financial collapse, a serious illness. It doesn't matter what it is . . . you have created it. Our journey is about recognising that everything in our life we have created for some reason, albeit we don't always know the reason until much later.

> *Thoughts create our words.*
> *Our words create our actions.*
> *Our actions create our life.*
> *Life creates our reality.*

If we are Aspects of God in human expression, why would things just happen to us randomly and against all our dreams and wishes? We are co-creators of our life.

Many of the things we have set up to happen in our lives are to complete a karmic contract. Many situations happen with other people in order for us to learn the lesson, which then brings the karma to a completion. Perhaps we have been trying to learn the lesson for several lifetimes but still have not "got it". In this case, similar situations or people will keep recurring in our life until we learn what we are supposed to. When this happens then we find ourselves moving forward and creating a better life.

If your life seems constantly in chaos, constantly in dramas of one kind or another, negative people and situations always in your face, perhaps you need to look for the reason. It is usually about cycling around and around in similar situations until you learn the lesson that is inherent in these situations.

Who's in charge?

*YOU* are.

However, before incarnating, you gave permission to your Higher Self and your guides, mentors and teachers in the higher realms, to keep showing you these people and situations, so you could have the opportunity to master the lessons.

Who's in control?

*YOU* are.

But you are always guided.

> *Wishful thinking is one of the reasons we allow ourselves to be led by outmoded default intentions. This refers to the habit we have of not paying attention to things, of not being bothered, of thinking that problems will sort themselves out in time. Wishful thinking is believing that one day everything will turn out okay without doing any inner work. When we hope to see our discomfort magically disappear we abdicate our role as programmers of our reality.*
>
> *. . . . From 'DNA Demystified' by Kishori Aird*

## CONSCIOUS vs SUB-CONSCIOUS

Our thoughts are conscious: we know what we are thinking and we are aware of what we are doing. Our words result from these thoughts. If we continually think that we are poor or useless or not good enough, this is what we become. If we continually think that we have abundance in our life, then that is what we create.

This conscious thought process is about being Self-Aware. This self-awareness of what we are thinking then allows us to take responsibility for our thoughts, slowly changing our negative thoughts into positive ones. When we have a negative thought we have about 9 seconds to delete that thought. Simply say to yourself "cancel, clear, or delete". Change to a positive thought. This is becoming aware of what we are thinking at all times.

Our conscious thoughts therefore are our manual control of life: our free will. We can choose what we think and what we say, which then results in our actions and thereby creates our reality. Our conscious thoughts and our free will can decide whether to continue with a negative habit or belief, or change to being positive and joyful.

We are not always aware of our sub-conscious beliefs until something triggers them.

Subconscious beliefs will always override conscious thoughts if we are not consciously self-aware. The subconscious is continually on "auto-pilot" and the minute we let our self-awareness of our thoughts disappear, the sub-conscious steps in and continues in our absence. This is a survival mechanism which serves us well. How many times would we crash the car while our thoughts have wandered off into some other aspect of our life. Have you ever arrived at a destination with absolutely no idea how you got there? This is the subconscious "auto-pilot" at work. We have to remain very aware of our conscious thoughts so we are in control of our life, and not giving power to those that are our negative subconscious beliefs.

---

**Some subconscious beliefs that affect our life:**

| | |
|---|---|
| I am a failure. | I can't get over the loss of my partner. |
| I am not good enough. | I am angry with people in my life. |
| I can't ever lose weight. | I get frustrated when things don't go my |
| way. | |
| I feel rejected | I never feel happy. |
| I will get cancer. | Nobody wants a relationship with me. |
| My body does not heal well. | I am old, or fat, or unattractive. |
| People don't like me. | Life is a struggle. |
| I have no friends. | Doctors are always right. |
| I'm always hungry. | Things always go wrong in my life. |
| I never win. | My boss never gives me a promotion. |
| I am scared of change. | The future is scary. |

Now take a minute to reflect and find the positive/opposites to each statement.

---

## AFFIRMATIONS AND MANTRAS

Many people believe affirmations work and in those cases they probably will to a certain point. However I could repeat over and over, every day of the year, that "I am wealthy", but if I have a sub-conscious vow of poverty, then the affirmation will not achieve anything until I clear the vow of poverty.

Affirmations are a way to change from negative thoughts to positive thoughts, but until you do something about your beliefs nothing will change. At best, it is usually just wishful thinking. Affirmations deny the inner work that must be done to achieve forward movement in life.

Mantras are different from beliefs and affirmations. They are used to still the mind and enter into a silence from where you can communicate with your spirit or with the non-physical realms. Transcendental Meditation uses mantras, and gives participants a word with no meaning and that does not exist in the dictionary. When using a mantra the mind does not get distracted by the meaning of the word.

# MANIFESTATION OF ABUNDANCE

*How much do you value yourself. How much do you believe you deserve abundance in your life. Abundance is your birthright, a state of grace. A lack of abundance is not loving self, not believing in the abundance of the universe.*

Abundance can be money, a house, holiday, business, a new job, and many other wonderful gifts and opportunities in our lives. Abundance operates on the higher frequencies of love. The universe will deliver abundance only if you are resonating within the higher frequency states of being.

However many people operate from the lower vibrating frequencies of negative emotions and these do not resonate with the things they desire. These negative emotions are the frequencies of fear, and fear will only bring to you that which you fear.

This again is the Law of Attraction. The resonances of fear based emotions will not enable manifestation of abundance.

So again, we need to take steps to clear our negative emotions and beliefs because they do not resonate with abundance.

Whatever your vibratory frequency, your state of resonance, is what you manifest.

Everything outside of us is a mirror of what is inside of us. So if you are manifesting poverty in your life, or confrontational situations in your life, or an inability to get a job etc., then look to the situations and people that surround you and they will reflect what you need to look at in yourself.

If you criticize people for varying reasons, then perhaps those reasons reflect who you are, more so than the other person. People unknowingly act as a mirror for our own attitudes.

When people talk about abundance, they are really talking about needing an abundance of money. However, money is usually the last thing we get. We first need to learn what abundance means, what manifestation is, and how to create our reality from a position of love.

Once we embark on our journey of light, the universe will help us out along the way. If we need money to pay the rent, the mortgage, power bill, have a holiday, start a new business or pay medical expenses, the universe will sometimes help us out with these urgent needs, either in the form of money or some other way of helping.

Perhaps if you have been evicted from your house and have nowhere to live, you may miraculously find someone offering you a place to stay. Someone might offer to help pay for your medical expenses. Sometimes when we need food or

*From a friend:*

*I wanted some new clothes, so went to have a look at the shops. I eventually decided that my money was more urgently needed to pay the bills so went home with no purchases.*

*When I got home I found a bag of clothes hanging on my back door. They were nearly new, exactly what I had wanted, and fitted me perfectly.*

*I had no idea where they had come from until the next day when a cousin rang to say she had been cleaning out her wardrobe and thought these may be of use to me to me.*

clothes, we may find exactly what we need at discounted prices, or someone may offer you clothes they no longer require.

Abundance from the universe does not necessarily come in the form of money.

True abundance is a STATE OF BEING and has very little to do with money. It is living in the higher frequencies of love and light where you manifest what you need. This happens by working from your heart, in co-creation with God/Universe.

If we are in the lower negative emotions we are not in the "state of being" that supports abundance. We may then feel like victims, powerless in the face of our poverty or the lack of goods and services that we require. It is not the universe punishing us, it is specifically that we are not resonating with the high frequencies that create abundance.

When we cannot manifest what we want, then we need to look at why. What are we doing, or not doing, that is promoting this lack of abundance?

## WHAT IS ABUNDANCE?

To many people it is money, a house, a new car, a holiday, etc. These are all materialistic things.

To spiritual people, those on their ascension journey, abundance comes in the form of love from family, friends and pets, from happiness, good health, peace of mind, pure food and water, beauty in art, music and nature, and fun and laughter. These are spiritual gifts and it is where this journey is leading all of us.

We cannot take material possessions with us when we die, but we certainly can and will take the spiritual gifts with us: the higher forms of abundance we have created in our life.

Society has become too materialistic where possessions mean more than spiritual gifts. We sometimes see where possessions are all-important after a family member has died and the family "fight over the spoils".

---

*From a friend:*

*I wanted to attend a conference but did not have the money to go. I put out the intent to the universe for the enrolment money I needed. When I went to the letterbox a couple of days later I found an envelope containing the exact amount of money I needed.*

*That was the first time I realised that we are truly provided for. I still do not know who did this or how the money appeared there. I had not told anyone about wanting to attend the conference.*

---

# THOUGHTS CREATE REALITY

*Thoughts are powerful.*
*Thoughts create universes, galaxies, planets, suns, worlds and civilizations.*
*Are your thoughts positive or negative?*

Here are some things we must consider when creating a better reality for ourselves:

## LOVE OF SELF:

*Love yourself more than you love anyone else,*
*then love everyone as much as you love yourself.*

This is the most important criteria for manifesting abundance in our lives. It is the movement on our spiritual journey that gradually re-instills this feeling of Self-love back into our lives. It is a criteria of the fifth dimension, where LOVE is the foundation of all life, as it is throughout the universe.

We have been taught through the ages that our body is unclean, dirty and that all acts of the physical body are disgusting. We therefore have a difficult time loving ourselves—truly loving ourselves and our body. We should enjoy this physical body that gives us life on earth, that provides a temple for the incarnation of our soul and spirit.

It is time to let go of all those distorted beliefs and love our body, perfect or imperfect, although there are no imperfections in the eyes of God. We must love our gender. Be the gender we came into form to experience, regardless of sexual preferences.

Stop all negative self-talk. Listen to how you treat yourself, what you say to yourself and how you act towards yourself. We are constantly telling ourselves we are stupid, useless or a failure. We convince ourselves we are unlovable, we are not beautiful, or we are not clever. When you continually say these things, your body feels unloved, and says "If you don't love me what is the point of my being here"? The body will set up an accident or illness in order to leave this life because you don't want the body.

Love your Body and Self, or you are going nowhere on this ascension journey.

## SERVICE:

Women have been conditioned to give to their family first, give to others, and always put Self last. Ultimately what happens is women become drained of energy, worn out, and perhaps die before they should.

Men have also been conditioned to be the breadwinner, to go to work to support the wife and family. They often work long hours at a job they don't enjoy, simply to "bring home the bread". Men then become tired and stressed, have a heart attack and die before they should.

It is time for us to realise we must put ourselves first and not feel guilty about it. Guilt is something that has been conditioned into us . . . to feel guilty about just about everything that we do or don't do.

It is a useless emotion and a waste of energy.

Unless we put our needs first, how can we have the energy and passion to help others? You are no good to anyone unless you are on top of your life. This is not selfish—it is imperative that we do this.

## MANIFESTING OUR NEEDS:

To manifest our needs we must stay away from negative thoughts and words. We need to drop the feelings of poverty consciousness and adopt the feelings of prosperity consciousness. We need to check on all subconscious beliefs to see if they support our desires.

To manifest, we need to intensely desire whatever it is; we need to make the choice and then the intent that it comes into our life. We need to keep an abstract focus on that, never wavering in that desire. We must take whatever action is required to help the end result. We can't get a job if we sit in a chair and do nothing.

Do not have expectations . . . miracles happen that may be quite different to what we are anticipating. Our expectations limit the result. Leave it up to our Higher Self and our teachers as to how and when it will manifest. We may get better than what we had hoped for!

We must believe that what we have asked for will manifest. Do not doubt. Doubt will negate the whole exercise and we will have to start again.

Understand that small needs can occur quickly while larger things take time. We need to learn acceptance and surrender to the higher plan of our destiny. What we want will manifest, but in its correct and divine timing, and we must learn patience.

Often people give up. They think their dreams are not going to manifest, so they give up, and perhaps go off on a different tangent to try and make something else happen in their life. Perhaps their original dream was just about to manifest, and they had given up! Divine timing of manifestations is always for our highest good. Perhaps we still have lessons to learn first.

Manifestations come from the highest levels: the higher vibrational frequencies. Do your vibrational frequencies resonate to that which you are desiring?

## WATCH YOUR WORDS:

Words are the action of your thoughts, and come back multiplied.

Do you like your thoughts and words coming back multiplied ten-fold?

Okay if they are good thoughts and dreams.

What if they are negative?

Do you really want abuse, or poverty, or illness, to come back multiplied ten-fold?

# MANIFESTING WEALTH

*To eradicate world poverty requires that we eradicate poverty from our individual consciousness. The state of our world rests solely on the collective consciousness of our thoughts and beliefs. If we feel poor, if we believe in our poverty, then we simply help to create it on a global level. We must let go of the belief in poverty and re-program our belief to one of prosperity consciousness. Only then are we assisting the world to eradicate poverty.*

Many times our inability to manifest abundance comes from our sub-conscious beliefs about money.

Firstly, we need to understand "who manifests this abundance?" "Who creates my reality?" So many people look to outsiders to solve their problems. Many people send endless prayers to God to solve their financial problems. Many expect their non-physical guides, angels or teachers to support them and give them the things they need. Perhaps some people wait for that bag of gold to land in their lap, to win the lotto, or inherit a fortune.

Sometimes in the past these have happened and so people continue to expect the same, always waiting for an outside force to come and save them.

However, our world is changing. The universe is changing, and we are approaching a change in consciousness that will see us manifesting our own abundance. The universe supports us and guides us in every way possible, but until you reach the levels of higher frequencies, they must and will leave us to sort out our problems on our own, including abundance. They cannot interfere with our free will and our free will choices, good or bad.

We must release old beliefs around money, and learn to manifest our own abundance.

We co-create abundance with the Universe and God, but "We Are God Also" and we therefore have the ability to create what we need. We are our own creators of our reality.

We need to investigate the beliefs that sit in our sub-conscious, unbeknown to us at a conscious level. These beliefs have come from earlier situations in our life, imprints from our parents and grandparents, and from many past lives.

**Some of our Subconscious beliefs about money:**

I am poor

I never have enough. I only ever have just enough.

I have taken a vow of poverty (from past lives).

Money corrupts. Money will corrupt me.

Money is evil. Money is the root of all evil.

The love of money is the root of all evil.

The less you have the more God loves you.

You must be poor to go to heaven.

I do not deserve abundance.

I am a sinner so I do not deserve abundance.

I am not worthy.

The rich get richer and the poor get poorer.

I have to work for every penny I earn.

People will be jealous of me and won't like me if I have money.

If I win the lotto everyone will hassle me for a share.

It is selfish to have too much money.

If I have too much money someone else has to go without.

If I have money someone will probably try and steal it.

Now take a moment and think about the opposites of these statements - look for the positives.

There are many more negative emotions, all of which will override our best intentions to create abundance. We need to replace these beliefs with positive beliefs.

Your beliefs about yourself also affect manifestation. If you suffer from low self-worth, low self-esteem, low self-confidence and don't love yourself, then these all play a role in the lack of abundance in your life.

Unfortunately society to this point has been conditioned to accept that money is the only way to live. Time to change this belief!

# A NEW MULTIDIMENSIONAL FUND

Our old beliefs about money include:

We need to have money in the bank or investment to provide safety and security. This makes us feel financially secure, particularly for future retirement, redundancy, or illness. This is a fear based security, and therefore will not work in the new economy we are creating. We need to learn to trust that our needs are taken care of.

We believe we need money in the bank for our purchases and feel this is the only way of operating. We don't know any other way to do it. We feel that to order goods without money on hand to pay for them is fraudulent.

We have been brainwashed into believing that it is acceptable to live on credit.

Our financial systems, including the banks, are in disarray as the old systems of working with money crumble, to be replaced by new systems. This crumbling of the old systems is forcing people to re-evaluate their ideas and beliefs about money. If a family has lost everything, it is necessary to take the view that the family is all alive and healthy and the only things that were lost were money or possessions.

It is interesting to watch people on TV after a disaster. Some are crying and bemoaning the fact that they have lost their possessions, while other people are so pleased that they have not lost any member of their family.

Money and possessions to many people are the most important things in their lives. However, in the higher dimensions these are irrelevant, as all needs are met in the instantaneous manifestation of them. We need to understand this is where we are heading. Lightworkers need to be an example to others.

On our Journey of Light we are moving into a new monetary system. This is an interdimensional system which will supply you with all your needs and wants.

The following are some of the issues involved:

Money or goods must not be hoarded. It then stagnates and this stops the flow of energy. Energy always wants to flow, and money is energy. It needs to keep circulating.

We must believe in this universal system. It works for all those operating in the higher vibrational frequencies. We must believe we have the ability to manifest our needs using this new system. We are co-creators with God. We can do it.

When we request something from this Universal Fund, we need to be open and flexible as to how and when items manifest. It may not always be what we expect, but it will always be for our higher good. Many times this will be better than what we actually hoped for.

The Higher Self is the manager of this Fund. It will check your request against your life blueprint to see if it fits into your Divine Plan. If it goes against your Plan then it will not manifest. If it is in alignment with your Plan then you will receive it, or something that aligns even better with your Plan.

After requesting something, always ask for a yes/no confirmation, otherwise you may be waiting for months for something that isn't going to manifest.

Sometimes the request is granted but the ego, or sub-conscious beliefs, stop it happening.

Requests will manifest according to Divine Timing, not our own linear version of time. Patience is often required. Many times the Universe says that just as our request is about to happen in our lives, we give up on the idea, which immediately stops the manifestation. Always keep in mind that it will eventually happen if you have a "yes" answer.

Only the items or money requested will be granted. No excess is given.

Prepare the groundwork if necessary, depending on what your request is. If there are steps you can take to help things happen, you must take them and not rely on the Universe to do everything. If you need a job, then you must prepare your CV, check out the job vacancies, send your CV out, and let people know you are looking for a job. These are steps you need to take to help the manifestation. It shows that you are serious about what you are wanting.

When you request something, you need to be operating from the heart: from the higher frequencies of love and light.

You must be grounded here on Earth—meaning the manifestation happens here in our physical world, not out in some astral plane where many people spend most of their time, simply because they don't like this world, and refuse to participate in it. Manifestations happen for us as humans on earth, not as humans having a spiritual experience outside of earth time.

Asking for these manifestations is about making intents during meditation or prayer.

# RELATIONSHIPS

*The internal equivalent to oxygen that we need in order to survive, is Love. Human relationships exist to produce love. When we pollute our relationships with unloving thoughts or unloving attitudes, we threaten our emotional survival.*

Human love is based on polarities, the intense desire and passion, but also intense fear and pain. These create the illusions of separation and limitation.

Unconditional love is free of these polarities and therefore there is no fear of being hurt by love. When you and your beloved are one, there is no sense of separation and no need for possessiveness or jealousy.

Human love prevents you from proceeding with your spiritual aspirations due to the constraints of the polarities. Unconditional Love between two people supports each to aspire to their highest goals and dreams while remaining at one with each other: individual but together.

## RELATIONSHIPS WITH PEOPLE

We have relationships with our partner, whether married or not, whether opposite sex or same sex. We establish relationships with parents, siblings, children, friends, colleagues and business associates. In some instances these are lifelong relationships and that is wonderful when two people can connect with such a close and caring bond, whether personal or business. For many people, relationships, especially romantic relationships, have been rocky and challenging paths, ultimately leading to a dissolution of the partnership.

This has happened for understandable reasons. We live in this world of duality and polarity. Here on earth the duality of energies have mostly been opposing energies, and this is why it has been so difficult to sustain long relationships. Instead of working as complementary energies we have been on opposing sides, always at loggerheads, always finding faults in the other instead of the positive contribution they can make to our lives, and we to theirs. This is a product of separation consciousness, finding ourselves separate to our partner instead of fully connected to them, mind, body and soul.

Our romantic relationships, and indeed all other relationships, have been built on a foundation of conditional love: I will love you, be your friend, be a good parent to you providing you are good to me, you help me do what I want, you earn the money, or you clean and cook for me, and many many other conditions we place, rather unsuspectingly, upon our personal or other relationships. Conditional love simply means you only love when the conditions are met. When we rebel in due course against these conditions, then the relationship hits rocky ground.

Romantic relationships and all partnerships in the future will be based on the Creator attribute of Unconditional Love. In 3D it has been impossible to fully experience unconditional love because the reality of 3D earth was built on a foundation of conditional love, so that we could in fact experience what it was like to be separate, emotionally separate, from others.

Having experienced that separation consciousness to the full, it is time to move into the 5D relationships of the future, and that is quite different to what we know at present. Relationships will be based very much on an equal balance of the two partners. One will represent the Divine Feminine energy and one will represent the Divine Masculine energy. Both will be individuals within a sacred union, supporting and encouraging each other in their individual endeavours, but always within a spiritual foundation of unconditional love.

My understanding is that marriage per se will be a choice, but not a necessary requirement of partnership. The marriage license of the past often constituted ownership. Couples may come together for a short time or long term depending on their choice and what they wish to learn and experience with each other. When they feel they have achieved what they wanted from the relationship they will mutually agree to move on.

Marriages will be a commitment between two people who wish to have children. They must take time to learn and understand the obligations and skills of parenting. It is a divine role, and a highly respected one within communities. Mother and Father, with a total love commitment, undertake the pregnancy, birthing and growth of their child with much attention given to the spiritual development of the child.

This is in stark contrast to the birth of many children on this planet in recent history. So many unplanned births, unwanted and abandoned children leading to the abuse we see so prevalent around the world. In the realms of the fifth dimension we will be in full control of our biology, and will either make the intent to have a child or not to have a child, and our body will respond in kind.

## RELATIONSHIP WITH SELF

Before you can undertake any romantic partnership of equal balance you must first develop a relationship with Self. Unless you do this, the next partnership will simply reflect the opposite faults of each of you just as in the past. So many people at present are looking for that "special" someone to have a relationship with, to share their life with. However, that "special" someone must initially be YOU. You cannot maintain a healthy relationship with anyone else until you have a healthy relationship with yourself.

To develop a relationship with Self, you must look deep within your subconscious and locate all the beliefs, attitudes and distortions that have prevented you from creating successful partnerships in the past. Look at what is inhibiting your movement into a healthy relationship with someone else.

Some of the distorted beliefs may have come from religious teachings. Religious doctrines have been about controlling women, keeping them subservient and submissive within a marriage they were not readily able to get out of, even if their male partner could do what he liked regarding affairs outside the marriage. However the vows made at the marriage ceremony did serve to control both men and women.

As you clear and become a partner with yourself, you develop a close relationship with your Higher Self and your inner God Self. This in turn brings you to a closer relationship with God and with life itself.

Many people are born into dysfunctional families, have experienced dysfunctional relationships, and have a dysfunctional relationship with God. They have dysfunctional attitudes towards life. These wounds must be healed.

We must become a clear channel with our own divinity in order to bring that to a relationship with an equal partner; one who has done the same work, therefore enabling the two to create a solid foundation for a long lasting and divine partnership.


## PARENTING

I am sure those of us on our spiritual journey are aware that the children of today are different. As Baby Boomers or early Lightworkers we have been different too. We have usually felt we don't fit in. Earth has not felt like home. We seem to have an underlying knowing that we do not come from earth, but from somewhere up in the stars.

The young children coming in now feel much the same way. They are arriving with much higher light quotients in their cells, much more of their Higher Self already downloaded into their DNA. In other words they are coming already partly ascended.

They are usually quite multidimensional already and are very intuitive and very creative. The rigid educational systems do not fit them at all. When they are made to conform, often they won't and this is when we see the rebellious side of them. They refuse to conform because they know better. They have such a knowing that they are fully attuned to the higher dimensions and simply cannot understand the reason for all the 3D stuff that surrounds them. They will see straight through their parents, teachers and anyone else. They can sense the lies and distortions of truth because they intuitively know the truth. They are often telepathic and can read your thoughts. If your thoughts do not coincide with your words they get very confused. They literally can't figure you out or what you are meaning.

It takes careful parenting of these children. They need to know that you understand them, or at least attempt to understand them. They want your support, your love, and most of all your help. They need boundaries so that they feel safe and protected within those boundaries that you as a parent establish.

They need to communicate their needs and their ideas without ridicule. Because of their higher light quotient they are creative and must be helped into projects that allow them to use this ability.

Because they are vibrating to a much higher frequency they do not tolerate dense food and heavily processed contaminated food. They often have food allergies and it is the wisdom of the parents that see these children eating the correct food. By living in a polluted environment, eating dense processed foods, and surviving in a negative home environment, these children will become sick, depressed or violent. This is not to judge parents, but to help parents see that they must find a new way to parent these beautiful children.

Their allergies may often stem from chemical sources, so be aware of chemicals in food, in the house and in personal use. Discontinue their use as much as possible from their life and their environment. Even such things as fly spray may be causing reactions.

If these young ones feel loved and nurtured, they bring to families the gift of joy, fun and laughter. They are here to lighten the load, to lighten the heavy lower vibrating frequencies of earth. It is a difficult job for them before they are mature enough to understand their role.

If the parents are too busy or too stressed to help these children, as teenagers they will begin to live on the outer edges of society, often feeling out of touch with the world. This can lead them to resort to drugs and alcohol to dull the feelings they have which do not match this world. In these cases they can feel isolated, unloved, failures, and that feeling of hopelessness can have sad and dangerous implications.

So having given birth to these children, parents must now take responsibility for doing everything they can to nurture these young ones to take their place in the new society as responsible adults helping to create the changes we need.

It is about creating the right relationship with these young ones. The more you can establish a good relationship with them while they are young, the easier the teenage years will be. Teenagers need to know they can trust you, as a parent, to be fair and reasonable.

## ROMANTIC RELATIONSHIPS

If you wish to establish a strong long term relationship with a new partner you must understand how energy works and how the vibrational frequencies of your cells magnetise to you a partner on the same frequency level. This means that if you are filled with anger, fear, depression, resentment and other negative emotions, then your vibrational frequency is at that lower level and you can only attract to yourself that same level of partner.

If you have done a lot of spiritual clearing work on yourself you probably won't be attracted to the lower vibrational energy of that person. If you do choose to have a relationship with that person, you will either lower your own signature energy level, or perhaps the relationship won't be long lasting.

When, and only when, you have done the clearing work on your negative emotions and beliefs, can you attract an equal partner to you at a higher spiritual level. You will both very quickly find a common bonding and respect.

Rather than just satisfying our sexual urges, we need to get back to the romancing of our partners. We should enjoy romantic gestures, or creating romantic situations. Even within a marriage there should still be the spontaneity of romance, and ladies, this does not just have to be overtures from the men. Women can also buy their partner flowers or chocolates or arrange a surprise outing. This way you make your relationship a happy and fulfilling one.

The relationships of the future will be one of sacred union; two fully balanced and clear spiritual beings who love and support the other unconditionally.

## BUSINESS RELATIONSHIPS

Future business will be conducted within a base of integrity and honesty, rather than a foundation of power, greed and control. So the meeting of a business partner and the conduct of that business will be very similar to the relationships we will build with anyone.

Businesses that function with the power base of greed will be disintegrating within the universal energies of love and light that are currently sweeping the planet. The fifth-dimensional energies will not tolerate any business or structure that is based on negative imprints.

Having developed a strong healthy relationship with Self, many people will then choose to work for themselves. However, strength and co-operation between like-minded business people will benefit all parties.

## SEXUALITY AND SENSUALITY

A dysfunctional attitude to life and our bodies has resulted in serious dysfunctional patterns of sexual behaviour. Churches have taught us that sex is dirty and sinful and should be repugnant to all women (but seemingly not to men!). We are born from the sin of sex, therefore we are sinners when born and our bodies are impure. This has created a fear of sex for many people and perhaps resulted in frigidity in some women.

Women have suffered sexual abuse and rape in many past lives and through our ancestors lives, and this pain is still carried today in the cellular memory.

During the last 50 years there has been a movement away from many conservative attitudes and constraints of past society resulting in a sexual freedom. This was helped by the arrival of contraceptives, which enabled women to express their sexuality without the fear of falling pregnant. However, this freedom arrived without the wisdom and understanding of female sexuality.

True sexual freedom comes from understanding that the female body represents the Divine Feminine energy of the Goddess. Each woman in her own right, in her body, is an expression of the Goddess. This is a sacred and beautiful energy which has been debased by the lustful society that has been enacted from the very freedom we have sought. The Divine Feminine energy is the energy of nurturance and compassion.

The men represent the Divine Masculine energy of God. This gives them the role of protector, provider, lover and friend.

In our move to fifth-dimensional living, each one of us will have an inner balance of the masculine and feminine energy, but represented by the gender we have chosen.

At this time in our evolution we as adults have failed to teach our young people the wisdom and understanding of sexual energy. They have looked to adults as role models and so often are mimicking the behaviour of their elders. Adults need to seriously look at their addictions and obsessions to alchohol, drugs and sex. It is time for adults to take the lead and create a beautiful society that we can be proud of.

When we connect with a partner sexually we receive an imprint of their DNA: an imprint of their emotional and mental energies. If the imprint of the sexual partner has a great deal of anger or fear, this is transmitted into your DNA, leaving you with more than just your stuff to clear.

In many cases the stronger masculine energy can drain the female of her life force energies. This energetic connection can remain within the auric field, enabling the stronger partner to continually feed off and drain the life force of the other.

Men are often sexual predators for this very reason: to drain the life force energy from the partner to boost their own energy field. In most instances this would not be apparent to either party. However, in the case of people involved in the Illuminati Matrix energies, this could and can be done quite purposefully. This is also why many older men wish to have sex with young beautiful women, because the young feminine life force energy is more pure, and this is what they consciously or unconsciously are seeking.

A word here about masturbation. This is something that has been designated by religions as a bad, even evil thing to do. The ascended masters tell us to release this distortion of the truth, as someone without a partner should feel no guilt associated with masturbation.

And what is sensuality?

It is the beautiful expression of love that happens between you and your loved one: a touch, a hug, a smile, a meeting of eyes, the holding of hands. In other words, just the pure happiness of having that special person at your side.

## CREATION ENERGY

Creation energy is sexual energy, one and the same. Creation energy through a sexual connection can create a new life.

The base chakra represents the Divine Masculine energy and the sacral chakra the Divine Feminine energy. These combine in a sexual encounter, and in a divine union of unconditional love these will activate what is known as the kundalini energy at the base of the spine. During the act of lovemaking this kundalini energy will move from the base chakra up the spine of both parties, igniting a flame of passion in each successive chakra. When it reaches the pineal gland in the head, the resultant orgasm of both parties will explode the kundalini energy out the crown chakra. This high frequency kundalini energy showers the auric fields of both partners with beautiful sparks of love and light.

The act of foreplay, or early lovemaking, should last some time allowing both parties, particularly the female, to reach the point where she will be fully immersed in her orgasm, which is often unfamiliar to many western women. After orgasm the couple should stay close together in this loving space they have created, in order for their respective auric fields to be strengthened by the cosmic energies they have released from their crown chakras into the auric field.

This kundalini energy we can say is our life force energy, but it is also creation energy. If the intent is to create a child, this act of creation will happen. At the point of conception the very high kundalini energy of both partners will merge and create a strong, spiritual, energy child, a child of light.

If you do not have a partner, or are not pursuing any sexual activity, you should be utilising the energies of the base and sacral chakras in a creative way. If this energy is not being used sexually you need to use it through some form of creativity, whether it be painting, dancing, sport, writing, or perhaps a business venture. It matters not as long as you are being creative in some way.

If this sexual energy is not used, or is suppressed in any way, perhaps by a stringent conservative upbringing, by fear, by religious teachings, then this energy must eventually find an outlet. This is when we see acts of violence, particularly those of a sexual nature. This suppression, as has happened in the celibates of churches, can also result in hidden, subversive sexual activities, because this is creation energy and needs to utilized. We cannot continue on this path of hidden sexual encounters in which those in control abuse their privileges.

## SOUL MATES

Soul mates are members of your earth, galactic or universal soul family. They can be any two people who come together to experience life in some way, perhaps karmic, perhaps fulfilling a dream they both have, or sometimes to help each other recognise and clear negative attitudes and beliefs.

These do not have to be romantic relationships although they may well be. They can be parent and child, siblings, friends, business partners. They can be short term or long term.

The more past lives you have had together, the more you know each other and therefore the closer the bond. Sometimes two soul mates can come together to complete a previous lifetime where they did not fulfill the aspirations and goals of that partnership.

## TWIN FLAMES

Twin flames are complementary energies, the mirror opposite of each other, or we might say, they are male and female forms that are both part of the one whole. It is often said they are two halves of the one soul.

These two people, as twin flames, come together to achieve something for the highest good of the whole. It is usually work that cannot be done singularly and is enhanced by their joining together on that mission.

Jesus and Mary Magdalen had a twin flame relationship, each one enhancing the spiritual aspects of the other, supporting each other through the highs and lows of their time.

In many life times, twin flames who are helping earth and humanity in their ascension have worked with one partner in physical form and one partner in non-physical form. It has helped keep the earthbound one safe and protected while doing the physical side of the work, and the other is able to direct and implement moves from the non-physical realms more easily.

Twin flames exist together to accomplish something that neither could do alone.

They can also exist as a romantic relationship and when that happens the connection and communication between the two is very apparent.

# PRACTICAL TOOLS

## BREATHWORK

*Breathe and let your body know you choose life.*
*Breathe and allow your body to heal and rejuvenate itself.*

Breathe . . . .
Breathe again . . . .
Breathe once more . . . .

For many years I followed the teachings of Ascended Master Tobias and he continually told us to keep breathing. Well . . . we do know that if we don't breathe we tend to die! That's obvious. What is not so obvious is the expanded understanding and importance of the breath.

The breath draws in oxygen and without it we would die. The breath draws in our life force energy, the interdimensional energy from the cosmos: from the sun, the moon, the planets, the stars and from Source. Without this we would also die. When we were born and took our first breath, it was the most important thing we would ever do. That was the breath of life, the acceptance of life. We could choose to take that breath or not, choose to live or choose to die.

We are familiar with the expression "the in-breath and out-breath of God", referring to the constant expansion and contraction of the universe. Deep breathing for the human is just the same. Breathe in, breathe out, contraction, expansion. Shamanism believes that the breath is the source of the balance of life. Ancient yogic teachings see the whole of life as governed by three forces: expansion, contraction and equilibrium.

When we are stressed, ill or in fear, we breathe from the upper part of our lungs. This does not allow enough oxygen or life force energy to be drawn into the lungs and body. When we have challenges, when we panic, or when we live in fear, we do not use the full capacity of our lungs. This means that the lower part of the lungs retains a lot of stale air containing carbon dioxide. This then impacts on the health and function of the lungs and the wellbeing of our cells. Oxygen and carbon dioxide are kept in balance by the breath. Shallow breathing also impacts on the acid/alkaline balance of our blood.

Sit up straight, shoulders back to open the chest out, and take a big breath in now, filling the lungs. When you think they are full, draw in some more. This is often called belly breathing because the abdomen should rise with the inhale. Hold this for a short time, then exhale through the mouth, mouth slightly open, and allow the expelling air to come out with a whooshing sound. When you think you have fully exhaled push some more out. This completely empties the lungs and then another big breath will fill them up with fresh air. Of course it is best to do this outside in unpolluted air, but wherever you do it you will experience benefits from doing this three times. Holding the breath between inhalation and exhalation is the point of equilibrium, the point where the body balances itself.

We cannot continue deep breathing like this as we would get light-headed and dizzy. However, our normal breathing should fill and empty the lungs completely.

The minute we have anxiety we flip to only using the top half of the lungs. This tends to increase the panic and fear, and the lower oxygen levels in the brain make it difficult to calm down and find a solution. Deep breathing relaxes the muscles and enables a slow down of the fear and anxiety. The muscles play a large part in breathing, and shallow breathing promotes the contraction of muscles with resultant elevated discomfort levels.

If we have headaches, muscle cramps and muscle pain, it can often be caused by poor breathing habits. Allergies can fall into this category because the muscles contract with allergic reactions. When any allergy or illness presents itself, the breathing will nearly always be shallow. Most functions of the bodily systems, and most illnesses, will all benefit from conscious breathwork.

Deep breathing assists in taking us to the inner realms of the subconscious and unconscious where negative experiences are held. Shallow breathing prevents this access. Perhaps the person does not wish, or is afraid, to delve into the negative experiences of the past. However, by not going there the person is unconsciously creating more ill health.

Conscious breathing offers a direct route to the negative emotions and beliefs held in the subconscious and unconscious.

One of the main benefits of deep breathing is that it keeps us centred and balanced. Shallow breathing creates more stress and keeps us in a state of imbalance. When a challenging situation arises, take a few moments to do some deep breathing, putting the focus on the heart chakra. Shallow breathing supports victim consciousness, poverty consciousness, feeling we have no control over our lives. If you want abundance in your life, start changing your breathing patterns. It is deep breathing and being centred that brings us into close communication with the higher realms.

Master Tobias always said there are far too many people walking around the planet half dead . . . and he meant this seriously in reference to only taking in half the breath required. By taking deep breaths you are choosing life, choosing to be here on earth, and choosing to live the dreams you incarnated with. By choosing to shallow breathe your way through life you are choosing illness and death.

Become a conscious breather and you will notice a difference in your life.

## USING BREATHWORK TO RELEASE

Meditation involves deep breathing to relax and calm the body and mind, and to release thoughts of the day and the outside world. Meditation brings in a connection with Mother Earth, our Higher Self, God or Creator Source, and our Guardian Angel or an Ascended Master. It then brings us into the centre of Self where we can access the inner child: in other words the negative traumas and emotions that we have experienced in the past, often as a young child.

By asking for assistance, we identify the negative experience that needs healing. There is no need to re-experience it, just to recognize what happened. It may have been a major trauma, it may have been a very subtle rebuke from a parent or teacher, or ridicule from a sibling or friend. The size of the trauma does not matter. At the time we were not able to process the hurt, particularly if we were young. As adults we can now look at the situation through mature eyes and gain a better understanding. We can look at the perpetrator and understand that that person did not know any better at the time. We need to forgive that person for hurting us.

We need to forgive ourselves for feeling this hurt that we have carried all our lives, affecting everything we have done ever since.

We need to acknowledge our anger, the anger that we suppressed at the time.

All these releases can be managed through the breath. Breathe in, and during the exhale make the intent to release the negative experience and the negative feelings. Make the intent that these negative feelings are cleared, transmuted into light and the cellular memory healed. Keep doing this for as long as it feels right. There will come a point when you know you have released everything to do with the situation and person or people involved.

During this process give thanks for the gift of the trauma, because from it you have learnt a valuable lesson and gained wisdom. The lesson may be forgiveness, freedom from anger, release of fears, or it may be acceptance. Whatever the lessons you envision, in other words the opposite energies of the trauma, draw those positive energies or beliefs into the body with the inbreath and send those new sensations around every cell of your body, re-programming the cells and DNA with the opposite of the trauma.

You can do this with any trauma, hurt, experience, situation, or people involved. Always make sure you transmute the negative energies into light, or send them to God. If not, those negative energies will simply find their way to someone else.

Always give thanks to the Masters, angels and other non-physical beings who have helped you work through this process.

*There are many humans who are not sure if they even want to be here, not sure if they wish to continue living this earth incarnation. Many humans feel like they are victims of life, having no control over life, having no creator abilities. But when you take the deep breath, the simplest of all things, it changes everything. It lets all the cells of your body know that you choose life. You choose to be here. And then life comes to you. It is that simple.*

# PSYCHIC ATTACKS

There are a lot of fears about psychic attacks. Who is attacking? Does it happen? How will it affect me? What can I do?

Fear, panic and anxiety set in and we begin to walk through life looking over our shoulder, worrying about all those people around us. Do they mean us harm? Are they a walking reptilian energy about to gobble us up, or whip us away to their spaceship?

The mind is often given a free-for-all in this area. The imagination is capable of running amok.

So let me make this clear . . . no-one can ever attack you unless you allow them to.

Well, that's good, you say. I won't give permission. Problem solved.

Unfortunately you give permission by living your life in fear. The negative, low vibrational frequency of fear will magnetically attract unwelcome energies to you.

Therefore the best way to prevent a psychic attack is to get out of the fear based life you may be living. If you are prone to worry, anxiety, stress, if you are overworked and overtired, or living in victim consciousness or poverty consciousness, you are allowing yourself to be open to receiving negative energies. If you have ill-health you can also be open to this problem.

When people have a psychic attack they often feel a threatening energy, perhaps a pain in an area of the body. They may have trouble breathing, depending on the attack itself. What causes this? It is a thought or intent directed at an individual, either consciously or unconsciously.

For example, if you do not like a person at work, you may have a thought wishing they would lose their job. If you focus on the person as you are thinking this, and continue to think about it for some time, it may surprise you to find that indeed they do lose their job. This can be an unconscious way of attacking someone with your thoughts. Sometimes it can be quite deliberate, with the intent to cause harm.

Please do not go into fear. This is not a common occurrence, because there must be a focus and an intent behind the thought. Random negative thoughts do not carry the same weight.

Many years ago, I felt a knife go in my back. A small sharp ladies dagger. I sensed the energy of the attack and realized immediately from whom it had come. The person was not happy with me and obviously was trying to "stab me in the back", metaphorically in a work sense, but the thoughts generated an energetic attack. Within minutes I had about 50 knives in my back. I held no fear or anger, and merely saw myself removing them and giving them back to the person with love and thanks for the lesson learned.

Negative words can often strike another person in the throat chakra, causing a constriction in the way they express themselves, or perhaps they may have a choking sensation. This attack is often done quite unconsciously, but does show us the power behind our thoughts and words.

There are dark energies, or energetic entities, that will seek to harm people, particularly those working for the light. These attacks may come in the form of feeling depression, anger, hatred, jealousy and so on. The attack will be the dark energies enhancing the negative emotions and fears of the individual, causing them to create havoc in their lives and the lives of all those around them. These dark energies will also enhance the feelings of victim consciousness or poverty consciousness.

These dark energies mainly come from thoughts in mass consciousness. You may believe that thoughts do not carry energy. They most certainly do and if any thoughts are not manifested into form or matter, they have been created and must therefore go somewhere. They go to mass consciousness, wherein lies the mass of negative thoughts that humanity has created for thousands of years. These thoughts continue to create havoc amongst our human minds until we take them on board and transmute them into light.

We can also have entity attachments, and this can be a negative thoughtform from mass consciousness that has grown into a larger entity and is looking for a body to house it. As negative energies they look for a human who is living a negative life, and they attach themselves to the energy field, or aura, of that person, and sometimes to the actual physical body. They can create havoc by trying to influence the thoughts of the human and convincing them to carry out harmful activities either to Self or others.

We also have soul attachments. When a person dies who has led a negative life, or has harmed people, or misused and abused energy, they often don't transition into the higher realms. They walk around as lost souls, and will attach themselves to an available human. This human will also be of lower vibrations and perhaps during a trauma such as an accident the lost soul can attach itself to the auric field. This can particularly happen if the human is bombed out on drugs or alcohol. They are leaving themselves wide open to an attachment. These attachments can often be angry and cause trouble for the human host. Sometimes friends and family sense the human as being different, perhaps a different personality seems to have emerged.

This situation can also happen during surgery when a patient is under anaesthetic. This opens up the auric field where attachments can happen. Within hospitals there are deaths where souls have not transitioned to the other side and have become trapped. The operating theatre gives them a chance to attach to a person who carries the lower vibrational energies. This is not said to create fear of operations. Instead it is about awareness. If you have an operation and feel different after recovery, perhaps heaviness, feeling disconnected, or displaying various negative emotions that would seem out of the ordinary, then you may have received an attachment. Visit an energy healer who is experienced in the work of removing entities. After removal you will find that your recovery takes a big stride forward.

In all cases, the human host must exist in a negative vibrational field. The dark energy or entity would not be able to attach themselves to a fearless Lightworker.

We are aware of the use of voodoo dolls in some primitive cultures. The perpetrator has harmful intent and focus behind the incantations to the doll. The people of these tribes live in fear, and it is the fear that kills, not the doll itself. It is the same with any curse or spell that is done to create harm. It is the fear that kills or maims. Fortunately we live in a western society where these activities are not part of our life.

Of course you might say now "What about the aliens? What about any of them landing here and having the intent to harm us?" This is not as likely to happen as people think. We already have the rebel Nibiruans in the fourth-dimensional realms who are certainly playing havoc in our lives, and have been for thousands of years, so outside interference is nothing new. There are of course the Greys, the extraterrestrial beings who mutilate cattle and occasionally abduct humans to check out their biology. These humans are usually returned unharmed, although emotionally frightened. There may be some unfriendly space visitors who land and do not have our best interests at heart, but it is over to us to use our intuition and our discernment, and not be in fear. They cannot harm you if you have no fear. Most of the so-called "aliens" will be our friends and family from the wider galactic community and so will be familiar to us.

It is useful to know how to deal with any unwelcome space visitors. As earth humans we are spiritually superior (and not in an egotistical way) to any of these aliens that might wish to harm us. If you stand without fear, and in the name of God ask them to leave, they must. If they do not, they can be transformed by your auric field into light. Many of them who see your light will not come close because they also have a fear of us, a fear of our light.

And what about "ghosts". These are souls who for whatever reason did not make it to the other side after death. Perhaps they were too frightened. Perhaps the death was traumatic and they refused to accept their death. Sometimes they did not want to transition to the other side because they wished to stay with family for some reason. The only problem here is that the family may move on in their life or ultimately die, and sadly that leaves the soul, or ghost, stuck in the in-between realms and not able to transition to the other side.

These souls are lost, confused and frightened. Some of them don't realise they are dead, some don't know where they are. They often live in the house they had in human life, and can become a nuisance by opening and shutting cupboard doors, banging doors, opening windows, and moving things in the house. Sometimes this is to get your attention, but of course most people can't see them and call the house haunted. If they think they are still alive, they can't understand why you are living in their house and this may make them angry.

Most of these souls do not wish to cause harm, they are just frustrated. Some of them can be angry and depending on their previous life, can occasionally be malevolent. This is not normally the case. They are just frightened of what is happening.

They don't become an entity attachment.

Just call your local "ghost busters" to move them over to the other side.

I want to move now to the most common of psychic attacks. The psychic attack on your own Self. I can imagine you crying out that that can't be right. How can we attack ourselves? Well, we do it often. We have emotional aspects of Self that we can call energies or entities. In metaphysical terms, these are Aspects: Aspects of Self. These are your buried negative emotions and fears that have risen to the surface of your conscious mind for you to address. When you think or speak nasty thoughts or words about yourself, they can come back to you as pain, or as an illness.

These Aspects need clearing, releasing, and healing. Often the only way they can get your attention is to attack you. They can do this in the form of illness or pain. You may feel a sharp ongoing pain without being able to identify the cause. They can and do attach themselves to your auric field or some part of your body, and cause havoc until you address their issues.

This may sound strange, but it is very real. So many people blame others for their psychic attack, when it is actually their own Aspects venting their anger and frustrations. They are parts of us trying to get our attention. Any suppressed feelings must be addressed during this ascension journey. We cannot carry these negativities into the fifth dimension. They must be cleared. The only alternative to that is we get sick, and perhaps ultimately die if they are not resolved.

The Medical System will try to bandaid the problem, hand out medications, or cut pieces out of the body, when it is simply an Aspect of Self that wants to be healed by the light.

*There is no place for blame, shame, anger and judgment of the energies you are ready to release. They have no meaning other than their experience in your life. You are responsible for their presence and you are responsible for their transformation. When humanity is ready, you will transmute all energies into their higher vibration and then there will be heaven on earth and the earth's healing and ascension will be completed.*

*. . . Archangel Uriel*

# PROTECTION

Protection . . . . What? Why? How? From whom?

As well the psychic attacks I have just written about, we are constantly surrounded by negative people and situations. Our family, friends and work colleagues are often depressed, angry, resentful, frustrated, and existing in victim and poverty consciousness. We only need to go to the supermarket, a local cafe, the picture theatre and even to church, to feel these emotions. These emotions affect us every day and we do need to protect ourselves from this onslaught. If we don't we can take on board someone's anger or sorrow, their fears, or perhaps their pain from an illness.

It is therefore important that we place an energy field of protection around us every day. This is as simple as taking those three deep breaths when we first awake or get up, and making the intent to God or our Guardian Angel to place a sphere of light around us to protect us from outside negative influences. Perhaps it is a ritual that you do in the shower each morning, or what you do when you are ready to leave the house. You must remember to do this each and every day.

Through the day, if you are faced with an intensity of negativity, or you are entering an environment that you know will be difficult or hostile, just quickly make the intent that your forcefield of protection is strengthened and maintained. You can ask for this forcefield to protect you from a particular person.

This field of protection is a higher vibration of light, and you can imagine being contained within a sphere of light, rather like sitting inside a lightbulb perhaps.

Remember the deep breathing. Shallow breathing will put you in a place of fear, so take the deep breaths when you feel a need to calm and balance your feelings.

Know that as you move through this ascension journey you are safe and protected at all times. Your Guardian Angel watches over you, and you always have the presence of angels, ascended masters, archangels and higher beings of light with you.

As an alternative to the sphere of light, I use a column of light. I make intent that a column of light comes down from God, comes down through my body, and continues through to connect with the core crystal of Mother Earth. I then ask for it to be widened, strengthened, and held in place throughout the day protecting me from any outside negative influences.

We also receive negative vibrations from the fluorescent lights in shopping malls, from strobe lighting, electro-magnetic frequencies of microwaves, televisions, cell phones and computers, and from chemical pollutants in the air. A force-field of protection will help in keeping these at bay, but it is wiser to stay away from these things if at all possible. Turn off electronic equipment you are not using.

It is also important to sever ties with anyone you are removing yourself from physically. Perhaps you are moving out of a relationship. Unless you have communicated well and intend to remain the best of friends, it is wise to meditate and visualise the connection cords between you both. These will be in place from their chakras to yours, and if not severed can continue an energetic connection whereby they can drain your energies. The other person, consciously or unconsciously, can draw on your life force energy leaving you feeling continually drained and tired. In meditation see these cords and make the intent that all the energy that belongs to you, you receive back, and all that which belongs to the other be returned to them. Ask Archangel Michael for his sword of truth and see yourself slicing through the remaining cords until they are all totally disconnected.

# MEDITATION AND PRAYERS

These two are actually the same. Whether you call it meditation or whether you call it prayer, the aim is to connect with the higher realms and the divinity of God. Many people pray to God, asking for something they need or want in their lives. These prayers can be superficial, merely asking God to solve their problems for them. "Please God give me this, then my life will be okay".

Deep meditation to commune with God or Spirit is akin to what I term divine prayer, an intense desire to connect with the Source of Life, that which we call God or perhaps Jesus.

Meditation and prayer can be for many reasons. It is a communion with God or Spirit to experience the feeling of Home, of the Unconditional Love of God. This brings peace of mind and meaning to life.

Meditation and prayer can be to find a solution to a problem in life. We call on God or the Archangels, the higher Beings of Light, to help us find a solution.

We can meditate to identify an issue that needs addressing. This can be a negative emotion or belief, or perhaps we are unsure what the blockage is and what its lesson might be. We use the outbreath to release the blockage and the inbreath to draw in its opposite of light.

We can meditate to move into past lives and revisit experiences to gain the knowledge and wisdom from them. We can meditate and move into the future and see the potentials that we placed there before we incarnated.

We can meditate to heal ourselves, using the breath to release the pain and to draw in the light of healing. In this we may speak with our Healing Angel and ask their assistance.

We can meditate simply to enter into the Silence. It is extremely beneficial to just "be" without the need for words and visions; just allowing the stillness to enter the mind and body through the breath.

We can meditate to visit other realms, other worlds, and other dimensions of awareness. We can move our consciousness into these other realms and speak with the higher Beings of Light, with the Ascended Masters, and with beings from other worlds. We can sit on the moon, dance around the heavens, spiral into the centre of the galaxy. All these are possible once we clear much of the third-dimensional dross away. This allows our consciousness to expand and travel the dimensions. If you are traveling into other dimensions always ask your Guardian Angel to accompany you. We are not yet aware of all that is out there, and perhaps need that reassurance of someone with us. Your level of consciousness needs to be able to move through the lower fourth dimension, what we call the lower astral planes where negative energies exist, and into the higher dimensions of light.

You can ask an Ascended Master to take you on a journey to the various Temples of Light to help you with your spiritual journey. You may receive wisdom or an initiation for the next step of your journey.

Deep divine prayer can give us the bliss of communion of God.

Meditation can offer us the freedom to travel the dimensions of the universe.

# GROUNDING

We live on earth, not in the heavens above, and it is therefore important that we stay grounded and connected to Earth. If we do not do this we can become "spaced out" or "floaty", our mind seemingly far away, and not functioning very well in our daily life. If you are not grounded manifestation cannot happen—you have moved yourself out of this time frame where the manifestation is expected. In effect you exist in another time/space continuum while your physical body remains in 3D.

People who live like this are living from their higher chakras, not utilizing their lower chakras, and this causes an imbalance in the physical body, possibly resulting in mental or physical illness.

If we travel the higher dimensions, our consciousness is at a much higher rate of vibration than our physical body. The consciousness can remain high even after the meditation or travel has finished. This causes serious issues between the physical body and its functioning mind.

When you return from meditation or deep prayer, or a group meeting where the energies have been high, you must ensure you are fully conscious and back in your physical body, connected with Mother Earth once more.

Make the intent to be fully grounded back in your body, back in the room and in this time frame. Rub your head, hands, legs and feet, have a glass of water, run water over your hands and feet, walk on the earth or grass, hug a tree, stand in the sea or river if these are close by and you are having trouble fully grounding.

Some crystals and even stones can be used as grounding tools. Keep them with you during the meditation with the intent that they keep you connected to earth.

Eating food that is deeply connected to the earth, such as a carrot or other root vegetable, can be grounding. Drinking tea with 1-2 teaspoons of sugar is also beneficial as sugar has a grounding effect.

When I am doing a deep meditation and travel, I send a cord deep in to the earth and hook it around an ancient log to keep me grounded. You can use this tool whenever you think you need to be kept grounded.

Being in nature is very grounding, and is a necessary requirement for those on a spiritual journey. Walk in the bush or sit by the sea or a river whenever possible and connect with energies of nature.

# INTUITION

What is intuition, that gut feeling that some of us have and some haven't?

Firstly, we all feel this intuition in different ways. It can be a gut feeling, it can come as words or visions, it can come as intense feelings that something is right or wrong, or it can just be a knowing. Some people get goose bumps, or a chill running up their spine.

People sometimes expect the voice of God to come booming down from the heavens . . . no such luck!

We must decide how our body communicates with us and it can be different for each of us. Intuition is a communication between cells and their DNA, the mind, the chakras, the auric field, and the Higher Self.

I have always said I am not intuitive and it took me a long time to come to terms with just knowing something, no feeling attached to it, just a knowing. It has taken me time to learn to trust what I know. Perhaps the strong feelings, voices or visions that people have act as confirmation of whatever it is. However, with knowing there is no such confirmation. I must just trust.

If you are unsure, you can ask for confirmation. Through your heart ask for validation to be presented to you three times. You can ask for it to be made loud and clear, and remember it may not come in words. Be open to the various forms of validation.

So, take note of how your body communicates with you and it may be different to your friends or members of your spiritual group.

Intuition is often felt when we meet a person for the first time, walk into a strange house, enter a workplace or gather with a group of people. Do the energies feel light and happy or do they feel heavy and negative? The first feeling, thought or knowing that comes into your mind is your intuition working, informing you of what is happening energetically. Trust that first feeling.

Intuition aligns with discernment. We must be discerning about people, places and events. We must rely on what our intuition is telling us and then use discernment to decide if we wish to move away or not, or how we will deal with the situation.

# DOWSING

If you feel very unsure of your intuitive abilities you can use a pendulum. If you are buying a pendulum it will be your choice as to what feels right (which is intuition). It can be anything, but most people go for a small clear glass orb or a crystal, often a clear quartz crystal. It can be something from nature, but needs to have some weight to make it hang.

When you first get a pendulum you need to programme it to your intentions. Hold it between the fingers of one hand hanging over your other palm (we have a strong healing chakra in each palm). Move the pendulum so that it moves back and forth over your palm. Tell the pendulum that this is the neutral position, and to show you this when it does not know the answer or that your question is not clear. Then move the pendulum so that it circles your palm in a clockwise direction. Tell it that this is a "yes" answer, the positive. Then move it so that it circles in an anti-clockwise direction and tell it that this is the negative answer, the "no".

Bless it and thank it for the work it will do for you.

Now you are ready to put a question to it and it must be a simple question requiring a yes or no answer. Hold the pendulum string between your thumb and forefinger very lightly and ask the question. I generally move it in a neutral swing just to get it started, and from there it will either move clockwise or anti-clockwise, giving you the answer.

The important thing is you must remove your mind from the question and answer. Make your mind neutral or you will influence the pendulum and perhaps get a false answer. It might be the answer you wanted, but it may not be correct. You have influenced the swing of the pendulum by your thoughts.

# BLESSINGS AND GRATITUDE

It behoves us all to be in a constant state of gratitude. Gratitude for all things in our life, for the gifts of experience and learning, even though they may be hard and painful, for the opportunities to move into greater self-mastery, and for gaining the freedom to create our dreams. There is a ten-fold fluid universe which functions by returning to you ten times more of what you think and create. If you are in gratitude for life, a good life returns itself to you ten-fold.

As we move up the levels of consciousness this return can be 100-fold or even more. If we exist in states of fear and negativity, then those too return to us 10-fold, perhaps 100-fold. The way to manifest your dreams is to live in the energies of gratitude.

Whatever you do each day, see the blessings in it. Whenever you walk in nature, be in gratitude for the love it bestows on you as you walk by.

Bless your food and drink before each meal. Bless the plants, animals, people and processes that have brought it before you. Without it you could not live in a physical body.

What about your friends and family? Sometimes we feel frustrated with them, and sometimes even angry, but if these people are truly your friends and your family who have your best interests at heart, then bless them each day for being part of your life.

Give blessings to Mother Earth and her kingdoms for nurturing you, give blessings to the Ascended Masters, Archangels and higher Beings of Light that walk the path with you every day. Give blessings to God and Goddess, to Spirit and the Spiritual Hierarchy that watches over our ascension journey.

---

*I've been homeless for half a century. The life of an exile is an unfortunate life, but I have always tried to cultivate a happy state of mind, appreciating the opportunities this existence without a settled home, far from all protocol, has offered me. This way I have been able to preserve my inner peace.*

*His Holiness the Dalai Lama*

---

# THE FUTURE

*"In the next two years, the love of power will begin to be displaced by the Power of Love. It will take time, but do not doubt it, for it is already in motion. It begins initially inside each of your hearts, and Dear Ones, that is happening now".*

.... *Archangel Metatron*

And so we end this book looking at the future. What will our future be? How will it evolve? What changes will happen? How will this affect us and our lives?

So many questions and perhaps very few answers.

We cannot accurately predict what the future will be because we are collectively creating it every moment of the day by our thoughts, our words, our actions, our desires and our focus.

If we stay in fear from the doom and gloom of some prophecies, then that is what our future will contain. We will create an Armageddon. But is that what we want? Of course not.

If we wish to move into the New Earth, the new Age of Golden Consciousness, one that will ultimately give us Heaven on Earth, and peace on earth, then that is what we must focus on. We must believe we can create it. We must participate in the process with positive thoughts.

We are what we believe we are. We are Masters. We originate from the Higher Realms. We are aspects of God incarnated in human form. We are powerful beyond measure. What then prevents us from creating the world that we have prayed and prayed for, for so long?

The only thing that prevents that is our fear. Our fear of change. Our fear of the unknown. Our fear of the future. Get over these hurdles and you can consciously take part in co-creating the world of our dreams.

## CHANGING THE OLD PARADIGMS

The systems of our world are going to crumble. Those that have been built on power, greed and control will disintegrate or be changed into a system with a foundation of love, compassion and wisdom. We have already seen some of the dismantling of the financial systems and an ongoing dissolution of the Illuminati Matrix control. This will continue for a number of years yet. Systems can't change overnight—it takes time but it will indeed happen. It has to happen, because we cannot take old third-dimensional systems into our fifth-dimensional New Earth.

We are seeing Mother Earth clearing toxic energies from her body. These take the form of earthquakes, volcanic eruptions, floods, droughts, tornados and tsunamis, and there will be many more to come. It is not about going into fear. It is about understanding that humans have wrought havoc on this earth, and now we feel the consequences of those actions.

Our weather and weather patterns will become more erratic. It is time to go with the flow of Mother Earth's cycles instead of continually fighting against her. Disruptive weather patterns may indicate that people need to move and set up home elsewhere.

We are going to see deserts returned to verdant green pastures and bush. Areas where there has been intensive agriculture may turn into deserts or lakes. Places where there has been no water, there may be rain and rivers once more. Some land areas will be devastated and people will need to move location, perhaps even country.

The seas will rise in some areas and lower in others. This is a natural water cycle of earth, and we see the changes as the earth moves on its axis to realign itself with the Galactic Centre.

Religions and churches will have to change their doctrines of control or lose their congregations. People will initially turn to the churches for help and understanding, but if that is not available in a way that gives them peace of mind, they will leave the churches and seek other avenues of wisdom.

Leaders will emerge in the next few years who will help the world adjust and move to fairer systems of government. Many more teachers and healers will move into their positions to help people cope, understand and to heal.

There will be an urgent need to move away from the polluting fossil fuels and into cleaner alternative methods of energy. This will halt the drilling for oil and the mining of the land for coal. Many of these changes will cause people to become redundant in their current jobs. There will be a need for self-employment, for creativity, and for self-sufficiency as food supplies become erratic.

All these changes will challenge our security and our belief in the foundations we have created for our lives. Remember, however, that these foundations have been built on fear and distorted truths. As I have stated, humans have an inherent fear of change and what it will mean for their lives. We live in the "uncomfortable" comfort zone because of that fear.

The time has come for us to move into the Higher Truths of the Universe and to become once more the Galactic citizens that we have always been.


## CREATING THE FUTURE

To help the world change and move into the New Earth we must clear the negative debris from our cells. Our thoughts, words and actions must become positive. We must heal the physical body. We must lift our vibrational frequencies to match the fifth dimension. We must become the future we desire.

To let go of the linear time that we have experienced in the third dimension, instead of seeing this straight line, imagine that you stand in the centre, in the "now" moment, and the future is around you. The future is no longer ahead of you, it exists all around you as potentials. In the present moment, this day, you change that future around you by your thoughts, words and actions. Your thoughts influence that reality we call "the future".

If you learn nothing else from this book, at least please take the understanding that indeed **"thoughts and beliefs create reality"**. If you deeply desire the world to have peace; if you deeply desire to live your dreams; if you deeply desire to live life as a higher being of wisdom, then make that intent to yourself and to God, and begin to live that way. Live that life as if it has already happened, and then indeed it will. It has to, because you are an Aspect of God. How could it be any different? You are a creator and a co-creator of worlds, and the one you are focusing on right now is this world we live in. This life we lead on Planet Earth.

Put your dreams and desires into the holographic template that we are creating for the New Earth, and then believe it will happen. Imagine if millions of Lightworkers around the world did that, which in fact they are. Our thoughts and our focus will influence the reality of the future.

It is how it works, dear people.

It is called . . . creation.

*We wish to leave you in this moment with these final thoughts. As the chaos upon your earth increases, do not be distressed. This is a natural process of shifting from one dimension into another. Spiritual mastery is the ability to deal with new situations in creative ways. Anything less than this is of no benefit. You must find new ways to deal with your life and what is happening in the world around you. The choices you make will determine your destiny. It is really that simple. As many around you spiral into despair and confusion, a strange opportunity opens. It is possible to ride the waves of change through the upcoming volatile periods of chaos with humour, grace and extraordinary growth. The power to do this does not come from the outside. It comes from the inside, but like a miner searching for gold you have to go digging. To find the treasure that will make you rich, in terms of spiritual qualities and an increased likelihood of surviving these times, requires searching on your part, not outside yourself, but inside yourself, for you already have what you need.*

*A message from the Hathors as channeled by Tom Kenyon 2010.*
*www.tomkenyon.com*

# CONCLUSION

And so this book containing my Truths comes to a close. Take what resonates with you and discard the rest.

I trust I have offered you new perceptions and that you will now continue your journey to discover the beautiful and very magnificent

Being of Light that you are.

Enjoy this lifetime because it is unique and very special. Know that even through the challenges, the Light always shines.

Dig deep and discover who you truly are.

My love and blessings are with all those who seek the Truth.

**Glenys-Kay**

# APPENDIX

## *CONNECT THROUGH THE HEART:*

*It is now time to come together. To embrace each other with open arms and to connect through the heart chakra. For centuries humans have connected through the heart with physicality and sexual attraction as the reason for coming together. Now it is time for the kundalini to rise, for this energy force to be used in a better and forceful way. To develop the DNA means a rising force, an awareness of what it is and what it means. The sexual energy is of the same ilk.*

*Your DNA is neutralised by both mental and physical inactivity and overactivity. To reconnect this means removing the layers of conditioning and genetic downplay, or more easily understood as the poisoning of the system by the hierarchy and those in power who wish the DNA to remain dormant for their purposes of control and misuse. While people are suppressed and depressed they are unable to access the light information that is available to them. To break free of conditioned sexuality and emotional conditioning enables the light information to once again be accessed.*

*This is a matter of choice. To choose to look at oneself as though in a mirror is the personal choice that can open the realms of reality. We watch with wonder as more choose to do this.*

*We are watching with excitement as earth moves into her last years of heavy vibration. What you each do to increase your vibrations and return them to their original blueprint is valuable to the earth and her evolution. Do not fear for there is no right or wrong. Just learning.*

*Safe and protected are you all.*

*With love and light*
*The Galactic Council and Lord Maitreya*

*Channeled by Deb, February 2010*

# LIFE IS LIKE A PACK OF CARDS

## It's not about the cards you are dealt, but how you play the game.

The card games of life are but a part of life, the importance, duration and participation is yours to decide. Deal not the cards from a pack of unknowns but deal from a pack of cards that are known as the results will be within your knowledge.

As I shuffle my cards in life I begin to realise that they have been mixed up with others' cards that have been placed with my pack that should not have been. It is like someone sneaked in and messed with the game before it started.

I need to know that it was because of past lives that I was given this life.
I need to realise that as I was before this life that I knew the cards were there before I entered the game.
As I played I discovered the value of the rogue cards and that was the moments when I said they could leave my game of life that I am playing today.
I welcome the beauty of the cards that bring love.
I welcome the understanding of the cards as I play them.
I realise as I do what value they have in my life.
I assess this on a daily basis and when I do, I see the ones that are repeating their appearance.
I ask if they are good or bad.
I ask what purpose they hold for me.
I ask shall I play or do I put them back today.
I ask if I know their value in my life.
I ask for the direction that they give and show me, to be made clear with other details.

The game is basic and yet advanced because the levels of play are variable.
The game depends on who is playing and how much value they get from their individual hand and the location from which they play.
I am in my own place, my partner across the table in a similar place, we both have different hands but need to play together.
The others around us in this particular game are against us, not because of true disharmony but just because that is what this particular card game implies with its rules.
We each create what is and this game is no different, the cards dealt are the cards that will be in play in the near future.
The other cards sit in the deck on the table and will be available very soon.
The hand is what we play and the table is what we display, in an order that gives reorder to our life.
New exciting times arrive the moment the partners play together with the same rhythm.

*Glenys-Kay*

*The moment of truth is when each card is placed in the order of play.*

*The others in the game are there to make the game more challenging.*
*The others have their own cards and depending on the game they can have the same card that pairs with another in the game, so even as we are different people, we can still hold the same cards for a time.*
*When cards come together they are joined.*
*When cards leave play they are finished for that round of the game and are now resting until the next time they are drawn from the pack of cards to be played.*

*If the game has all unique cards that hold singular meanings but different weights, we know the order of play is by the best card for the sequence that is dictated by the order in which we sit around the game.*

*If once again we are a single individual playing, we will play for the highest and best return for our self.*
*If we are playing in a partnership we will be playing for our joint highest and best return.*
*It becomes fun the moment we do not know the cards that the partner holds and have to play alongside with an open mind of what they have and of course the skill they have in playing the cards.*
*There are some helpful benefits as when we know the game, we also know what cards are within the pack.*
*The order that the game asks to be played by the rules and also by the outcomes required, is how we as an individual learn to play.*
*The ultimate finish to each Set that is played is to win.*
*The challenge is in how we play with what goes before us and what comes after us.*

*Laugh along the way. Laugh within the play. Laugh at the end of the day.*

*Relief is in the order, and benefit is in the structure.*
*It is up to us as individuals and partnerships to play the best we can with what cards are dealt to us this particular lifetime.*
*There is a new shuffle each time we are ready.*
*The new or the regular people we play with allow us to choose how we play.*
*Variety sits on the knee of the person who moves around, and consistency sits on the knee of the person who stays in one place and grounds.*
*Neither or either are right or wrong, they just are.*
*Enjoy the games, take the moments of loss or gain.*
*Know how to hold the face that does not give away your place.*
*Be at peace on the outside, but know the chaos on the inside is just for the time that the game is played.*
*As reality steps in, realistically games are games, and we start and stop when we know the value of what we are experiencing.*
*We can stop when we know the final value.*
*To set limits is wise.*

*To have boundaries is common sense.*
*To be in control is your right, as being in the game gives you your learning.*
*You choose what is hard work and how long to be there.*
*When you realise what is easy work and how much this ease will create a better outcome for you, this will show you how to be open to more than just this game.*
*You will also see other aspects of life around the game.*

*My cards are now beginning to make more sense as the shuffle is done and wayward cards disposed of.*
*I am excited about the new pack.*
*It is reduced in size but now the remaining cards are becoming enhanced in spirit.*
*The essence of these cards is what attracts me to play with them.*
*The belief that I know what I am doing is mine to monitor.*
*The facts of what becomes displayed are mine to acknowledge and to deal with as I can.*
*Supporters are behind and beside me to help.*

*Ultimately I am who plays.*
*Ultimately I want to play the easy way.*
*Ultimately I have to live with the results.*

*So as I go to my new cards I pray, bless, affirm my intentions.*
*I plan, prepare, play my games.*
*I believe, balance, and become my choices.*
*How exciting!*
*I realise the value of the greetings on arrival before play.*
*I realise the energy within the play.*
*I realise the farewells on departure from play.*

*As I walk away I know the final conclusion, and accept what that means to me as an individual.*
*I observe what it means to others in the game and I support what it means to my partner, because we had a closer association than other players in the game.*
*I can extend myself to a little more than observation because that is the universal rules that the game gives us.*
*Sometimes I want to walk away as the partner shows colours of disharmony, but as I see the whole picture I know that the colours come and go, and I know as each hand is dealt and as each hand is played that it is the development and the improvement that will show the potentials of the game to ALL who play.*

*Each day, each game, each hand, becomes the total sum of what we are here in the now moment to live with and to survive with and to begin to build on.*
*Decisions give direction and delays give detours.*
*Just as we play our highest of the lowest cards first or last, it is our individual skill that will see our thrill!*

*Glenys-Kay*

*Forgive the moments of grief.*
*Forgive the moments of surprise!*
*Forgive what is not right, accept it for what it was, for it will no longer assist you to reach for your new heights.*

*Channeled by Gail, 2010.*

# *A STORY FROM A FRIEND:*

*I was looking to move home and when I was shown a particular house for sale I experienced something quite amazing. We walked through the house and out the ranchslider on to the deck and then walked on down to the end of the lawn. When I turned and looked back at the house there was this giant American Indian, about 12' tall, dressed in buckskin breeches and waistcoat, the usual type of dress, and he was standing on the deck. His height was above the roofline. He was standing with his arms folded and shaking his head at me.*

*I went absolutely white, and as I was seeing him out my physical eyes I rubbed them several times and looked again hoping that it was just my imagination and that he would have disappeared. However he was still standing there. There was a dog playing outside and it went and sat down at this giant man's feet. The dog knew he was there! Oh goodness.*

*I did get the feeling he was telling me not to buy the house, but I was literally gobsmacked.*

*We had to go up on the deck and pass him to get back through the house. When I got close enough somehow I managed to find the courage to reach out and touch his leg (my level!) to see if he felt real. He did!*

*I was still white and was driven home to go straight to bed for a couple of hours to get over the shock. I have seen a lot of things over many years and didn't think I could be shocked any more, but this one certainly took me by surprise.*

# A NEW EARTH "ILLUMINATION" MOMENT

*When I recently had to move out of my rented unit, I was led to a lovely big house in the country with, however, a very high rental. I was pushed into trusting that I was divinely guided and that it would be okay despite my misgivings about being able to pay the rent. I strengthened my belief and trust in divine guidance and moved in. After a death ceremony and a rebirth, this move was to take me into my new life, new me, and a new way of being.*

*To make sure I was able to pay the rent I instigated a series of new courses and teachings. None of these eventuated because I received absolutely no interest from people. This seriously challenged my belief and trust.*

*I practised what I teach . . . that is to always remain centred in the heart, breathing deeply to relax and keep away the irrational fears and disillusionment. I had some understanding of why it was happening but not enough to bury the fears for good.*

*I realised that the past paradigm would have been for me to panic and go into fear, probably ranting and raving at the injustice of it, perhaps even the stupidity of the higher realms for leading me here. However, I could see that my new paradigm was to breathe, stay calm and balanced and see the situation from a higher perspective of wisdom. There was a challenge in this, and a lesson. The old me had left but it was still a struggle to relate to the new me and a new way of viewing life.*

*It took me some time to get the "aha" moment.*

*Our old paradigm, old life, old world, was based on money. We were controlled by the economy, social systems, and we had to go out to work simply to pay the bills. So the old foundation was built on and around money.*

*The new paradigm, the new way of living, in other words, the New Earth, has a different foundation. It does not, and will not, function around a foundation of money.*

*The foundation of the 5D New Earth is one of Love, Wisdom, Truth and Freedom. These were my beliefs that I teach, and I was challenged to bring them into my daily living.*

*The 5D New Earth is NOT about money!*

*Aha!*

*We must believe and trust in our divinity, in our ability to manifest our needs with all the support and help from our friends in the higher realms.*

*That is the ONLY way we will exist on the New Earth!*

*And so it is that we of the Lightworker movement learn to have a foot in both worlds. We are truly straddling the dimensions of 3D and 5D, living in the realms of love, wisdom, truth and freedom, but able to also manifest the needs of the 3D world around us without going into fear.*

*. . . Glenys-Kay, 2010*

# *WORK IS LOVE*

*Work is love made visible.*

*If you cannot work with love but only with distaste, it is better than you should leave your work and sit at the gate of the temple and take alms from those who work with joy.*

*If you bake bread with indifference, you bake a bitter bread that feeds but half a man's hunger.*

*If you begrudge the crushing of the grapes, your grudge distils a poison in the wine.*

*If you sing as an angel and love not the singing, you muffle man's ears to the voices of the day and the night.*

*All work is empty save when there is love.*

*When you work with love you bind yourself to yourself, to one another and to God.*

*And what is it to work with love?*

*It is to weave the cloth with threads drawn from your heart, even as if your beloved were to wear that cloth.*

*It is to build a house with affection, even as if your beloved were to dwell in that house.*

*It is to sow seeds with tenderness and reap the harvest with joy, even as if your beloved were to eat the fruit.*

*It is to charge all things with a breath of your own spirit.*

*"The Prophet" by Kahlil Gibran 1923*

# AN INTERVIEW WITH GOD

### *"So you would like to interview me?" God asked.*

*"If you have the time" I said.*

*God smiled. "My time is eternity. What questions do you have in mind for me?"*

*"What surprises you most about humankind?"*

*God answered . . . "That they get bored with childhood, they rush to grow up, and then long to be children again."*

*"That they lose their health to make money . . . and then lose their money to restore their health."*

*"That by thinking anxiously about the future, they forget the present, such that they live in neither the present nor the future."*

*"That they live as if they will never die, and die as though they had never lived."*

*God's hand took mine and we were silent for a while.*

*And then I asked . . . "As a parent, what are some of life's lessons you want your children to learn?"*

*"To learn they cannot make anyone love them. All they can do is let themselves be loved."*

*"To learn that it is not good to compare themselves to others."*

*"To learn to forgive by practicing forgiveness".*

*"To learn that it only takes a few seconds to open profound wounds in those they love, and it can take many years to heal them."*

*"To learn that a rich person is not one who has the most, but is one who needs the least."*

*"To learn that there are people who love them dearly, but simply have not yet learned how to express or show their feelings."*

*"To learn that two people can look at the same thing and see it differently."*

*"To learn that it is not enough that they forgive one another, but they must also forgive themselves."*

*"Thank you for your time," I said humbly. "Is there anything else you would like your children to know?"*

*God smiled and said, "Just know that I am here . . . always."*

*Author and origin unknown*

# ONE DAY AT A TIME:

*Stand tall, start fresh, let go of guilt*
*Don't look back, take an inventory*
*Make amends, trust others*
*Believe in yourself, discover God's love*
*Appreciate your specialness.*
*Accept your humanness, ask for help*
*Trust enough to take*
*Have the courage to change*
*Accept the unchangeable*
*Be patient, keep promises*
*Bury regret, discard hate*
*Transcend self-doubt.*
*Don't dwell on the past*
*Love each moment, live each day*
*Build a better tomorrow*
*Open your heart, explore your soul*
*Expect the best*
*Let miracles happen*

*Origin and author unknown*

# ACKNOWLEDGMENTS

The section on Cosmic Laws, and also the Planetary Energies, have been referenced from the work of Ascended Masters Kuthumi-Agrippa and Mary Magdalen, channeled by Michelle Manders. For more information, channels, seminars and tours visit www.palaceofpeace.net

The section on 12-strand DNA has been referenced from the work of Kryon channeled by Lee Carroll. For further information read 'Kryon Book 12: The Twelve Layers of DNA' published by Platinum Publishing House 2010, or visit www.kryon.com

The section on The Seven Rays of Initiation have been referenced from the book 'The Seven Sacred Flames' by Aurelia Louise Jones, published by Mount Shasta Light Publishing 2007. For further information and free articles visit www.lemurianconnection.com

Excerpts from Dr Ulric Williams have been taken from the book 'New Zealand's Greatest Doctor: Ulric Williams' compiled by Brenda Sampson, published by Zealand Publishing House and available from www.healthhouse.co.nz

Quotations from Lord/Archangel Metatron have been channeled by James Tyberonn. For more information and free channels visit www.earth-keeper.com

Quotations from Ascended Master Ramtha have been channeled by J Z Knight. For more information on Ramtha's School of Enlightenment visit www.ramtha.com

Quotations from Mother Mary channeled by Judith Coates, have been taken from the January 2011 article 'Starseeds of the Future'. For further articles visit www.oakbridge.org

Quotation from The Sirian High Council has been channeled by Patricia Cori, taken from her book 'The Cosmos of Soul', published by North Atlantic Books, 2007. For further information visit www.sirianrevelations.net

Quotation from High Priest Adama of Telos was channeled by Aurelia Louise Jones and taken from his article 'The Wake Up Call'. For further information and free channels visit www.lemurianconnection.com

Quotation from the Pleiadian High Council has been channeled by Lauren C. Gorgo. For further information visit www.thinkwithyourheart.com

Quotation from Mary Magdalen channeled by Tom Kenyon has been taken from the book 'The Magdalen Manuscript' by Tom Kenyon and Judi Sion, first published by Orb Communications 2002, reprinted by Sounds True Inc. 2006.

*Quotation from The Hathors channeled by Tom Kenyon was taken from the article 'The Holon of Balance and the Holon of Healing', March 2005. For further information, free channels and articles visit www. tomkenyon.com*

*Quotation from Adamus Saint-Germain channeled by Geoffrey Hoppe has been taken from the 'Next' series, 'Tools for 2011 and Beyond', Jan 2011. For further information and free channels visit www.crimsoncircle.com*

*Quotation from Archangel Uriel has been channeled by Jennifer Hoffman. For further information and channels from Archangel Uriel visit www.urielheals.com*

*Quotation from Professor Masaru Emoto taken from page 132 of 'The Secret Life of Water' by Masaru Emoto, originally published in English by Beyond Words Publishing, a division of Simon & Schuster Ltd. For more information on the work of Professor Emoto visit www.masaru-emoto.net/english or www.myhado.com*

*Quotation from Kishori Aird has been taken from her book 'DNA Demystified Vol 1'. For further information on the Kishori Institute visit www.kishori.org*

*For further information on the work of Dr Dietrich Klinghardt MD, PhD, visit www.klinghardtacademy.com*